THE GITA FOR A GLOBAL WORLD

Rohit Chopra is Professor of Communication at Santa Clara University. His research centres on global media and identity, digital media, and the relationship between media, memory and violence. He is the author of *The Virtual Hindu Rashtra: Saffron Nationalism and New Media* (HarperCollins, 2019) and *Technology and Nationalism in India: Cultural Negotiations from Colonialism to Cyberspace* (Cambria, 2008), and co-editor of *Global Media, Culture, and Identity: Theory, Cases, and Approaches* (Routledge, 2011). Rohit also writes extensively in a journalistic capacity on media, politics and culture in global contexts. An expert on the role of social media in fomenting sectarian violence, he works with non-profits, think tanks, and technology and media firms on developing strategies to combat the negative effects of social media. Rohit is also the co-founder and co-host of the India Explained podcast, a conversation on matters related to India (www.soundcloud.com/indiaexplained).

Praise for *The Gita for a Global World*

'In the current political environment of intolerance and bigotry, it's urgent for scholars and teachers to reclaim salient texts and engage them in a manner that is at once informed and critical. Rohit Chopra's reading of the Bhagavad Gita is an example of how to put the humanities to work in keeping alive the practices of public reason and democratic debate.'

> – Ananya Vajpeyi, Fellow at the Centre for the Study of Developing Societies and author of *Righteous Republic: The Political Foundations of Modern India*

'*The Gita for a Global World* takes a lucid and fair assessment of the ethical opportunities afforded by the Bhagavad Gita and applies them to contemporary crises created by globalisation. Prof. Chopra offers astute cross-cultural comparisons and a fascinating investigation into how ideas are constructed, communicated (both technologically and politically), and acted out in global public life. *The Gita for a Global World* takes one of the world's masterpieces of philosophy and religion, and gives it new life in the twenty-first century.'

> – Robert Geraci, Professor of Religious Studies, Manhattan College, and author of *Futures of Artificial Intelligence: Perspectives from India and the US*

'Chopra reveals a nuanced approach to texts, where you do not accept or reject them because they conform to your worldview or not. He seems to value the importance of texts which present continuity of tradition and which have served as a meeting point for generations in society. Tradition is important, but a tradition that is constantly interrogated.'

> – Parsa Venkateshwar Rao Jr, *The Wire*

'Chopra is a remarkable scholar, and it shows. Laced with astute philosophical and political commentary, his writing is marked by a fluidity of thought and words.'

> – Sukhda Tatke, *Open*

THE GITA FOR A GLOBAL WORLD

ETHICAL ACTION IN AN AGE OF FLUX

ROHIT CHOPRA

cntxt

First published by Context, an imprint of Westland Publications Private Limited, in 2021

Published by Context, an imprint of Westland Books, a division of Nasadiya Technologies Private Limited, in 2023

No. 269/2B, First Floor, 'Irai Arul', Vimalraj Street, Nethaji Nagar, Alapakkam Main Road, Maduravoyal, Chennai 600095

Westland, the Westland logo, Context and the Context logo are the trademarks of Nasadiya Technologies Private Limited, or its affiliates.

ISBN: 9789357768009

10 9 8 7 6 5 4 3 2 1

Typeset by SÜRYA, New Delhi
Printed at Parksons Graphics Pvt. Ltd

For my parents,
Jagat Pal Chopra and Urvashi Chopra

Contents

1

INTRODUCTION

Reading the Gita in a Global Age

It is a sign of the universal relevance and enduringly enigmatic character of a book when it speaks compellingly to opposing concerns, when it is invoked in the defence of radically varied principles, and when it means vastly different things to different people. So it is with the Bhagavad Gita.

For Mahatma Gandhi, the force behind the greatest non-violent political movement of the twentieth century—the Indian anti-colonial revolution against British imperial rule in the subcontinent—the Gita was a source of spiritual plenitude, an anchor in which to ground his philosophical approach to political action and the basis for his understanding of human existence itself. Introduced to the text by theosophist friends in London while a student of law, no book, arguably, influenced Gandhi as much as the Gita.[1] In Gandhi's reading, 'the battlefield of Kurukshetra [was] located in every human soul, where the perennial conflict between good and evil occurs without end.'[2] Gandhi's interpretation of the Gita is pessimistic in its tragic vision of life as endless *agon* or struggle, but it is also hopeful in offering itself as a spiritual guide to wage that battle.

While Gandhi knew the entire text of the Gita intimately, two ideas from the book shaped his politics and personality in especially powerful ways: the concept of *nishkama karma*, or action without desire for reward, and the notion of struggle, internal and external, as a fundamental principle of existence that the ethical self was obligated to constantly navigate. His repeated insistence that the means of anti-colonial resistance mattered as much as the ends and his lack of hesitation in pointing out the ethical failures of his countrymen as willingly as he identified the evils of British colonialism were consistent with these principles. Gandhi's decision to halt the non-cooperation movement shortly after the Chauri Chaura incident on 4 February 1922 stands out as a particularly significant example of how these two ideas from the Gita shaped his thought and practice. At Chauri Chaura, following conflict with the police, a group of political activists set fire to the local police station, killing the twenty-three policemen inside. Dismayed by the violence, Gandhi called off the civil disobedience movement on 12 February 1922.[3]

In another invocation of the Gita, Robert Oppenheimer, the mind behind the American atomic bomb programme, quoted the words 'Now I am become Death, the destroyer of worlds' from the text, on witnessing the first test of a nuclear weapon in 1945.[4] The phrase ominously foretold the cataclysmic devastation that the bombs dropped on Hiroshima and Nagasaki would cause barely weeks later, when the United States would attack Japan in retaliation for the bombing of Pearl Harbour.

Oppenheimer's words were apposite; humanity had not witnessed anything in scale and scope like the annihilation caused by the nuclear explosions.

A report on Tokyo Radio described the uniformly unimaginable character of the destruction, which went well beyond the conventions of warfare, killing civilians, flattening the cities and sowing the seeds for decades of suffering among the surviving residents of Hiroshima and Nagasaki: 'The impact of the bomb was so terrific that practically all living things—human and animal—were literally seared to death by the tremendous heat and pressure set up by the blast ... All the dead and injured were burned beyond recognition. Those outdoors were burned to death, while those indoors were killed by the indescribable pressure and heat.'[5] The death toll, including both immediate deaths and those who died later from the horrific effects of the radiation, is estimated to be around 200,000 people. Oppenheimer's choice of words from the Gita anticipated the total obliteration of Hiroshima and Nagasaki, of humans and animals, living beings and inanimate objects alike. They speak to the capacity of violence to reshape the world, evoking the fearsome, godlike omnipotence of those who can unleash such force. The words serve as a reminder that the Gita, among its many interpretations, has also been used to justify violence in the service of a cause, a reading that is the very antithesis of how Gandhi viewed the book.

For those who may not be familiar with it, the Bhagavad Gita is a 700-verse text from the great Hindu epic, the Mahabharata. In his sparkling and condensed prose rendition of the epic, the illustrious Indian writer R.K. Narayan notes that the story of the Mahabharata would have been familiar to audiences in 1500 BC.[6] Running 100,000 stanzas in length, the story of the Mahabharata centres on a familiar and familial theme: the conflict between two branches of a warrior clan—the Pandavas and their kinsmen, the Kauravas—which inevitably leads to a battle for dynastic control between the two sides.

Narayan points out that the vast text of the Mahabharata is punctuated by philosophical discussions, of which the Gita is one.[7] The setting of the Gita is the imminent theatre of the battle of Kurukshetra, where the Pandava and Kaurava armies are set to clash. Arjuna, the Pandava prince, and a renowned warrior, is immobilised by doubt and stricken by anguish at the prospect of having to fight his kinsmen. Dejected, he lays down his bow, announcing his decision not to do battle. It falls on Krishna, his charioteer—who will eventually be revealed as an embodiment of divinity—to convince Arjuna of the need to fight. The Bhagavad Gita is an account of the discussion that ensues between the two about the necessity of waging war. It is simultaneously a treatise on action, morality, duty and kinship. In the Mahabharata, the Gita is conveyed to Dhritarashtra, the blind king and father of the Kauravas, by his charioteer, Sanjaya. Though not present at the scene of the action, Sanjaya is gifted with divine vision and can see what occurs on the battlefield. He duly conveys events as they transpire to Dhritarashtra. In reading the Gita, we experience the events in the text in the same mediated fashion, the technique of narration at a remove anachronistically similar to the narrative voice-overs of today's documentaries, cinema and television shows.

There is considerable debate among scholars about whether the Gita was originally a part of the Mahabharata and central to the epic or a later addition.[8] Brockington describes the two viable scholarly perspectives on the matter thus: 'either [the Gita] is an integral part of the *Mahabharata* and directed pragmatically to Arjuna's situation, or it is a later insertion (which includes the possibility of a later expansion of a brief original) developing a philosophically and theologically significant message from its *Mahabharata* context.'[9] I suggest that we can treat these interludes to the Mahabharata, of which the Gita is one, as possessing a curious double status: possible digressions but nonetheless essential to the story. Scholars may object that this apparent resolution actually results in inconsistencies in the text, in that the theological and philosophical ideas presented in the Gita contradict perspectives articulated elsewhere in the Mahabharata.[10] Yet, one can argue that the cultural practice of treating the Gita as inseparable from the Mahabharata and reading it as such is what has made the Gita a fundamental part of the Mahabharata even if it can be meaningfully seen as autonomous—for what text exists without communities of readers, practices of reading and contexts of reception? As Narayan observes, episodes of the Mahabharata like the Gita 'could be termed "asides," but no reader of *The Mahabharata* in India would miss any part of it'.[11] Part of the Mahabharata in the form of such an 'aside', the Gita is also a self-contained text that distills key philosophical ideas from the epic. In the narrative universe of the Mahabharata, these ideas from the Gita are woven into the dramatic twists and turns of the plot, threaded into events involving family and honour, jealousy and competitiveness, desire and anger, love and rejection, hubris, folly and sacrifice, betrayal and vengeance, conniving and compassion. In its examination of important philosophical notions, such as ethical action, duty and wisdom, the Gita functions as a reflexive aspect of the larger text, a meta-commentary on the deepest animating impulses of the epic.

Though they may seem abstract and distant from the compulsions of reality, the thoughts, views and ideas articulated in the Gita cannot be divorced from the brute realities of war and power that run through the Mahabharata. Arjuna and Krishna do not have the luxury or the unhurried time to debate for the sake of debate. The action, that is, the conversation between the two, occurs in the tense moments before a battle, and any decision that Arjuna takes—whether he chooses to fight or not—will bear immediate practical consequences. These ideas are explored in a dialogic model between Arjuna and Krishna in a chariot, a space that is neither entirely public nor entirely private. Arjuna's doubt and Krishna's wisdom belong to both the private and public realms by belonging wholly to neither. The actions that Arjuna will take, likewise, are both matters of public import and consequence and deeply personal decisions.

Beyond its relationship to historic figures like Gandhi and Oppenheimer, both of whose actions changed the course of world history, the Gita has been, and continues to be, encountered by countless people the world over in myriad ways. The Gita is ubiquitous in Indian social life, its insights woven into daily routines, its quotes inscribed on the flapping plastic curtains of autorickshaws, proclaimed on posters everywhere and emblazoned in the lobbies of corporate houses. In a characteristically incisive observation, the scholar and poet A.K. Ramanujan notes that no Hindu ever reads the Mahabharata for the first time.[12] Indeed, I cannot recall a time when I have not known of the Gita or of the characters of Arjuna and Krishna, just as I cannot tell when exactly sayings from the Gita first entered my consciousness. I remember my father quoting the dictum most closely identified with the book, of the virtue of effort without seeking reward, a sentiment that seemed directly at odds with practically everything that the culture of middle-class India of the 1980s stood for, given its soul-crushing, unhealthy competitiveness. 'Whatever has happened is for the good, whatever is happening is for the good, whatever will happen will also be for the good': I have a memory of seeing this sentiment from the Gita, in roughly similar phrasing, etched in a wooden plaque above a photocopier at a stationery shop in my neighbourhood in Mumbai, words that struck me as simultaneously optimistic and fatalistic, a stubborn contradictoriness that I would later find in other arguments in the book too.

An essential part of Indian identity, of Indian popular culture and of India's image of itself, the Gita manifests itself in many forms across various media. It showed up at my home in several editions: a Hindi translation published by a local North Delhi press that my grandparents brought with them when they visited us in the different cities in which we lived across India;

in a children's book in English on Indian religious deities; as a volume of Amar Chitra Katha, the comic book series that was my unofficial introduction to so much about Indian history, religion, culture and mythology. Inexpensive audio tapes of recitations from the Gita, along with other devotional offerings, could be found at any music store or stall on the sidewalk in markets in Delhi, Calcutta and Mumbai, mingling with offerings from popular Western artistes and songs from Hindi cinema. At handicraft stores, brass renderings of the most famous tableau from the Gita, depicting Krishna and Arjuna seated in a horse-drawn chariot or rath, were as ubiquitous as models of the Taj Mahal or statues of the Gautama Buddha. I remember the reference to the Gita in a song from the film *Yudh* endlessly playing on tape recorders and radios in public spaces in the mid-1980s, a time when listening to the songs of Hindi cinema was one of the few modes of entertainment commonly enjoyed by most Indian social classes. The song, *Yudh Kar*, literally 'Do Battle' or more loosely 'Go Fight!', includes the lines, '*Krishan ne kaha Arjun se / Na pyaar jataa dushman se / Yudh kar*'. Translating to 'Krishna said to Arjuna / Don't express love for your enemy / Go battle', the lines reduce and misrepresent—in classic Bollywood style—the complexity of Arjuna's anguish and torment at the prospect of having to fight his kinsmen to an unseemly fondness for the enemy.

The Gita travelled across private and public thresholds, inhabiting spaces of work and leisure. Outside my school in Calcutta in the 1980s, a host of itinerant vendors would set up shop each day around the time the school day got done. Along with the fruit seller, the jhal-muri wala and the ice-candy man, an enterprising mobile salesman would set up a display of posters. While waiting for my school bus, I would marvel at the dazzling arrangement of popular visual art spread out like a feast for the eyes. There, rubbing shoulders with scenes of the Alps, images of Wham, Madonna and Michael Jackson, red Ferraris and yellow Lamborghinis, cricketers and Bollywood actors, were posters with renditions of several scenes from the Gita: Krishna with the *sudarshan chakra*, Krishna and Arjuna in his chariot, Krishna bathed in divine light, his face radiating serenity, while a kneeling Arjuna gazed up awestruck at him. The bright colours of the posters, with their impossibly blue skies, radiant golds and reds, and bold, ornate text, were captivating, drawing on lineages of Indian sacred art but reflecting popular Indian aesthetic idioms as well. Other gods and goddesses, Kali and Durga, Rama and Vishnu, housed in their own posters, kept Arjuna and Krishna company as did mortals like the cricketer Kapil Dev, who was worshipped by some 750 million Indians for captaining India to an improbable victory in the 1983 one-day cricket world championship.[13]

The Gita also boasts a powerful global presence, arguably more so than any other Indian text. Familiar to Western thinkers from the eighteenth century onwards, the book has taken on an independent life beyond Indian borders, akin to the sayings of Rumi, the *Tao Te Ching*, Omar Khayyam's *Rubaiyat*, the *One Thousand and One Nights* or, more recently, the aphoristic wisdom of spiritual pop stars like Paulo Coelho, the Dalai Lama and Deepak Chopra.[14] The writer and literary critic Amit Chaudhuri argues that the fact that we do not know the authors of texts like the Gita and the Upanishads is precisely what has made them central to traditions of Western literary and intellectual modernity, an episode in the history of cross-cultural influence that still needs to be excavated and written about.[15] These ancient Indian texts fit well with the modernist literary critical paradigm of reading texts unyoked from biography and freed from the assumption of a central authorial consciousness and intentionality as sources of textual meaning. In an astute, speculative bit of genealogical detective work, Chaudhuri traces the concept of disinterestedness as a philosophical and literary trope in the Western intellectual tradition to the influence of the Gita following its translation into European languages. The Gita's impact is clearer on some figures like Matthew Arnold than it is on others, such as Immanuel Kant. However, there is a strong case to be made for the widespread influence of the Gita's idea of detachment-with-commitment on the concept of disinterestedness, as aesthetic quality, sensibility or critical stance, in the work of a whole host of modern European thinkers. Krishna's way of reading life, though the seemingly paradoxical notion of disinterested sincerity, becomes a technique for grappling with, apprehending and framing the reality of a text.

In the twentieth century, no individual did more to popularise the Gita than Abhay Charan De, known more widely as A.C. Bhaktivedanta Swami Prabhupada, the founder of ISKCON or the International Society for Krishna Consciousness. I have seen followers of the movement, or Hare Krishnas as they are commonly called, in cities of three continents. As a graduate student at Emory University in Atlanta in the early 2000s, I had the odd experience of being subjected to a relentless bout of proselytisation by a Hare Krishna on my university campus, during which interaction he tried to sell me a copy of the Gita. I was amused to see that the edition, which the Hare Krishna was pitching to me at $15, had been published in Dadar in Mumbai with a listed price of ₹150. Given the anxieties among conservative Hindus about proponents of Christianity seeking to slyly convert unsuspecting Hindus to their faith, it was richly ironic that one of the two persons who tried to convert me in all my years in the American Deep South—the heart of hellfire-and-brimstone evangelical Christianity in the US, with its rants about harvesting pagan souls and the evils of polytheism—was an American Hindu pitching an international brand of Hinduism.[16]

Online commercial websites, like the global behemoth Amazon, list numerous editions of the Gita, including the well-known translations and commentaries by Edwin Arnold, Sarvepalli Radhakrishnan, Swami Prabhupada, Eknath Easwaran, and Winthrop Sargent, as well as any number of books about the Mahabharata, Hindu philosophical thought and Indian religions and mythology. On websites like eBay and Etsy, vintage dealers, individuals and small businesses from everywhere, including India, Bulgaria, France and the United Kingdom, sell statues, carvings and posters of scenes and characters from the Gita, not all of which are sourced from or made in India. Beyond the sale of items associated with the Gita, there are scores of websites dedicated to the exegesis of the text itself, largely set up by non-specialists. On online forums like Reddit and Quora, discussions abound about the provenance of the text, the merits and demerits of particular translations, the place of the Gita in Hinduism and the meanings of ideas in the book. The Gita is an essential part of the discourse of global Hinduism, a powerful symbol of pan-Hindu identity and diasporic Hindu communities. Hindu temples in many overseas locations host regular lectures on the Gita. Since the 1960s, a whole host of self-styled Hindu godmen have found a ready global market for their spiritual wares—Maharishi Mahesh Yogi, who served as a spiritual advisor to the Beatles and introduced transcendental meditation to the West, is perhaps still the best known of them. In that venerable tradition, jet-setting godmen in the present continue to dispense wisdom to Silicon Valley billionaires, assorted oligarchs and non-resident Indian (NRI) communities. The Gita serves as one of the ready sources to which they turn, processing its insights into massively diluted and easily digestible, if often erroneous, nuggets of oriental spiritual insight. In 2011, the Bhagavad Gita became the subject of a controversial trial in Russia, when the Russian Hare Krishna community successfully sued to have the book stopped from being placed on a list of banned extremist books.[17]

It is fitting that in the present, as has been the case in the past, the Gita is the subject of endless discussions and that a great many people are in conversation with it. The book is 'what the Indian Sanskrit tradition calls a *samvada*—a dialogue or conversation, in which options for action are explored, the meanings of those potential actions weighed carefully and teachings given'.[18] The conversation between the mortal Arjuna and Krishna travels across a vast terrain of complicated themes, categorised under eighteen teachings. While the Gita may take as a point of departure the issue of whether to wage war or not, its significance far exceeds that question. 'The dialogue between Krishna and Arjuna,' as Davis notes, 'goes far beyond a rationale for war.' The rich discourse of the Gita consists of the examination of a wide and varied range of ideas, concepts and ethical dilemmas: the morality of engaging in war versus the ethics of abstaining from violence; our obligations towards those close to us in contrast to our actions towards those whom we do not know; how we behave towards those we perceive to be like us as opposed to our behaviour towards those whom we see and who see themselves as different from us; how the value of disinterested action, separated from any desire to control outcomes, measures up against the commitment towards particular goals; renunciation versus disinterestedness; and the nature of the individual, transient self versus an abiding collective spirit of which the singular self is a manifestation.

This book seeks to bring the Bhagavad Gita into a dialogue with our times. It asks how the insights of an old Indian text might apply to the condition of living in a global world, especially one wrought by the formidable challenges that we face today. At first mention, the very premise may strike one as incongruous, just as it might for similar texts from other cultural and religious traditions. What could the Gita, a nonmodern text, tell us about the particular phase of contemporary existence we call globalised life or global capitalist modernity?[19] Our forms of life today, after all, are profoundly different from those prevalent during the times when the Gita, by any of the accounts of its genesis, would have been composed. The issue here is not that different historical contexts cannot be meaningfully compared or that ideas from one time and place cannot travel to another, but whether the differences might be so vast that any such inquiry means little beyond pure intellectual speculation.

For all their diversity, our vocations, identities, daily routines, choices of leisure and entertainment, relationships with friends and family and modes of communication are tied largely to the structure of capitalist modernity—even if that structure takes varied, uneven and highly localised forms across the world. As a basic definition that will suffice here, we can understand capitalism as a highly intricate and complex system centred on the accumulation of profit, wherein resources are allegedly allocated based on perceived value to the system. Modernity is a specific historical condition, woven intimately with industrialised and post-industrialised capitalist life. The term and concept also denotes a form of human subjectivity, a particular orientation or dispensation through which we define and understand ourselves, others and the world at large.[20] Modern values include the ideals of justice, equality and liberty; the ideal modern subject is one who possesses individual freedom and rights, is empowered to author his or her own life, and is free to transact his or her labour in return for compensation from other individuals or organisations. In its most commonly used meaning, globalisation denotes a set of ongoing processes, set into motion in the aftermath of the Second World War, through which the world has become more integrated economically, politically, technologically and culturally. Over the past few decades, globalisation has radically reshaped every aspect of our lives, whether they are our ways of communicating, shopping, experiencing culture, getting the news, working, earning money or making friends.

The political economy of global capitalist modernity shapes our subjectivities, dictates our life choices, and colours the ideological meanings of freedom, faith, family and self. In turn, the system of global capitalism is perpetuated and sustained by our practices. Regardless of race, gender, sexual orientation or nationality, we live our lives according to the range of possibilities that this larger structure offers us, based on the economic, cultural, educational and social capital we possess.[21] To state the obvious, the more resources we possess, whether in terms of money, educational qualifications, social connections, status or privilege, the better the opportunities available to us and the more choices and freedom we have in determining the course of our life. Those who fall outside the structure of global capitalism—the 'wretched of the earth', in Frantz Fanon's powerful phrase—are marginalised and exploited, while a complex apparatus of corporations, nation-states, global media systems and experts on 'development' seeks to ultimately bring this large segment of humanity into its ambit as productive, efficient individuals with modern sensibilities.[22]

To note that the majority of the world's population generally lives under the structures of the condition of capitalist modernity is not to suggest that it is the only mode of social life in the present, an inevitable state of affairs, or a necessarily superior way of life to other paradigms of social existence. There are areas of the world where capitalist modernity is not the dominant paradigm of social existence. Something of the older ways of life, not reducible to the transactional form of social interaction required by capitalist modernity, survives in any number of cultures. Groups that seem to be able to live with some degree of insulation from contemporary globalised capitalism include remote, indigenous tribes living in isolation and protected by national and international laws, such as in the Amazon basin or in the Andaman and Nicobar Islands; small communities that have held on to their ways of life, with strategic adaptations and concessions to the demands of modern life, like the Amish in the US; and, ironically, the ultra-wealthy, who have benefited handsomely enough from the opportunities offered by global capitalism so as to be able to live free from its compulsions. Yet, even these three groups are not entirely exempt from the pressures of global capitalism, of course. Indigenous groups, for instance, have had their habitats destroyed by environmental degradation caused by industrial processes such as mining and by the illicit economy of poaching that, like the drug trade or human trafficking, represents the underbelly of legitimate capitalist enterprise. Communities who interact with modern society while seeking to preserve a nonmodern way of life have to continually negotiate the pressures of an ever-encroaching force in a deeply unequal battle.

While the trends associated with globalisation have generally proceeded along the trajectory of greater integration of different regions of the world and different global systems, even with some setbacks and reversals, the last few years have witnessed an unusual degree of turbulence in these processes. We may not consciously identify or think of ourselves as global citizens, a term that, frankly, sounds pompous, clichéd and more than a little hollow. We may be sceptical of the very idea of cosmopolitanism, a word often understood as connoting a sophisticated global sensibility. We may prefer to see our lives as grounded in our local identities, practices and rituals, even as we watch cinema made in Japan and Korea, on a global digital streaming platform like Netflix, aspire to travel to India, study in the US or vacation in Switzerland. Those left out by globalisation, in the developed and developing world alike, have often reacted against it, seeking consolation in the simplistic certitudes of religious fundamentalism and terrorism or projecting their anger and frustration against minorities, refugees and immigrants. In the US, there has been no clearer example of this trend than the unexpected election victory of Donald Trump in the 2016 presidential elections. Bucking all trends, Trump defeated Hillary Clinton by running a toxic campaign based on a deeply racialised nationalism, reinforced by an extensive Russian disinformation drive on Facebook. Among the constituencies that cast their lot with Trump were voters from America's 'rust belt', regions that were once prosperous centres of American manufacturing but had long since fallen into a state of decrepitude following the decline of the industrial sector in the 1980s. America's shift to a post-industrial service economy and its increased reliance on overseas manufacturing, directly implicated in the endless economic winter of the rust belt, is both a consequence and a cause of globalisation. States like Michigan, now a part of the belt, had voted Democrat in the previous six US presidential elections. The Democrats, after all, were the party more closely associated with labour rights, unions and welfare programmes, in contrast to the Republicans who emphasised the free market, low taxes and light regulation. Yet, in 2016, Trump was able to tap into the sense, prevalent in parts of Michigan and similar regions in other states, that the working people of these communities had been sold out by their leaders, Democrats and Republicans alike, through deals like the North American Free Trade Agreement (NAFTA), which left American businesses unable to compete with Mexico or Canada, and by the processes of globalisation in general, which had shifted American jobs to China, India, the Philippines and other locations. While Joe Biden has prevailed over Trump in the 2020 US presidential elections, the sizeable numbers who still voted for Trump in the industrial belt should indicate that these sentiments continue to hold real power in the minds of many Americans.

One of the main arguments of this book is that such developments represent neither a reversal nor a significant disruption of the logic of globalisation, but are reflective of a particular phase in globalisation that I term 'crisis globalisation'. In this phase of globalisation, economic precariousness, political instability, existential uncertainty and a general condition of vulnerability play a much more prominent role than they did previously. The characteristics and effects of crisis globalisation are all around us.

In the economic realm, setting aside periodic and expected cyclical downturns and recessions, developments in global capitalism have concentrated massive amounts of wealth in the hands of a few technology and media firms, like Amazon, Google, Apple and Facebook. At the same time, the number of jobs in previously stable professions has dipped precipitously, falling prey to the contract labour model of the gig economy.[23] The global spread of democracy, once thought inevitable, is on pause for a complex set of reasons, including the rise of terrorism, the erosion of an international commitment to rights brought on by the US-led 'war on terror', a political lurch towards the right in numerous countries, more of which are led by strongmen with authoritarian tendencies, and a widespread feeling among large sections of the population in many nations that neither values of democracy, inclusion and openness to immigrants nor pro-globalisation economic policies have served them well. The impact of climate change, which respects no national boundaries, can be seen across the globe, manifesting itself in unpredictable and savage hurricanes, raging fires and rising seasonal temperatures that are increasingly making many cities and towns fundamentally uninhabitable for part of the year. As I write this, the state of California in the US is struggling to control twenty-eight wildfires, which have scorched 3.2 million acres of land, killed two dozen people, and show no sign of letting up.[24] The cause of the fires, a predictable annual occurrence in the state now, is near unanimously accepted by experts as climate change. The impact of these wildfires, which has been most tragically felt at the local level in terms of the loss of lives, destruction of homes and livelihoods, and devastation caused to families, communities and towns, goes beyond the state of California. Anything that affects California, the world's tenth largest economy, will necessarily affect the world.

Uncontrolled and haphazard industrial development, accompanied by an unrelenting exploitation of the natural world, has extracted a heavy cost—not just in the form of the devastation of wildlife, depletion of resources and dangerous levels of pollution but now, alarmingly, through a pandemic that has brought the world to its knees. In 2021, we close in on a year of battling COVID-19, which, as of the end of 2020, had infected around ninety million people and killed nearly two million.[25] It has disrupted the course of life everywhere, sending countries into lockdown, devastating economies, halting travel, causing workplaces and schools to close, and forcing the unnaturalness of social isolation on a species whose essential nature it is to be social.[26] Initially thought to be contracted by humans in China through inter-species transmission, the virus has hijacked transnational flows of people travelling for business, leisure, education, migration and refuge in blazing across the globe. Business travellers, tourists and members of diasporic families visiting China brought it to Silicon Valley and the East Coast in the US as well as to Europe, while wealthy Indian tourists carried it from Europe to the densely overpopulated Indian metros of Delhi and Mumbai. The virus spread through other routes as well, such as an international religious gathering at the headquarters of the Islamic organisation, the Tablighi Jamaat, in Delhi in mid-March 2020, at which 4,500 people from all over the world had congregated at one location, and a local gathering at which an infected 'super-spreader' Sikh preacher who had returned to India from Italy and Germany spoke at a Sikh festival attended by some 10,000 people in early March of the year.[27] These events are proof of how religious practices and events in India, as in many other parts of the world, are now deeply intertwined with global networks. The events also reflect how the trajectories of the COVID-19 virus' spread are inseparable from the dynamics of globalisation. As the fundamental logic of organisation of the present-day world, globalisation is what has enabled the virus to spread as far and wide as it has and at the speed with which it has. A year since we first learned of the existence of COVID-19, we miraculously do have several vaccines that promise to be very effective, but we will have to live with the virus as a permanent reality in our lives for a good while as, indeed, with the possibility of other pandemics in the future.[28]

Despite these obstacles in the path of the ongoing processes of globalisation, our lives, for better or worse, continue to be shaped by it. Though we experience the impact of the economic, social, political and cultural forces associated with globalisation intimately, their causes are often far removed from us. The disorientation of being at the mercy of forces one cannot see, unsettling as it is, is compounded when we are in the midst of the maelstrom that we face now. This book asks what guidance the Gita might be able to offer us in light of the situation of crisis globalisation in which we find ourselves. It does so without assuming that the Gita will or can easily provide ready answers to our dilemmas. Instead, the book examines the Gita as an ethical treatise that addresses several fundamental issues that may not necessarily be unique to our age but are possibly invested with an enhanced relevance at this historical moment.

What is the meaning of action in the face of uncertainty? It is neither healthy nor viable to worry about every possible event or every possible outcome of an action. To borrow metaphors from mythology and religion, such an approach is likely to turn us to stone or salt, immobilised and frozen into inaction or ready to crumble under the slightest pressure. And yet, it is a perfectly legitimate desire to want some sense of stability in which to ground one's existence. In times when difference is treated as dangerous and those seen as visibly different face the threat of exclusion and violence, the question of how we behave towards our fellow humans also takes on a special urgency. Who are our kin? Who are Others? What is the nature of our obligations towards our fellow beings? This is a question that takes on a heightened salience in light of the kinds of identities and differences—national, cultural, religious, sexual, ethnic, caste, racial, gendered, bodily and others—that we, as individuals and communities, assert, negotiate and encounter today, perhaps at a scale unprecedented in human history. Of equal import is the matter of war, both literal and metaphorical. What sense do we make of the relentless wars being waged today between state and non-state actors? What norms or codes should govern the wars of the twenty-first century? Are the costs that they extract from us worth it? Are these wars inevitable? And what approach do we take to fighting battles with adversaries like the COVID-19 coronavirus? Or those waged for the cause of social justice? The abiding significance of these kinds of questions is perhaps why the Gita has spoken compellingly to readers across two millennia, since it was written in the first or second century CE.[29]

Like any other text, religious or secular, the Gita may not provide easy or immediate answers to such questions. But it may give us a way to struggle with them, and show us a way to find the answers for ourselves. If war is a near constant of human existence, whether understood as the struggle of the soul, the fight for justice, political and ideological clashes, or military conflict between nations, then the Gita has something to say about it. 'Kurukshetra,' Davis points out, 'is both a particular field of battle and perpetual field of *dharma*, or righteousness.'[30] While the setting of the Gita is an actual field of battle, the battlefield in the text refers to any struggle we may face in life. If living in a state of crisis, with the threat of global warming, pervasive pollution and economic upheavals is part of our reality, the Gita does have something valuable to contribute to how we negotiate and understand that state of affairs. It has likely done the same for readers across the centuries, in times of crisis or otherwise.

Shakespeare, the scholar Jan Kott persuades us in his influential book, is our contemporary.[31] *Ran*, Kurosawa's masterful interpretation of *King Lear*, and *Omkaara*, Vishal Bhardwaj's gripping rendition of *Othello* set against the backdrop of a nexus of caste, politics and crime in Uttar Pradesh, strongly endorse Kott's thesis. Greek tragedy moves us and leaves us chilled to the bone, its landscapes of desolation strangely familiar, the savagery and horrors of its violence painfully current. The writings of Marx or the meditations of Marcus Aurelius affect us with an immediacy and intimacy that we may not experience in more recent, run-of-the-mill texts that are set in contexts much more well known to us. In Italo Calvino's *Invisible Cities*, the traveller Marco Polo describes all the cities to which he has travelled to the emperor Kublai Khan. I find Calvino's masterpiece to ring more true of Mumbai than any novel which takes the great Indian metropolis as its literal setting.

Works likes the ones named here are representative of particular traditions, yet also possess a life beyond them. The Gita shares this quality of transcending historical and geographical context with other great texts, whether of religious or secular provenance. Davis has described this quality as the 'doubleness of the Bhagavad Gita—its historical specificity and its continuing, even eternal, life'.[32] Truly, over the course of its long and ongoing life, the Gita has meant an astonishing number of things to an astonishing number of people. The interlocutors of the text include 'medieval Brahmin scholars and Krishna devotees, British colonial scholars, German romantics, globe-trotting Hindu gurus, Indian anticolonial freedom fighters, Western students, and spiritual seekers', all of whom have 'engaged in new dialogues with the Gita'.[33] Architects of war and apostles of peace, ordinary folk and extraordinary people, atheists and believers alike have found the Gita a source of wisdom, guidance and consolation, a powerful instrument of justification for troubling actions or a bulwark for weathering storms of doubt.

In a number of cases, the meaning of a word, Wittgenstein tells us, 'is its use in the language'.[34] We may extend this dictum to the meaning of texts. The Gita, Davis suggests, 'is internally complex and ambiguous enough to have spoken differing truths to different audiences, as suited to their diverse situations and expectations'.[35] Flood and Martin, similarly, point out that 'the *Bhagavad Gita* is a dialogue, rather than a work of systematic philosophy, and so the meanings of the text are not self-evident. As a result, the *Gita* has been interpreted in many ways and used in support of a number of different philosophical and political ideas, from pacifism to aggressive nationalism, from philosophical monism to theism.'[36] In a justly famous essay, A.K. Ramanujan suggests that the existence of numerous versions of the Ramayana means that no single version of the text should be considered authoritative.[37] Each of the 300 or 3,000 versions of the Hindu epic *is* the Ramayana. There may not be as many versions of the Gita, a text not close to the size of an epic since it is but a part of one, but there is no dearth of readings of the relatively slender 700-verse poem. Inseparable from the innumerable interpretations that flower from its aesthetic, political and philosophical richness, the Gita is an infinite text, its meanings endlessly refracting as it speaks to readers across time and space.

It is in the spirit of an ordinary reader, one among many, that I approach the Gita. Nonetheless, it would be disingenuous to claim that my reading is not informed by my vocation as an academic, specifically, as a scholar with interdisciplinary training focused on the study of globalisation, media and culture and a student of the humanities versed in the methods of close reading, formalist literary analysis and contextual readings of texts as products of history, society and culture. I have been studying contemporary forms of Hindu nationalism, especially as they interact with and take shape in media, for close to two decades. This book is informed by my experience of observing the intersections of Hinduism—as text, politics and authority—and media in Indian and global political and cultural spaces. Through the many commentaries on it, in its hundreds of translations, in the untranslatability of its key concepts and terms, the Gita has proliferated to be able to accommodate widely divergent readings and analyses, from the materialist and historicist to the philological and philosophical, from the nativist to the universalist, from Gandhi's fundamentally allegorical interpretation of the text to vulgar Hindu nationalist readings which claim that Krishna's words in the Gita are proof of ancient Indian knowledge of nuclear weapons. My reading is one more among these. My exploration of the Gita also bears the hope that the nonmodern, as a sensibility, a way of life, an ethical framework or a mode of consciousness, can exist alongside the modern or even within it. Having lived in India, it is difficult not to feel, existentially and experientially, that something of the nonmodern ethos of earlier times has survived into the present of Indian life.[38] Perhaps it survives elsewhere too and that may have been one reason, among many no doubt, why the Gita has meant something to so many audiences in so many times and places.

The Gita which I read in this book can be viewed as a composite version, consisting in varying measure of several editions that have been published over the course of more than a hundred years. I draw on Gandhi's Gujarati translation of the Gita and his other writings on the text, as well as more recent editions such as those by Barbara Stoler Miller, Laurie Patton, and Gavin Flood and Charles Martin.[39] I also refer to the bilingual translation of the Gita in English and Hindi by Alok Bhalla and Chandra Prakash Deval that accompanies late-seventeenth-century miniature paintings of scenes from the Gita by the artist Allah Baksh. Two editions of the Mahabharata, by R.K. Narayan and John D. Smith, respectively, have been immensely valuable in providing a contextual elaboration and elucidation of aspects of the Gita.[40]

Translation, at its best, is an act of democracy. Each translation to which I refer conveys the power and complexity of the Gita in a unique and distinct manner, compelling in its telling and imbued with its own rare music. And yet, as the first principle of literary interpretation holds, this does not mean that anything and everything can be read into the Gita. There are readings that are more or less relatively true to a text and those that a text cannot accommodate or bear. I have tried to be true to the text in my engagement with it, drawing attention to those moments in the text where I have found it stubbornly unyielding or elusive in its answers. All readings of any text ultimately remain partial, because the situations in which we read texts change and because we ourselves change as readers over time. You cannot step twice into the same river, says the ancient Greek philosopher Heraclitus. You cannot, one might similarly say, step twice into the same text—and if there were ever a text that could be described as a river, it is the Gita.

There is a major, immediate challenge that the Gita presents the reader. Much of the text is written at a very high level of abstraction and centres on debates about a range of themes—the self and the world, action and non-action, desire and renunciation—between different Indian philosophical traditions. What could these passages, in their narrow, specific manifestations in the text, tell us about the challenges we face today, at this moment, in this world, as individuals and members of many communities? What could they tell us about global warming and violence, inequality and suffering, pandemics and the savage oppression of vulnerable groups? In negotiating this challenge, I have sought to follow the example of some of the most well-known readers of the Gita, who have reframed the book as a statement of principles or ideas that are not constrained by the philosophical debates of a particular cultural tradition.

The paradoxes of the text, for example, the unresolved tension between action and non-action, or the idea of commitment to a cause and the imperative of preserving an existing hierarchical order, likely stem from these philosophical debates. Yet, the value of these paradoxes extends beyond the debates, bearing significance for how we should think about and respond to urgent political and social issues of the present. The scholar D.C. Mathur suggests, for instance, that from the point of view of radical social change, the Gita must strike us as a conservative text, an insight that is consistent with the Gita's affirmation of the four-fold varna or caste system as a reflection of a desirable social order.[41] And yet for Indian intellectuals grappling with the question of what British colonial rule reflected about the nature of Indian society, the Gita represented a radical call to action out of stupor for reforming Hindu and Indian society and freeing the nation from the yoke of British imperialism. Patton notes that the Gita was considered subversive enough by British colonial authorities that anyone found in possession of more than one copy of the book was deemed a terrorist.[42] To this end, paradoxes of the kind noted above can be seen as productive in helping us think through what constitutes an appropriate response to a given state of affairs and the merits and demerits of different courses of action to address the situation in question.

My reading of the place of the Gita in our world is divided into five chapters, including this introduction. The next chapter elaborates the idea and condition of crisis globalisation, or the present state of globalisation. The following three chapters address the questions, respectively, of: action in the face of uncertainty, difference and war. I investigate each area with a focus on how its meanings have been reshaped by the condition of crisis globalisation.[43] A brief coda, which concludes the book, examines Gandhi as a reader of the Gita in light of the realities of crisis globalisation. Gandhi is the single most significant interpreter of the Gita in our times, though, as Patton points out, he was 'not a textual interpreter' but a seeker of moral truth, who looked to the book for inspiration and guidance.[44] In the same vein, in the concluding chapter I consider whether the broad moral lessons of the Gita that Gandhi found so powerful can tell us something about the challenges facing us today.

My method is to identify in the Gita a set of ethical, moral and analytic principles—not all necessarily in harmony with each other—to see if and how these can help us grapple with the major existential questions of war, difference and uncertainty that confront us as a global community. I should clarify that in no way is this a self-help or motivational book, a category that seems to be booming in India thanks to entrepreneurs of the self, assorted godmen who claim to have the ear of some celestial being or another, or celebrities who have suddenly discovered spirituality along with numerology, astrology and the tarot. The book does not seek to provide a list of distilled answers or principles that can serve as precepts for magically generating solutions to all problems. Taking a cue from Wittgenstein's dictum of philosophy as a means to an end, I have tried to use the text as an instrument that can help navigate some of the intractable difficulties of our complicated, and intertwined, global lives. While we share these struggles in varying degrees of overlap with a number of groups, what all of us have in common is the experience of struggle itself. Loss, heartbreak, frustration, disappointment and alienation are perhaps more universal than their opposites. Whether we accept them as inevitable, attempt to rationalise them in terms of some larger philosophical, religious or metaphysical framework, or seek to make changes to reduce the possibility of being disappointed or hurt by such experiences again, we have no choice but to keep living our lives. The emperor-philosopher Marcus Aurelius advised stoic acceptance in his well-known dictum, 'all things soon pass away', from which the title of George Harrison's 1970 album, *All Things Must Pass*, is taken.[45] In response to the increasingly visible threat of authoritarianism in the 1930s, the Italian Marxist Antonio Gramsci came up with phrase 'pessimism of the intellect, optimism of the will', as a motto by which to persevere in the face of such alarming changes.[46] The Gita, too, may have something of value to tell us with respect to how we go about facing adversity under difficult conditions.

I have also deliberately chosen to read the Gita through a resolutely non-religious frame. My own beliefs and religious identity or lack of the same are irrelevant to this choice. A critical believer or an atheist alike may come up with compelling readings of the same text. As a matter of methodological principle, though, reading a text as the voice of divinity or as a manifestation of transcendental religious, spiritual or mystical principles forecloses the interpretive possibilities that it offers. If we were to use the mystery of divinity, or whatever name we wish to give it, as a heuristic principle, any and every argument and its opposite could be attributed to such an explanatory framework. I do not consider such readings, when I have come across them with reference to religious texts from various traditions, to be particularly insightful or illuminating. Wittgenstein inaugurates his landmark work, the *Tractatus Logico-Philosophicus*, with the proposition that the world 'is all that is the case'.[47] By this, Wittgenstein means that reality does not exist beyond the empirical world, so philosophy should keep its feet firmly grounded in it. Of course, the nature of that world is still up for grabs, philosophically speaking, but Wittgenstein is asking us here to start and stay with the world in seeking to understand and illuminate it. One cannot completely escape engagement with the metaphysics of the Gita, but I have tried to focus on what the Gita may illuminate about the world as we mortals encounter it not as the gods have known it.

A final motivation for engaging with the text is to counter, in whatever small way, the co-option of the Gita and other texts considered canonical in Hinduism by the Hindu Right. Since well before the election victory of the Bharatiya Janata Party (BJP) in 2014, an event that has unleashed an aggressive and frighteningly vicious majoritarian religious nationalism in India, the Hindu Right has sought to control practically every aspect of the public and private forms alike of Hindu faith, tradition and culture. Hinduism, in the view of the Hindu Right, is the property of Hindus, but Hindus of a certain type. Its truest followers and believers, and, consequently, its real guardians, are not Hindus in all their diversity, but Hindu nationalists or adherents of the ideology of Hindutva. In the *weltanschauung* of the Hindu Right, any criticism of Hinduism, real or imagined, is designated as an act of heresy. Whether in states like Gujarat, long considered the laboratory of Hindutva, in universities all over India, or in the Indian-American diaspora, the Hindu Right has established a violent monopoly over the control, production and circulation of knowledge about Hinduism. This has resulted in revisionist accounts of Indian history being authorised as the immutable truth in school textbooks in BJP-controlled states. This revisionist historiography abounds in narratives of Hindus as perennial heroes and victims and Muslims as pillaging invaders, aliens and rapacious villains. Scholars, Indian and non-Indian, such as Romila Thapar, one of India's greatest historians, and Jeffrey Kripal, an Indologist, have been maligned as anti-Hindu or 'Hinduphobic' and threatened or attacked for works alleged to be disrespectful to Hinduism and Hindus.[48] Essays considered subversive and questioning of a monolithic, reductive vision of Hinduism, such as the one by Ramanujan that questions the very possibility of a single, authoritative version of the Ramayana, have been forcibly removed from university syllabi, under pressure from Hindu right-wing groups like the Vishwa Hindu Parishad (VHP). Like other visible and iconic symbols of Hinduism, the Gita has been transformed into an object of contestation between a majoritarian Hindu nationalist project and alternate imaginings of India. The text is a Kurukshetra of its own, the site of a battle between, on the one hand, those who would insist on controlling the right to determine who can interpret it and, on the other hand, those who do not see the text as the exclusive possession of one faith, group or ideology.

I believe that the Gita's significance exceeds its Hindu provenance, for its sayings have been secularised as a kind of everyday wisdom in Indian life. Yet, the Gita has also functioned historically as a hegemonic Hindu text for Indian caste minorities and non-Hindus, one that embodies not only the possibilities of liberation, emancipation and freedom but also their opposite. This is especially pronounced now, given the entrenchment of Hindu nationalism as a reason of society and state in India. I have, personally, always known the Gita in its secular ubiquity—while growing up in India, as a graduate student navigating my way in a foreign land, as a child, parent and friend, as a human being who has experienced joy and sorrow, struggle and fulfilment, failure and its opposite. But that is just my experience, which is not inseparable from my privileged caste, religious, class and cultural identity both in India and as a member of a privileged Hindu and Indian diaspora, even if I may not strongly feel the affective pull of any of these ascribed identities. In presenting my arguments about the relevance of the Gita, I do not in any way wish to suggest that it is obligatory on the part of any Indian or non-Indian to find solace, wisdom, joy or enlightenment in the book. The interpretive insights that emerge from my reading are not in any way meant to be prescriptive. With these considerations, I hope that this book makes a statement, even if modest, that the Gita predates, and hopefully will outlast, the virus of Hindu nationalism, even though it may have been co-opted by the Hindu Right for their project of violently reshaping normative ideas of Indian identity in a majoritarian Hindu mould.

2

CRISIS GLOBALISATION

The Current World Order and
How We Got Here

Globalisation on the run?

'The era of globalism is over,' says Genichi Mitsuhashi, the world's first, and so far only, person to hold a master's degree in ninja studies, though he does not provide detailed reasons for his intriguing conclusion beyond an assertion that the world is 'not global, but local'.[1] Mitsuhashi's view would seem to be intuitively borne out at this time when many aspects of our existence that are dependent on global economic, cultural and technological arrangements have been upended by the COVID-19 pandemic. Yet, even if one were to grant his claim about globalism the status of a modicum of truth, our recent ninja studies graduate, Mitsuhashi, is guilty of assuming that the local is immune from and opposed to the global. For local life almost everywhere on the surface of the earth is shaped deeply by what happens elsewhere, even if the intricate webs that connect what happens in far-flung locations are not visible. If global systems of commerce, community and communication are affected by any event, whether war, a hurricane, a public health catastrophe or an economic disaster anywhere, then the consequences are widely experienced at the local level. This is simply a function of the fact that we already live in a globalised world, even if the processes that got us here and the resulting reality have been uneven, exclusionary and violent.[2]

Whether we are in an era of globalism or localism, we find ourselves in a state of deep crisis. Life as we knew it barely a year ago—local, national or global, in person or online—is on permanent pause and is unlikely to return to that state. The most powerful proof of this altered reality lies in the interruptions to global flows of trade, technology, skilled workers, travellers and capital caused by COVID-19. The virus has impacted life on the ground everywhere, from villages and small towns to great megacities and metropolises, with not even Antarctica spared. First to rear its head in major world cities which saw travel to and from China, COVID-19 has reached previously untouched parts of rural India. A draconian shutdown imposed by the Indian government in the early phase of the spread of the virus meant that massive numbers of labourers, daily wage earners and transient workers in cities like Mumbai and Delhi were forced to return to their homes in rural India because of a loss of employment.[3] In the absence of adequate transport and support provided by the Indian state, they had to undertake long and brutal journeys by foot. The virus caused such upheavals everywhere it struck, triggering deep social dislocation, straining hospitals and morgues to their limits, creating sudden populations of refugees and armies of the unemployed. In every location, from New York to unnamed villages in nearly every continent, it was the vulnerable—the elderly, the afflicted, the poor, those working on the frontlines—who were hit the hardest.

On 17 March 2020, London Breed, the mayor of San Francisco, the city I call home, issued a shelter-in-place order that strictly limited people's movements and social interaction.[4]

In a matter of days, the order brought life in San Francisco, a vibrant, bustling and global city in every sense of the word, to a grinding halt. Justly renowned for its cosmopolitan and urbane culture, home to leading global media and technology corporations, and a major international tourist destination, the city suddenly mutated into a ghost town. Downtown San Francisco, an exciting smorgasbord of flagship designer stores, cafes and Michelin-starred restaurants, futuristic-looking offices of start-ups, and spanking new steel-and-glass buildings born of the recent tech boom, now appeared utterly forlorn. Cloaked in the same eerie silence, their sidewalks shorn of shoppers and tourists alike, bustling neighbourhoods like Valencia in the Mission District looked like settings from dystopian science fiction films like *Blade Runner*, with their storefronts boarded up and streets sprayed with graffiti and trash.

Like many cities across the US, San Francisco was also afflicted by shortages of hand sanitiser, disinfecting wipes, toilet paper and paper kitchen towels that lasted for weeks. The lines of anxious shoppers snaking around grocery stores depleted stocks of groceries as soon as they were replenished. For the first time in over twenty years of living in America, I noticed empty shelves in supermarkets as well as in the local mom-and-pop store in my neighbourhood. I was reminded of the perennial shortages of food and goods in the India of the 1980s in which I grew up, although the American idea of a shortage is remarkably different from the Indian version. Unused to seeing supermarket shelves bare, coupled with a uniquely apocalyptic strain in the American imagination, which fears that doomsday is always around the corner, Americans loaded up their SUVs and crammed their basements full with buckets of bleach, bundles of toilet paper and cans of beans.[5] Somewhat bizarrely, gun sales also shot up, possibly out of exaggerated fears that looters would break into homes to steal Bounty paper towels and carefully stashed bottles of Purell hand sanitiser.

If the immediate cause for the paucity of goods was panic buying by the freaked-out inhabitants of the city and hoarding by unscrupulous sorts looking to make a quick profit, the deeper underlying reason was the global impact of the ongoing COVID-19 pandemic. The ensuing explosion of empty store shelves across the nation possibly made the situation of scarcity appear a trifle more dire than it really was. But the shortages were real, a function of the fragility of global supply chains and bottlenecks that had clogged up the flow of trade because of the wildly divergent and globally uncoordinated responses of members of the international community to the crisis. That these disruptions in global supply chains had affected the availability of the essential products consumed by every household was cause enough for worry; more alarming was the fact that in a highly interdependent and globally integrated economy, countries like the US found themselves facing an acute shortage of essential personal protective equipment like the masks required by medical personnel and medicines like hydroxychloroquine, an immunosuppressant that had briefly seemed to show some promise among high-risk patients afflicted with the virus before medical studies revealed that the drug did not really provide any benefits. Far from acting in any coordinated way, or as part of a comity of entities, nations began a petty competitive scramble for procuring masks and securing rights from pharmaceutical companies for any successful future vaccines or treatments. Trump managed to arm-twist Narendra Modi, the Indian prime minister, into promising the US hydroxychloroquine supplies, almost immediately after Modi had grandly declared that he was banning the export of the drug to ensure Indians had priority of access to it.[6] Though the details are murky, Trump, in a brazen move, also allegedly tried to buy access to a vaccine being developed by CureVac, a German firm.[7] American manufacturers of masks, on the other hand, were selling them to the highest international bidder, while medical personnel in the US were reduced to reusing masks because of a shortage at home.[8]

The policy response to the public health crisis reflected the same pattern. Whether Sweden, the US, India, New Zealand, China or Vietnam, each nation tackled the problem in its own particular, and often stumbling, way. The policies of each government and the response of the public in each society were more a reflection of a national culture than of a global consciousness or a commitment to global responsibility. For instance, in the US, the resistance to initiatives to shut down cities or states and, more recently, the vociferous opposition to wearing masks, notably in conservative or Republican-dominated areas, has typically been couched in the language of individual rights and liberty and opposition to government overreach and tyranny.[9] The analogy is bizarre, of course; not wearing a mask is more akin to driving drunk, an act that endangers others as much or more than it does oneself. Yet, an incendiary mix of rabid right-wing media personalities like Tucker Carlson, trolls who specialise in circulating fake news, and sceptics like the rank-and-file of the anti-vaccination constituency that believes that the virus is a hoax has compounded the difficulty of getting the pandemic under control. Conspiracy theories about the 'deep state', a trope deployed by Trump to feed the constant right-wing populist frenzy that is grist to his mill, have fed the hostility to the US government's own policies.[10]

'The Paranoid Style in American Politics' is the memorable title and theme of a landmark essay by historian Richard Hofstatder, in which he describes the inclination of Americans to believe in utterly unrealistic theories about the machinations of secret forces controlling their lives.[11] What makes this peculiarly American style of common-sense political understanding important, according to Hofstatder, is not that there are vast numbers of paranoid people who believe and spread such theories. Rather, as Hofstatder notes, 'it is the use of paranoid modes of expression by more or less normal people that makes the phenomenon significant.'[12] In an almost perfect illustration of Hofstadter's thesis, large numbers of Americans have found an ideal object for paranoia in the story of the virus, in its mysterious origins, in the unpredictable logic of the factors determining its spread and, equally, in the responses of local and state authorities to the rapidly proliferating cases of infections and deaths resulting from it. By one account, the number of rumours and conspiracies related to the coronavirus exceed 2,000, and an astonishing 25 per cent of American adults think there is some truth to the conspiracy theory that the virus is the result of a planned project.[13]

The internet, the cauldron in which such conspiracy theories are fed and kept boiling, has given a fresh boost of energy to the paranoid style of American politics, with online paranoia representing a special and new form of the malaise. Social media platforms, and Facebook in particular, have played a central role in incubating and facilitating the spread of such conspiracies. The polarising nature of social media only exacerbates the speed and scale of false information, readily lapped up by willing believers.[14] The 'infodemic' of false news about the virus, as one journalist put it, parallels the spread of the virus itself in scale and reach.[15] In an alarming development in the same vein, COVID-19 conspiracy theories have now merged with the online QAnon movement, 'a wide-ranging, unfounded conspiracy theory that says that President Trump is waging a secret war against elite Satan-worshipping paedophiles in government, business and the media'.[16] With widespread suspicion among Americans regarding the motives of their own government and their penchant for seeing the presence of shadowy international cabals out to subvert American greatness—much like the trope of the 'foreign hand' in socialist India that was conveniently blamed by political parties for every shortcoming, failing or scandal—it was unlikely that the majority of Americans would have responded to any public health or policy measure recommended by a global body like the World Health Organization. Likewise, for the average American who saw the shutting down of businesses, bans on gatherings of large numbers of people, and orders not to invite people over to their homes as violations of their fundamental and constitutionally guaranteed rights, what China, Singapore or New Zealand did was utterly irrelevant, even if these nations had managed to get the initial outbreak of the virus under control.[17]

In the US, dog whistle attempts to blame China, President Donald Trump's description of COVID-19 as a Chinese disease, and the outbreak of anti-Asian racist attacks showed that along with the pandemic and the malaise of fake news, widespread xenophobic sentiment was a third plague afflicting the body politic, mixed in with the widespread anxieties and fears engendered by the virus.[18] In a classically irrational reaction, people everywhere seemed to assume that those familiar to them, whether as family members, friends or inhabitants of their local communities, would somehow be less prone to infecting them with the virus. The unknown stranger became marked as the embodiment of danger, and the greater the distance between the stranger and the self, the greater the danger he or she represented. This likely explains why, as cities reopened after lockdowns, people did not comply with rules to avoid congregating in large numbers, and promptly proceeded to meet family members and friends at social events, barbecues and picnics. In the American imagination, the virus was initially associated with China and, then, with the cosmopolitan, ethnically diverse and global city of New York, at first the most severely afflicted region of the US. In right-wing media rhetoric, New York's diversity, population density and liberal outlook—all hallmarks of a thriving global metropolis and the product of a remarkably long and rich history of immigration—were responsible for its plight.[19] The racist discourse, reprehensible in itself, was made worse by the fact that ethnic and racial minorities and migrants in New York were the worst hit by the pandemic, a pattern that repeated itself across the US and in countries around the world, from Sweden to Lebanon, India to China.[20] Some of the more petty-minded behaviours in response to the crisis, such as suspicion of outsiders and the ostracism or exclusion of populations seen as possible carriers of the virus, were not unique to the American context, manifesting themselves as much in globally connected areas as in remote rural locations across the world. A turn towards inwardness and a hardening of the distinction between 'us' and 'them' emerged visibly as an unfortunate consequence and side effect of the policy measures of containment taken by official and state authorities in many a country.

Such developments seem to portend a rapid slowing down of the generally steady progress of globalisation over the last few decades and, at the very least, compel us to ask some important questions. Are these the first steps of the retreat of globalisation; a return to the high noon of the sovereign nation-state and the hard border? Have we reached a kind of tipping point, which has been slowly building up for a while, and from here on, will we witness a receding of the tide of globalisation? Although the global financial crisis of 2007–2008 did not halt the march of economic globalisation for any lengthy period of time, the crisis took a permanent toll on many of the poor and vulnerable. Despite the boom in the 2010s that followed the recovery, income inequality significantly worsened in the decade, another failure of the promise of globalisation to lift all boats. In my neck of the woods, so to speak, in just the last several years, highly prosperous locations across the Bay Area, including San Francisco, Berkeley and Mountain View, have seen parallel cities of the homeless take root along with a frenzy of new residential and commercial construction, escalating home prices and a general increase in prosperity. The contrast between the haves and have-nots is starkly inescapable, the latter living in rows of mobile vehicles parked permanently on city streets, sheltering in tents that are clustered together in parks, under flyovers and off highways, or just hunkering down day after day on sidewalks or in recessed doorways. The Bay Area has also seen many middle-income and lower-income inhabitants of its cities evicted and displaced despite generally good protections for renters in several cities in the region. The chief cause of the changed political economy of the area is the boom in the technology sector, which has resulted in massive flows of capital into the region and an influx of wealthy professionals hired by Google, Salesforce, Amazon, Facebook and the like. These changes, in turn, have led to soaring rents and considerable increases in the cost of living, pushing out large numbers of residents of the cities into distant suburbs or away from the state altogether.[21] Those who now stand to lose their jobs because of the impact of COVID-19 on their industries will be adding to a sizeable population of the disenfranchised in the Bay Area, who have already been living in a condition of precariousness. The increase in inequality threatens to lead to more disaffection with globalisation as the larger, enabling structural framework for this state of affairs.

Trump himself has stoked anti-globalisation sentiments and benefited from them politically, despite the fact that he continues to profit handsomely from globalisation. His anti-globalisation measures have been successful in tapping into the nationalist sentiment of a disenfranchised, largely White, non-college-educated population that perceives itself as excluded from the benefits that old and new elites, minorities and skilled migrant workers in STEM (science, technology, engineering and mathematics) fields have reaped. Globalisation, associated in the popular American imagination with open borders, free trade agreements and an influx of skilled migrants from India and China who very visibly appear comfortably off, has been an easy target, one that Trump has fully exploited in his protectionist rhetoric. However, while Trump's theatrics of rejecting globalisation to play to his support base may have been strategically amplified to exploit the isolationist and nationalist turn brought on by the global pandemic, they have not led to a resurgence of US manufacturing at the cost of China. His populist measures, including the imposition of tariffs on goods from a number of the trading partners of the US, have not stopped leading US-headquartered technology firms from proceeding with their blistering pace of expansion in several countries. Yet, Trump's actions have been symbolically powerful, enabling him to claim that unlike his adversaries, and even colleagues in the Republican party, he does put America over principles of free trade.[22]

In a nutshell, this is the contradiction that we are living through everywhere at this moment. Our way of life is too deeply dependent on the processes of globalisation for us to extricate ourselves from it in any meaningful manner—yet, globalisation appears threatening enough that we seem to instinctively recoil from it, seeking shelter in a more stable, simpler way of life. The problem, of course, is that inasmuch as we seek a nostalgic return to some earlier model of social life, that longed-for world is likely a romantic idealisation that may never have existed. But even otherwise, the turn inward, of which one prime example is Brexit or Britain's decision to leave the European Union, does not necessarily mean that we are witnessing a shift away from the drive towards further global integration. In the aftermath of Brexit, Britain may no longer employ as many Indian-origin doctors or migrants from Europe, but it will still have to trade with India and continental Europe. Global problems like the COVID-19 pandemic and climate change require innovative global solutions and cooperation across borders on an unprecedented scale, and international health organisations, nation-states and corporations are trying to work out such arrangements. Global technologies like Zoom have enabled employees of corporations, universities and governments to work effectively within and across national borders without being constrained by distance. The technology sector, dependent on skilled migrant labour, reliant on global markets and constantly seeking expansion into new markets, has strongly benefited from the pandemic. Online platforms, products and tools have helped people with their work, leisure activities and social relationships. While we are seeing a rejection of some aspects of globalisation, we are also perhaps simultaneously witnessing the unconscious adoption and endorsement of a range of other global practices, a redefinition of priorities within a globalised zeitgeist and a rearrangement of the architecture of globalisation. A brief tour of some of the meanings of globalisation can help illuminate and contextualise what the current situation portends for some of its possible future directions.

Globalisation: A brief sketch

The term globalisation is typically used in two ways: as a historically specific condition that emerges at a distinct point of time in world history; and as a process or dynamic to describe the logic of a particular world order, such as the one we currently find ourselves in. In its simplest sense, globalisation refers to any action that involves travelling across or transcending some natural boundary of limit, such as the political boundary of the modern nation-state. According to Lechner and Boli, the editors of a significant anthology on globalisation, the term 'refers to the processes by which more people across large distances become connected in more and different ways'.[23] Lule, the author of the textbook that I use for my undergraduate 'Media in a Global World' course, proposes an even more basic working definition: 'globalisation is anytime anyone does anything anywhere across borders.'[24] Globalisation is not just a one-way flow from West to non-West though it is often criticised—or, in some cases, valorised—as the equivalent of Westernisation or Americanisation. Even if the West, or America, is a dominant player in charting the course of globalisation, it is hard to conceive of a globalised world without China and, in recent years, India. 'Made in China' is likely one of the most common bits of information one is likely to see on products that one purchases in the US and, increasingly, in India, notwithstanding the political tensions between China and these countries. Generic drugs manufactured in India help communities in the US, Brazil and South Africa. Cinema from Mexico, Iran or Spain finds audiences of cinephiles everywhere. Indian Hindi-language popular cinema or Bollywood films are wildly popular in Nigeria and West Asia, and in the decades following Indian independence were eagerly watched in the Soviet Union.[25] It is hard to find a small town in America that does not have a Chinese restaurant, just as sushi is now part of the international palate.

The basic definition offered by Lule and the slightly more elaborate one offered by Lechner and Boli conceptualise globalisation as an impulse or action, not necessarily unique to one historical era, that has expressed itself with varying force in different time periods. Yet, of course, for things to happen across borders, people need to be able to travel across them and be able to communicate instantly across vast distances. They need to be able to buy and sell things in countries other than their own and they need to enjoy food, music and sport from other cultures, incorporating elements of the same into their own lives, cultural forms and practices. These kinds of global exchanges have been made possible by technological inventions and advances, whether the printing press, telegraph, satellite television or the internet—though not necessarily determined by them in any simple or direct way—that have emerged at different points in the trajectory of recorded human history. Economic and political factors, whether the impulse of religious or imperial expansion, the motivation to discover the source of spices or find fantastic lands and treasures, or the will to dominate and civilise supposedly inferior cultures, have also facilitated the spread of globalisation.

Historians, sociologists and other scholars of globalisation tend to differ in their views on whether any particular period of history has been more significant than others in generating the conditions that have led to the globalised world of the present. Historians consider the roots of globalisation to lie variously in the pre-modern era of the great trade routes that spanned the sea and land, the age of early modern exploration and discovery, the era of European colonialism and imperialism, or the high noon of the industrial revolution in the Western world of the nineteenth century. These differing accounts amount to a range of scholarly perspectives on what may be called a long history of globalisation.[26] In the sense in which it is more commonly used, however, the term refers to its shorter, more recent history—that of the accelerated exchange of knowledge, information, people, culture and capital across the world that kicked off in roughly the second half of the twentieth century. These exchanges, uneven as they have been, include the movement across national boundaries of highly skilled migrant workers, tourists, and undocumented migrants and refugees seeking to make a better life in distant places. They include the unfettered movement of capital across the borders of nation-states. They encompass the transportation, circulation and consumption of goods and services in different national settings, whether material objects like clothes, electronics, ceramics and furniture, or digital products like YouTube videos or films on Netflix. They include political conflict and political cooperation, the fruitful exchange and cross-fertilisation of some ideas and the rejection of others.

Digital transmissions of culture, capital, information and knowledge, in particular, are a crucial part of the rise of the 'network society', in sociologist Manuel Castells's well-known theorisation, having transformed the nature of work, entertainment, communication and social interaction.[27] The internet is the most powerful symbol and vector of the network society, and Castells views it as responsible for this new paradigm of global social organisation. Castells describes the global space or structure enabled by the internet as a *space of flows*, a metaphor that accurately captures the dynamic, intricate and complex nature of the dizzying economic, social, cultural, political, technological and ideological entanglements of a global world.[28] It is this form of globalisation, in the second, more proximate sense, that we experience more intimately and powerfully than the longer arc of globalisation, although, of course, the longer histories of globalisation have provided the basis for its more recent trajectories. And, to be sure, our ways of life are also influenced by the longer histories of globalisation, to the point where we don't recognise the traces of those histories in how we eat, dress, talk, think and behave.

In his pithy book on globalisation, *Runaway World*, the noted sociologist Anthony Giddens draws attention to the remarkable transformation of the word 'globalisation' from obscurity to ubiquity.[29] A little-used term for much of the second half of the twentieth century, by 1990 the word had entered the lexicon of public conversation. In the India of the early 1990s, following the process of economic 'liberalisation' or the set of reforms inaugurated in 1991 aimed at integrating the Indian economy into the world economy, the word 'globalisation' popped up with remarkable frequency in the English-language print media. Articles breathlessly and relentlessly spoke of a global India, India finally entering the global economy, India embarking on the path of becoming the next global superpower, and the like. India, in this narrative, had previously been isolated from a rapidly globalising world, and had been denied a chance to play its natural role in shaping the future of the global world order. Now, it would rightfully take its place alongside first-world titans in charting the course of this brave new world, dutifully proceeding to fulfil its destiny. Some three decades later, it is debatable whether India has arrived as global superpower or is still stuck in limbo; an emerging power that will never quite fully emerge, much like a butterfly only half out of its cocoon and unable to fully wriggle free. What is undeniable, though, is the transformation of Indian economy and society since the onset of liberalisation and globalisation in the early 1990s.[30] Though some classes and sections of society, such as the professional and emerging middle classes and the wealthy industrial-political class, have captured the lion's share of the gains, the impact of globalisation and liberalisation, both positive and negative, has been felt across Indian society, in sectors as wide ranging as education, finance, Hindi cinema, life insurance, automobiles and the media. Indian politicians may still wear khadi kurta pajamas and cotton sarees but the dark glasses and watches that they sport to accessorise these humble fabrics are made by sought-after designer and luxury brands like Bulgari and Hublot.

In one account of the story of globalisation, advances in media and communication technologies in the 1960s, such as satellite television, have been key drivers of the phenomenon. The most well-known evangelist of this perspective is the Canadian futurist Marshall McLuhan, the man credited with articulating the concept of the 'global village' to explain the impact of electronic media in bringing people across the world closer to each other.[31] Electronic media, in McLuhan's view, has ushered in a radically altered social reality as well a new cognitive sensibility to comprehend this new reality. Globalisation, as Anthony Giddens points out, has often been treated as no more than its economic dimension by both its advocates and detractors. Giddens argues that this view represents a fundamental misunderstanding of globalisation, and that its cultural and social dimensions, such as its impact on ideas of the family and tradition, as well as its relationship to developments in information and communication technologies, need to be seen as equally significant in terms of their influence on the world. Globalisation affects these non-economic aspects of human existence directly, and not just through the second-order consequences of economic change.

Though precipitated by the COVID-19 pandemic, the roadblocks to globalisation and the opposition to it are not trends that have emerged from nowhere. Resistance to, and criticism of, globalisation by a diverse group of constituencies have been constant features of its history, shadowing its path from early days. Writing of the demonstrations against the World Trade Organization (WTO), such as during the landmark 1999 Seattle protests, the journalist Gregory Scrugg notes that the delegates of the WTO were faced by 'an estimated 50,000 to 70,000 protesters who feared the ill effects of globalization—a coalition including environmentalists, labor unions, indigenous groups, international NGOs, and students'.[32] Ironically, the opposition to globalisation, such as the regular protests at the World Economic Forum and the demonstrations against the WTO were themselves global events, mobilising protesters from many countries and garnering attention the world over.[33] The World Social Forum, an answer of sorts to the World Economic Forum, brings critics of globalisation from all across the world together in a single location. Similarly, following the invention of the World Wide Web and the Web 2.0 revolution in communications and media, anti-globalisation activists have used the same tools and technologies as those they consider their adversaries.

For at least the last two decades, the entry of US-headquartered multinational corporations like McDonald's and Kentucky Fried Chicken, seen as symbols of an American cultural imperialism that now calls itself by the name of globalisation, have elicited strong reactions in countries ranging from India to France and Chile to Iraq.[34] Scholars, including those who generally see globalisation as a force for good, have long sounded alarm bells about its role in increasing economic inequality and exacerbating the digital divide between those who are tapped into global information networks and those who are left out of them.[35] The economic benefits provided by globalisation have not always translated into social stability or cultural enrichment for many people within and across societies. In the Indian context, economically vulnerable groups and senior citizens now have to contend with the vagaries of a market-based economy, often disproportionately bearing the risks of such a system without being able to avail of its benefits. And while the charge of Western or US media being an instrument of cultural imperialism may seem a trifle exaggerated, it is worth noting that even a resilient cultural industry like Bollywood has had to adapt to the pressures and influences of Hollywood. This may not be an entirely bad thing for Bollywood, with regard to production values, technical competence or aesthetic sensibility, but for other cultural forms, whether the art of indigenous communities, labour-intensive artisanal techniques, or Indian classical music, the challenges of competing with multiplayer internet-based games, the American music and film industries and international television shows available on streaming services are formidable.

Crisis globalisation

I propose that what seems to be a rejection of globalisation or, at least, a retreat from it is in fact a new normative condition of a phenomenon that I term 'crisis globalisation'. Some degree of uncertainty, instability and unpredictability is inherent in globalisation. After all, a phenomenon that is dependent on and, in turn, powers massive movements of people, information, ideas, technological products, money and financial products, will necessarily be dynamic and subject to some degree of instability. The idea of globalisation being in flux or in crisis has been explored by several commentators in academia, business, policymaking and the like.[36] The end of globalisation has been repeatedly pronounced as well—and quite loudly in the last year.[37] The point that I am making here is different from these perspectives: my argument takes as axiomatic the fact that globalisation will endure while proposing that the experience of globalisation will involve a significantly higher degree of uncertainty and instability for a much larger cross section of humanity than before.

The crises we are experiencing at present, then, whether climate change or the COVID-19 pandemic, do not represent a reversal of globalisation or even a body blow to it. Rather, they signal that we are in the midst of a new and distinct phase of globalisation. This form of globalisation will almost certainly lead to a reformulation of the structural logic of globalisation as we have known it till now—changing the terms on which countries negotiate free trade, ushering in new and effective models of cooperation on some issues like global public health, but retreating from collaboration on others. We may be able to control or manage some of the problems we face, for example, by finding a range of effective treatments for COVID-19, while getting other difficulties, like the existential crisis of climate change or the political problems in West Asia, under control may be harder. The condition of crisis globalisation is likely to persist even when we manage to return to a generally more stable state of affairs. This has to do not just with the turmoil caused by COVID-19 but also with a somewhat longer history of crisis that has haunted globalisation like an unwanted guest or an obdurate ghost that simply refuses to leave.

Beyond scholarly and policy critiques and a history of anti-globalisation activism, the ideas, practices and policies associated with globalisation have appeared to be on the proverbial back foot since well before the COVID-19 pandemic started burning through the world population. During the last decade or thereabouts, in country after country, we have seen the evisceration of international initiatives to ensure more inclusive policies for workers, migrants and refugees, the weakening of multilateral institutions and efforts to address issues pertaining to climate change, human rights and democracy, and the undermining of a commitment to a sensibility of openness. The retreat from globalisation has been accompanied by the rise of authoritarian leaders whose parochial ideologies have fanned the flames of xenophobia and played to majoritarian nationalist fears and impulses about foreigners and minorities. Leaders such as India's Narendra Modi, Hungary's Viktor Orbán, Turkey's Recep Erdoğan and America's Donald Trump have all loudly spewed the rhetoric of cultural exceptionalism, rejecting the idea that the nation-state is bound by any commitment to a larger global community or to international standards of human rights. In a vicious spiral, these developments, in turn, have further attenuated the spread of the more salutary aspects of globalisation and prevented its benefits from reaching a wide section of the population in each of these countries.

Tempting as it may be to reach such a conclusion, these changes should not be taken as confirmation of the naive thesis of 'the clash of civilisations', advanced by Samuel Huntington close to three decades ago. Huntingon's theory proposed that globalisation would lead to a battle between seven or eight unique civilisational entities, each with its own distinct characteristics, namely, the Western, Confucian, Islamic, Japanese, Hindu, Slavic-Orthodox and African.[38] Huntington's central argument is, at once, reductive and ethnocentric, unable to break out of the trap of Western exceptionalism and superiority as much as it is unable to conceptualise of cultures beyond essentialist cultural, behavioural and psychological characteristics that apparently hold true for huge numbers of people. What we are seeing in the realm of globalisation is neither such a clash nor the inability of the rest of the world to accept supposedly superior Western values that are deserving of universal adoption. The unmitigated disaster of the US-led 'war on terror', the resurgence of xenophobia in western Europe, including its ugly heritage of anti-Semitism, Trump's policies regarding undocumented migrants and his encouragement of White supremacy, and the Little Englander mean-spiritedness of Boris Johnson's bumbling out of Europe should put paid to any claim of the superiority of Western civilisational values or the robustness of liberal Western values and institutions.

My argument is that the changes reflective of crisis globalisation are the product of a confluence of events and developments in disparate spheres, each with its own historical trajectory. These include the environmental degradation caused by rapacious economic and industrial development, the rise of terrorism, the US-led wars in retaliation to the attacks of 11 September 2001 and the unexpectedly complicated impact of social media on democracy and civic life. We are currently confronted by a global pandemic, the COVID-19 crisis, which, as of the end of 2020, had killed almost two million people.[39] The spread of COVID-19—a scenario that till now has been the stuff of apocalyptic films and fiction, the morbid fantasies of doomsayers, and what have turned out to be the prescient worries of scientists and technologists—brought life to a standstill across vast swathes of the world. An early, nightmarish phase of exponentially increasing infections, rapidly climbing daily deaths, overburdened hospitals struggling to keep up with severely afflicted patients and shortages of medical equipment gave way to the eerie silences of suddenly forlorn cities, plummeting job losses, shuttered economies and a general feeling of existential dread in which time itself blurred into an inchoate expanse without beginning or end. A brief period of attempting to return to normalcy saw a rapid spike in cases in many parts of the world, including in countries that had appeared to have bested the threat, resulting in a second round of lockdowns and the same apocalyptic scenes of illness, strained hospitals and morgues with no space for the bodies of the deceased. The fear endemic to the surrealist theatre in which we have found ourselves as unwitting actors this last year has been compounded by the fact that we have had to confront an unknown enemy—one that has continually surprised, eluded and frustrated us. Armed now with several vaccines that, against all odds, have proven to be remarkably effective, we can hope for a semblance of normalcy and dream of the consolations of routine again, but the virus remains far from conquered. Waiting to go back to the world we knew but a year ago is like waiting for Godot.

The third of the coronavirus illnesses to plague the world in the last decade, after SARS and MERS, and so far the worst, the COVID-19 contagion is, in part, an environmental consequence of the untrammelled economic and industrial development on which our modern society is founded.[40] While its exact origins remain unclear, it is known that the virus jumped species to humans from an animal, possibly, though not certainly, a bat, snake or pangolin.[41] The immediate source of the infection of a human may have been a wet market in Wuhan, China, but the broader condition of possibility for the interspecies transmission of the virus is the devastation of animal habitats, which has brought bats, known carriers of viruses dangerous to humans, into proximity with the latter.[42] The erosion of natural barriers that somehow worked to protect humans from zoonotic viruses is a result of 'development', a kind of collective stand-in term for the social, economic and technological processes that have created the modern world, carving it into a rich, developed, largely Western world and a poorer, developing, largely non-Western remnant.

Development is central to modern nation-building and to modernity itself, a project that all nations are expected to undertake as a kind of secular theological obligation, to ensure economic progress, leaps in education and healthcare, better standards of living for their citizens and, ideally, the establishment and strengthening of democratic institutions that protect the rights, well-being and dignity of those citizens. Yet, modernity, whether it has been linked to democracy or not, whether capitalist or socialist, in the developed or the developing world, has come at a massive cost, perhaps even a Faustian bargain. Idealistic conceptions of a pre-modern world are, no doubt, politically regressive romantic fictions, with their endorsements of hierarchical social orders, opposition to rational forms of knowledge and antipathy to egalitarianism. But the project of modernity has created its own forms of violence and exploitation, engendered its own hierarchies and, crucially, has placed humans in a radically exploitative and adversarial relationship with nature. Modern technology, Martin Heidegger suggests in an illuminating essay, frames the world according to the logic of a 'standing-reserve', a potential source to be exploited.[43] A river now becomes reframed as a means to the end of a dam that is a source of energy to serve human beings. The event of the Holocaust, the sociologist

Zygmunt Bauman argues, embodied all the cherished principles of modernity: 'to conceive of such an idea separately from the engineering approach to society, the belief in the artificiality of social order, institution of expertise and the practice of scientific management of human setting and interaction. For these reasons, *the exterminatory version of anti-Semitism ought to be seen as a thoroughly modern phenomenon; that is, something which could occur only in an advanced state of modernity.*'[44] Gandhi, in his radical text *Hind Swaraj*, offered a similarly trenchant critique of Western modernity, significantly centred on its political and technological aspects.[45] For Gandhi, a technological development like the railways had disrupted the natural rhythms of human life, which were as dependent on the limitations of humans as on their abilities. In providing humans with a means for overcoming their limitations, technology, in Gandhi's view, paved the way for the abasement of what was human about humans, dislocating them from their organic place in the world. In destroying the relationship of the self with nature, technology separated the self from itself.

If the war against an invisible, microscopic enemy preoccupies us now, the world for the last two decades has been enmeshed in wars against itself, where the enemy has been the human, especially the human who is visibly different, whether in terms of culture, religion, race, ethnicity or nationality. The invasions of Afghanistan and Iraq by a US-led coalition, in violation of international law, in the aftermath of the terrorist attacks of 11 September 2001 on America, have resulted in widespread devastation in both countries and destabilised the entire arc from the Khyber Pakhtunkhwa province of Pakistan to the fringe of West Asia. During the same period, Islamist fundamentalist groups like ISIS and Lashkar-e-Taiba have launched a spate of horrific terrorist attacks in countries and cities across the globe, including Paris, London, Barcelona and Mumbai. Spectacular in their savagery, these attacks have clearly been meant to psychologically maim and terrify as well as take lives.

After the fall of the Berlin Wall in 1989 and the collapse of communism, a common view held that we were at the 'end of history', in the sense that there were no major ideological divides left that could cleave the world anymore.[46] In the words of Francis Fukuyama, credited with coining the phrase, the conquest over communism signalled 'the end-point of mankind's ideological evolution and the universalization of Western liberal democracy as the final form of human government'.[47] The liberal democratic nation-state, in this view, was now firmly and definitively established as the axiomatic political unit of world society, with the spirit of history itself ensuring its inevitable spread.[48] Fukuyama's misplaced confidence and somewhat premature pronouncement was based on a wildly utopian hope, itself anchored in a naive reading of Hegel. But even sceptics of Fukuyama's theory could not have imagined or anticipated the events of 11 September 2001 and the new order that would begin to take shape following that radical moment of rupture. Far from finding itself at the end of history, the world some two decades later finds itself in a new, and unfamiliar, epoch, one marked by instability, violence, the rise of the surveillance state and dangerously unpredictable natural catastrophes caused by global warming. States have become more powerful against the individual and their respective citizenries, yet remain helpless against the cataclysmic vagaries of nature or unpredictable acts of violence by individuals or groups who are motivated by radical ideological causes, whether Islamic fundamentalism, Hindu nationalism or White supremacy.

The new world order has also been marked by a radical fear of difference, of those who speak, look and seem to behave differently from majorities, from those who signify a 'normal' way of life, or those taken to be the natural citizens of a country or inhabitants of a place. The fear of those who are different from an assumed norm, whether Muslims in India, Ahmadis in Pakistan, Uighurs in China or African Americans in the US, is not new to humanity, but it has reared its head with an unexpected viciousness in the post-9/11 sociopolitical landscape. The sense of permanently being under siege, fed and fully exploited by democratic states and dictatorial strongmen alike, in conjunction with economic insecurity and a rise in inequality, has led to an alarming rise in xenophobia and anti-minority violence. It has been accompanied by a resurgence of a narrow, insecure nationalism everywhere from the US to India, from Turkey to Hungary and setbacks to democracy through a centralisation of power, weakening of institutions that hold authorities accountable, attacks on the press and a culture of demonising dissent as unpatriotic and treasonous.

The authors of this new global rulebook are many: Donald Trump, whose unexpected election victory in 2016 was prefaced and followed by a rash of assaults on racial minorities across the US; Vladimir Putin, whose continuing chokehold on Russia is tantamount to a slow strangling of democracy; Hindu nationalist hardliner Narendra Modi, whose sweep into power in India in 2014 was promptly followed by a barrage of attacks by the Hindu Right on minorities, dissenters and critics of his government. Europe's demons, never entirely buried, have reared their ugly heads in the form of a resurgence of incidents of antisemitism and White supremacist expressions of rage and hostility against Muslims and other immigrants and refugees from West Asia.[49] The challenges of integration encountered by these communities and the cultural anxiety that migrant populations from Syria, South Asia, Turkey or Algeria often evoke in majority groups in European countries conjure up the spectre of deeply racialised assumptions at work in these societies about who counts as the ideal, genuine or authentic citizen.

I had the unfortunate experience of witnessing this first-hand, when, in 2016, a few months before the shock election of Donald Trump in the US presidential election, a White woman screamed racial abuse at my son and me in the aisle of a supermarket that I frequently visit in San Francisco, a city that prides itself on its radically liberal and inclusive culture. Regardless of whether Trump's ugly rhetoric in the months leading up to his election actively promoted and led to a fresh outpouring of racism or simply gave a go-ahead to racists who had been barely holding their tongues all this while, his victory dramatically lowered the bar for what was considered acceptable behaviour and speech in public. Sentiments that would have rightly been considered beyond the pale soon ceased to shock, whether in the statements uttered by politicians, the pronouncements of media pundits, or the rants and conspiracies mouthed by lay Trump supporters on social media. Assertions of pride in White identity, which are nothing other than barely concealed declarations of White supremacist ideology, overt hostility to and racism against African Americans, attacks on minorities of colour on grounds of nationalism and the pervasive incidents of American citizens or immigrants of Mexican, Indian, Chinese and Filipino origin being told they did not really belong to America—all of this steadily became part of a new normal.[50]

As the US grappled with the toll of COVID-19, cities across the nation also saw widespread protests against police brutality, following the death of George Floyd, a forty-six-year-old African American man, at the hands of the Minneapolis police on 25 May 2020.[51] Violence against African Americans is, tragically, as old as the American republic, with the stain of slavery indelibly marked on the nation since its birth. But the Trump presidency saw a relentless stoking of the banal racism that characterises American life, the US president's efforts reaping results in the form of White supremacist rallies, the emergence and newfound legitimacy of the alt-Right and an alarming rise in racist hate speech online. This was the spark which lit the fire, with the long-standing problems of racial profiling and police violence against African Americans provoking a national outpouring of outrage. The virulence of the new racism of the Trump era may not have directly caused the death of George Floyd, but no doubt played a role in contributing to it. The US was convulsed with protests, mostly peaceful but with enough incidents of violence to warrant curfews in many of America's major cities. For a week around the end of May, San Francisco city residents were under orders to stay indoors from 8 p.m. to 5 a.m., a situation reminiscent of the India of the 1980s and 1990s in which I came of age. Though some protesters were guilty of smashing stores and looting, the violence was also traced to White nationalists and supremacists seeking to disrupt the protests and provoke the police into responding aggressively to peaceful protesters.[52] That these fires were fanned by the US president through social media should give us pause about claims that the internet and social media have strengthened community and connection, an assertion that is central to the self-congratulatory rhetoric of Silicon Valley culture and the self-image of forums like Twitter and Facebook.

A similar story has played out for the last six and a half years in India, since the election in 2014 of Narendra Modi, the hard-line Hindu leader of the majoritarian Hindu nationalist BJP. Modi secured power with an astonishing majority, a feat that he would go on to repeat in the next general election that followed in 2019. Modi, his right-hand man, Amit Shah, extremist leaders like Ajay Bisht—who goes by the moniker Yogi Adityanath, and currently holds the post of chief minister of Uttar Pradesh, the northern Indian state—a number of Hindu right-wing groups, including well-known players like the VHP and Bajrang Dal, as well as new, bit players that have mushroomed overnight, have all contributed to the relentless climate of anxiety and fear under which Indian minorities have to live. Terrorised by vigilante assaults and mob lynchings, accused of disloyalty to the nation and subject to routine humiliations, minorities, in particular Dalits and Muslims, have found themselves under constant threat, whether in the abusive spaces of Twitter that are dominated by Hindu right-wing trolls or on the streets of India's villages, small towns and large metros.[53] And, as has been the case with White supremacists in the US, social media platforms and networks, especially Facebook, WhatsApp and Twitter, have been used to deadly effect by the Hindu Right.[54]

Our world, then, is not quite Marshall McLuhan's somewhat romantic idea of the global village—a single community brought together by revolutions in electronic communication.[55] It is not quite the haven of cosmopolitanism outlined in Kant's vision of world society nor the utopia envisioned by the cheerleaders of the World Wide Web, in which differences of race, class, gender and national origin are whisked away into nothingness by the virtual nature of the internet.[56] Globalisation has not succeeded in guaranteeing more people across the world greater opportunities, stability and security, even if, in the view of its most ardent advocates, it has led to a significant alleviation of extreme poverty.[57] If it has improved the life chances of many, globalisation has also forced others into a position of chronic insecurity.

The seductive notion of the world as a global village, even if simplistic, captures one small truth, though: that our lives are deeply connected, even if not quite in the salubrious and rosy manner that McLuhan had predicted and hoped for. The ongoing COVID-19 pandemic, the global financial crisis of 2007–2008 that was triggered by bets on subprime mortgages in the American housing market, and the terrorist attacks that have scarred so many of the great cities of the world during the last two decades have all driven home the fact that in the age of globalisation our fates are intertwined in unfathomable ways that manifest themselves in unpredictable forms. The natural immunity to the economic and political actions of other nations provided by the isolationism of the Cold War era and the monopoly of the nation-state over the flow of information, goods and even ideas is no longer a feasible reality. A decision by a group of traders in London can effectively erase someone's pension fund halfway across the world. A cyberattack on key internet sites can throw a spanner into the working day of millions of people. A terrorist attack by a group like Al-Qaeda reverberates across the globe, through the lives that it claims, the actions it compels states to take in response, and through the other radicalised individuals and terrorist groups that it inspires.

By no means am I suggesting that globalisation or, arguably, its most powerful symbol, the internet, have had no benefits or are largely responsible for miring the world in this darkness. Far from it. Aside from the naiveté and incoherence of such a claim, part of the challenge in understanding, let alone addressing, the economic, social, cultural or political effects of globalisation or the impact of the internet is the fact that their positive attributes are so closely tied to their negative ones. The ease of international travel for much of the world's population across much of the globe for tourism, business or education and the economic interdependence of major economic powers were both contributing factors to the wildfire-like spread of the COVID-19 virus everywhere from December 2019 to March 2020, before countries temporarily closed their borders. The ability of labour to move across national boundaries in common markets like the European Union, a source of economic prosperity for countries like Germany and Britain, and the demand for highly skilled workers in technology in the US are also a cause of resentment against foreigners in these countries. The unprecedented flows of information, data, media and cultural products made possible by the internet have been accompanied by the rise of fake news, conspiracy theories, the manipulation of democratic processes by troll farms and the unethical monetisation of countless aspects of our lives by large technology firms.

For example, any changes in Facebook's algorithms, user interface or design deeply affect how inhabitants are presented with and consume information, what information surfaces to the fore on their screens and what kinds of information enter the public sphere—from the smallest local networks to conversations that circulate in global space.[58] With 2.6 billion active users, who in turn are connected with more people through various other networks, Facebook is able to affect the lives of a truly mind-boggling number of people. The social media platform's policies regarding what kinds of speech it allows to be posted and shared on its platform, which are determined by its leadership in the US, have had a strong impact on everyday political and social relations as well as on formal political events like elections in many countries. The most well-known example of the abuse of Facebook in this regard is the generally accepted fact of Russian interference in the US 2016 elections and the subsequent worry that this would be repeated in the 2020 elections in the country.[59] Fake news on WhatsApp, the social networking application owned by Facebook, has been a scourge in countries like Brazil and India, playing the same role as it has in the US, in mobilising and empowering political extremists.[60] In a more ominous manifestation of their power, these platforms have been used to incite violence against minorities in India, Myanmar and Sri Lanka.[61]

Given that the positive and negative aspects of globalisation are deeply related, it is not possible to simply pluck out and retain the good about globalisation while discarding the bad. And given that the economic, political and social structures of the world that we inhabit have been significantly shaped by the dynamics of globalisation, it is not a process that can be undone such that the world resets to an earlier prelapsarian pre-globalised state. The phenomenon of crisis globalisation itself has already resulted in some changes that are likely to persist, whether at the level of the individual or that of the state and beyond. Crisis globalisation, for instance, has transformed the logic of warfare by state and non-state actors. In the realm of selfhood, public and private, thanks to the highly mediated, quasi-public nature of reflection, expression and communication brought about by social media, we have been confronted with the limits of our certitudes and the fallacious nature of our assumptions about human behaviour. The explosion of forms of self-definition in global virtual spaces tells us that our received truths about being human cannot accommodate those expressions of identity that subvert norms about national belonging, gender or the body. Our economic destinies as inhabitants of particular countries are that much more exposed to what happens elsewhere now. In terms of geopolitical realities, lives in many parts of the world, fragile at the best of times, now face new dangers such as unmanned drones that can be controlled remotely from a bunker in Utah. These realities compel us to think of what it means to live with uncertainty, in conditions of precariousness or war, literal and metaphorical, how to recognise and respect difference, and how to behave, make decisions and believe—in a word, how to *act*. These are the very themes to which the Gita speaks, with respect to its own time and beyond. In the chapters that follow, I will try to hear and understand what the Gita has to say to us about these and related in matters in our own times.

3

BEYOND SELFISHNESS

Action and Uncertainty in the
Age of Crisis Globalisation

Introduction: *Nishkama karma* in a modern world

Perhaps the most challenging concept in the Gita is contained in
the term *nishkama karma*, which can be translated as 'desireless
action', 'action separated from outcomes' or 'disinterested
action'. It is a phrase that I heard often while growing up in India:
work hard without worrying about the fruits of your labour or,
as expressed in conversational Hindi, *karm karo lekin phal ki
chinta mat karo*. No doubt, many Indians across generations
have heard the phrase on more than one occasion, whether as
motivation, admonition or, apropos of nothing, as gyaan, the
much-dreaded wisdom that everyone in India, from uncles to
nosy neighbourhood aunties, the local shopkeeper to a stranger
on a bus, is willing to freely dispense at the drop of a hat. As
folksy advice, the phrase makes intuitive sense, exhorting one
to get on with one's business without lapsing into existential
angst about the meaning of life, the purpose of the universe
and the like. The other part of the saying, though—that is, the
caution to set aside concern or worry about the results of one's

efforts—strikes one, in contrast, as somewhat counter-intuitive and a wee bit hypocritical.

For one, the very point of modern existence is fundamentally related to results and outcomes: in other words, the fruit of one's labour. Modern citizens and subjects are supposed to be productive and efficient, geared towards optimising their output in not just the realm of work but all aspects of their lives, from running households to excelling at a hobby, from parenting to checking off a bucket list of life goals. The two great diagnosticians of modernity, Marx and Foucault, would concur. In Marx's writings, the exploitation of workers by those who control the means of production ensues from the goal of, first, ensuring that the workers produce more and, secondly, through the appropriation of the fruits of their labour.[1] Control of the means of production, whether in the case of Nike factories or Facebook, is also an outcome or goal that motivates the actions of the bourgeoisie or the capitalist class. Foucault's notion of governmentality refers to the use of techniques of rationalisation to shape the behaviours, attitudes and practices of a people. Li defines the concept of 'government', in Foucault, as 'the attempt to shape human conduct by calculated means'.[2] Governmentality, is a 'distinct, government rationality' aimed at the betterment or improvement of populations.[3] Both analyses of modernity agree that as a framework for existence it is essentially goal-oriented, its idea of freedom paradoxically inseparable from the cultivation of a certain prescriptive notion of the ideal self.

Consistent with the thrust of the project of modernity, the dominant economic philosophy of our age of capitalist modernity is based on the idea that individuals are rational beings who seek to maximise their self-interest, directing their energies in a manner that brings them the rewards that they wish for. In the Indian context, other than the elite, who possess the rarified levels of wealth to live without concern for the consequences of their actions, or the abjectly poor, who struggle to eke out a living, hoping to make it to the next day, every action of those in the great mass of the middle is oriented towards some result or another. At least in the India in which I grew up, no college student had the luxury of taking a year off to discover oneself by bumming around the world, like the hippies, the Beat Poets and Steve Jobs had done. The goal of college was not discovery of the self, either. It was to figure out what you had a shot at, for making something of a life for yourself. The local shopkeeper who might have shared the nugget of wisdom from the Gita very much had a goal: increasing his profit. The retired uncle holding forth on the philosophical riches of the Gita was busy trying to engineer a wedding to cadge an Omega or Rolex watch from the grateful parents of the bride or bridegroom, should his matchmaking efforts come to fruition. The neighbourhood aunties showing off their piety by quoting the Gita were always on the hunt for the latest bit of local gossip floating around; not a laudable goal by any means, but a goal nevertheless.

Indeed, whenever and wherever I have encountered the proposition of *nishkama karma*, within or outside India, it has always struck me as somewhat incongruous with reality. Is not the very point of most, if not all, kinds of action the achievement or realisation of particular and desired outcomes? Scoring a pair of sneakers, saving to get the car of one's dreams, securing a spot in a college of one's choice, landing a plum job, getting a promotion and the corner office, buying a house, building a good life, travelling to new and exciting destinations, trying out unusual experiences like bungee jumping, sampling the first Alphonso mangoes of the season or tasting new foods—these are the things that constitute the very stuff of existence. We try to achieve one goal after another to construct the story of our lives, even if we do not know what plot twists lie ahead. Even sticking to the familiar, if we are complete creatures of routine, and structuring our actions around that goal involves directing our energies towards a particular outcome. In times of adversity, following the advice of the Beatles, we may just let things be till we see an answer, but we still hold out hope for revelation or at least for a glimmer of light that illuminates a path to a beneficial outcome.[4]

It seems logical that outcomes do not just give meaning to our actions but to our very lives, indicating how we might structure our existence. Goals and outcomes help us make sense of both significant and banal aspects of our lives. Our lives are shaped by major aspirations: pursuing an educational course in a prestigious university overseas, planning a wedding at a special locale, deciding when to have a child, choosing a location where to retire. In equal measure, our lives are shaped by smaller goals and quotidian practices, such as eating healthier and getting a modicum of exercise each day, learning to cook a new dish or eking out time to read a book, the pursuit of which gives substance to the everyday. A life without goals is a life without purpose, and any person stuck in such a life would seem to share the predicament of stasis experienced by the ancient mariner in Coleridge's poem: 'Day after day, day after day, / we stuck nor breath nor motion / As idle as a painted ship upon a painted ocean.'[5] A purgatory of sorts then, surely, to live a life without goals?

Interestingly, the ruptures caused by COVID-19 to our practices and routines, as we are forced to live under lockdowns and shelter-in-place orders and work from home, have resulted in many of us experiencing a sense of being trapped in a world in which the concept of time has lost its meaning.[6] Deprived of our routines, time stretches out endlessly, and habitual actions that we performed without thought now seem strange and unnatural. Our realities have become visible as socially constructed rather than natural and inevitable, our comfortable knowledge of them now defamiliarised. Discombobulated and disoriented, forced into social isolation by the law of the land and the tyranny of an unpredictable adversary, we have to live with the possibility that our loved ones are at risk or that we may need to be quarantined from them, should we or they contract the virus. We are struck by how necessary these social structures—of daily, weekly and annual routines, our small and large goals, the division of our life into work and leisure—are to our sense of a coherent and meaningful life, even if before the coronavirus changed everything, we chafed at the constraints that the same human-made structures imposed on us. It seems perfectly legitimate to ask, then, in what sense the Gita's insights about selfless action without reward hold with respect to the realities of Indian life, or modern life anywhere, really.

Nishkama karma in the Gita

The concept of *nishkama karma* is voiced in the second teaching of the Gita by Krishna. An anguished and dejected Arjuna has made up his mind that he will not fight against his family members. He lays down his bow, declaring his intention to abstain from battle. In his response to Arjuna's plight, Krishna voices this thought:

> Be intent on action,
> not on the fruits of action;
> avoid attraction to the fruits
> and attachment to inaction[7]

Interestingly, in his translation, Davis uses the stronger word 'bondage' for attachment and links it to the concept of desire. This idea, Davis notes, stems from theories of action from older philosophical traditions in India: 'Religious philosophers of various schools (Buddhist and Jain as well as Hindu) identified desire, the primary motivation for action, to be a fundamental problem. Undertaking an act out of desire, they maintained, leads to bondage.'[8] The term 'bondage' and its philosophical lineage of attachment to desire further complicate the relationship of the concept of *nishkama karma* to capitalist modernity. Desire is central to capitalism, turning wants into needs, driving the engine of consumption and leaving us perennially thirsting for more. The doctrine of *nishkama karma* would seem to call for an abdication, not just of the principle of capitalism but of the pleasures of material fulfilment altogether.

It is in persuading Arjuna of the necessity of going to war that Krishna communicates the doctrine of selfless or desireless action to him. Arjuna should neither worry about the 'fruits of action', that is, the bloodshed and disruption of the social order that will be caused by war, nor should Arjuna fall prey to the temptation of inaction by resorting to the option of not fighting at all.[9] The argument about inaction not being an option is complementary to the idea of *nishkama karma* and follows logically from it. The commonsensical understanding of the phrase, expressed in the colloquial Hindi idiom shared above, contains both elements of the proposition. *Karm karo.* You have to act. Not doing so is not a choice. *Lekin phal ki chinta mat karo.* But act without any anxiety about the results. You cannot sidestep the onerous task of not worrying about consequences by seeking recourse in inaction.

A sceptical reading of Krishna's words suggests itself here. Krishna is trying to convince Arjuna to fight. To achieve this goal, he needs to persuade Arjuna that the Pandava warrior will not be responsible for the deaths and chaos that will result from his decision to fight against his kinsmen. Reading Krishna's words through a hermeneutic of suspicion raises a number of questions about the scope of the doctrine and highlights a possible contradiction in Krishna's own objectives in articulating the idea.[10] Does the doctrine of *nishkama karma* apply only to the imminent battle of Kurukshetra, despite it being presented by Krishna as a universal philosophical truth? Does the idea operate more at the register of rhetoric or polemic than as reasoned argument whose claim to truth will stand tests of validity? Is there a fundamental paradox in Krishna's very act of proposing the doctrine of *nishkama karma*? For, in doing so, is he not trying to shape the outcome of the battle of Kurukshetra by ensuring that a great warrior like Arjuna will indeed take to the battlefield to fight? Is Krishna not also trying to control, in advance, the impact of going to battle on Arjuna's psyche, by seeking to absolve him in advance of any guilt he may feel about the deaths of his family members, whether his compatriots or adversaries, in war? Is the argument that Krishna makes merely a strategic tool to get Arjuna to slough off the despondency and doubt that the Pandava feels so he can lift up his bow?

Certainly, one can pursue a radically sceptical and deconstructive reading of the idea of *nishkama karma*.[11] My argument, however, is that the Gita's concept of *nishkama karma* or desireless action is most fruitfully understood in light of a distinction between *the desire to control outcomes* and a profound *awareness of the possible consequences of one's actions*. In choosing a course of action, we must relinquish even the illusion that the action can lead to a particular outcome, while keeping in mind the impact that the action may have on our fellow beings and the world. Meaningful action, according to the interpretation that I propose, requires that we engage in both kinds of commitments at the same time. The belief that we have some control over outcomes, whether by virtue of our individual actions or as part of a collective, in our positions as figures of authority in a public domain, in the power that we exercise over others, or as ordinary persons, reflects nothing more than folly and arrogance. Abandoning that misguided hubris and acting in the knowledge that whatever we choose to do or not to do bears implications for those other than our own selves can serve as a beacon for us as we make our way through the world. This dual imperative of letting go of worries about outcomes but weighing the consequences of our actions before undertaking any action can function as an effective overarching philosophical framework for our daily existence. The value of such a framework should be obvious in a world in which our lives are constantly in the process of being linked to larger numbers of people, many a times in ways which we cannot envision.

The elusive character of *karma*

It makes sense to begin an examination of the concept of *nishkama karma* with the more fundamental idea of *karma*. An engagement with the idea of *karma,* in turn, can help us think through the relationship of *nishkama karma* to several other concepts that are present in the Gita, including *dharma* (duty or sacred duty), *bhakti* (devotion) and *jñāna* (knowledge).[12] Ubiquitous in Indian life, these are terms whose meanings have been sedimented in the popular collective imagination over centuries, a palimpsest that continues to inflect the stories we live and tell. Despite their complex and multilayered character, one can grasp the sense in which the terms are used, thanks to the tacit historical, social and cultural knowledge that comes from the experience of having lived in a society shaped by these concepts of work, obligation, duty and the like. The meanings of these terms exceed the roles they play in texts associated with religion, philosophy or myth, having been extended to the mundane, the profane and the humorous. Consider that fans and acolytes of Narendra Modi are widely called bhakts, not just in the parlance of social media but in mainstream media as well. Gyaan, the Hindi term for *jñāna*, has expanded in scope of meaning to refer not just to gainfully earned and meaningful wisdom or knowledge but also to its ironic opposites such as bogus information, fake news and phoney, unsolicited advice.

Yet, finding precise equivalents for these terms in a language like English is not a simple task. *Karma*, like *dharma*, is an apt example in its resistance to a translation that is both accurate and concise. No single word in English captures the many depths and resonances of its meaning. Its uses in Hindi are likely closer to those in the Sanskrit of the Gita and other texts. In Hindi, the word is part of a constellation of similarly untranslatable terms whose meanings inform each other, a semantic web that the word as used in English lacks. As someone who is bilingual in English and Hindi, and with basic comprehension of a couple of other Indian languages, the term *karma* generates a somewhat different set of associations for me in English than it does in Indian languages. In its uses in the English language, *karma* is strongly associated the idea of destiny and, as Patton notes, with fortune or good luck.[13] The word is also vaguely evocative of Volkswagen hippie vans painted in psychedelic designs, bumper sticker witticisms like 'my karma ran over my dogma' and the popular 1980s song *Karma Chameleon*. In Hindi, in contrast, I find the word suggestive of a number of meanings: work, action and, more narrowly, righteous action and obligatory action. In the way that I understand and use it, it is contiguous with the term *dharma*, that is, duty or moral obligation. Finally, in Hindi, the word *karma*, as I see it, incorporates an idea of constraint and agency; *karma* is exercised or undertaken in a partially determined field of possibilities. While I have always thought of *karma* separately from any conception of the afterlife—a natural interpretive bias rooted in my own beliefs and politics, no doubt—the term does bear those meanings as well.

Scholars concur that the main, and obvious, meaning of the term *karma* is action.[14] Yet, as Patton observes, *karma* 'is far more complex than simply a single deed, or moment of agency. Rather it denotes both the pattern of actions in one's life, the ways in which one leads one's life according to one's station in life, and the pattern of action and consequence that keeps us in the cycle of death and rebirth.'[15] Davis, in his brief genealogy of the word, notes that in 'classical India, [...] karma had also come to refer to the persisting moral consequences of action ... Many envisioned karma as a residue that adhered to a person's self or soul, like some kind of opaque grime that obscured its intrinsic clarity'.[16] *Karma*, in sum, applies both to the singular act and to a set of predictable behaviours or actions—for that is what a pattern is. The latter may be interpreted as a cumulative accretion of practices, manifested as habitual, unthinking acts that become the mark of the self and of identity. *Karma* is the action taken in this world, yet bears consequences for the fate of future selves. *Karma* is our baggage from this life and earlier ones, but *karma* is also the means for liberating oneself from the burden of having to carry that baggage. *Karma* tells us we have the choice to shape our future fate and free the self, albeit in terms of a metaphysical idea of freedom from the condition of being, but the word also carries deterministic connotations, for the arena in which we exercise our *karma* in this life is dependent on our *karma* in our previous life. These complexities borne by the word are consistent with Krishna's view of the relationship between *karma* and *dharma* or action and duty. Though Krishna proposes that one's *dharma* or sacred duty must be in synchronicity with the action one takes and both *dharma* and action must be in harmony with a larger cosmic order, the arguments in the Gita do not necessarily rule out individual human agency. Some degree of choice must be available for the action that a person takes to be meaningful at all. Action is significant precisely because it resonates with a larger principle of order while being undertaken of one's own volition.

Krishna himself admits that the concept of *karma* is not easy to understand. As he says, 'What is action? What is inaction? / Even the poets were confused.'[17] Despite his promise to Arjuna—'what I shall teach you of action / shall free you of misfortune'—Krishna does not necessarily make it any easier for us in the text.[18] In passages in the fourth teaching, chapter or discourse, Krishna reveals that action and inaction or non-action are not binary opposites; one can exist within the other, and the ability to identify this relationship is the sign of wisdom, understanding and enlightenment, as is the ability to tell good actions from bad ones.[19] For every situation, there is a right course of action and a wrong course of action and a stance that qualifies as inaction. Yet, these possible courses of action or choices do not possess an ontological reality that is independent of the person who will undertake the action. The relationship between the concepts of *karma* or action and *dharma* or duty makes itself apparent here. What is the correct course of action for one individual may not be so for another. Fighting is the right action for Arjuna, since he 'must follow his own nature as well as his class duty', the latter relating to his obligations as a member of the warrior caste, and act accordingly.[20]

In the advice that he gives Arjuna about duty, obligation and action, Krishna recommends a philosophy and way of being in the world. To live is to act but one must maintain an attitude of detachment from anything that might steer one away from the right course of action in any situation that one might encounter in life. Nothing in the verse presents an excuse or justification for inaction, in case the slothful want to marshal it in defence of never responding to anything. Detachment from the results of one's actions does not entail retreating from the world and living like a hermit, nor does it call for a solipsistic inward turn that requires ignoring the world. But, in some circumstances, paradoxically, doing nothing may be the correct form of action to take. Inaction, accordingly, is not to be conflated with non-action, if we ascribe the latter term to a meaningful non-response.

Krishna also counsels Arjuna, and us, about the relationship of reality, embodied in different orientations of the self, to the principle of action. Krishna offers a taxonomy of three kinds of men, each embodying one of the *gunas* and each characterised by the kinds of action to which they are prone. Of the three qualities or *gunas* of nature or reality, *sattva* or purity is the quality of the highest order, the path to happiness and enlightenment. *Tamas*—variously translated as 'darkness' and 'dark inertia'—is the most harmful, and has disastrous effects when amplified within the self, leading to indolence and delusion.[21] *Rajas* or passion, placed between the two qualities, results, somewhat cryptically, to 'attachment' or 'connection' to action.[22] The man of of purity has discipline, lucidity and equanimity, and engages dispassionately in action, without being chained to any outcome. The passionate man is motivated by particular ends and is therefore prone to being misguided, greedy and lustful in what he does. The indolent, deluded man, trapped in claustrophobic stasis, has no capacity to engage positively with the world. The word 'action' here is possibly used in two senses: one, in the broad sense of any kind of engagement with the world, and second, in the narrower sense of impulsive action driven by unthinking desire.

Pointing to the consequences of action that is linked to attachment, Krishna says that this kind of action imprisons the world, and exhorts Arjuna to engage in action as 'sacrifice'. One way to understand this argument is to consider it in terms of the impact that actions motivated by narrow or limited outcomes have on the world; in that such actions may bend the world to the will of a person or in light of a certain goal, the world will become that much more inhospitable to others. Action as sacrifice, in contrast, is action undertaken selflessly, without an ulterior motive or reward in mind. By implication, such action liberates the world.[23]

Juxtaposing these theories of action, we can see the practical value of *yoga,* or discipline, for action in the Gita. In the sixth teaching, Krishna tells Arjuna that it requires both renunciation and discipline to act in the right manner.[24] However, earlier, in the fifth chapter or teaching, Krishna has clarified that 'discipline in action / surpasses renunciation in action' or 'the *yoga* of action is better than renunciation'.[25] In the eighteenth chapter, Krishna makes another distinction, that between renunciation and relinquishment. Renunciation is defined as 'giving up actions based on desire'.[26] Relinquishment, in contrast, is giving up the 'fruit of all actions'.[27] In the hierarchy of affect and sentiments, then, action trumps renunciation, which, in turn, trumps relinquishment. Action freed from outcomes stands as the highest value; doing is superior to not doing. Giving up actions that are yoked to outcome stands as an intermediate value, superior to giving up the fruits or outcomes that result from actions.

Nishkama karma through the lens of outcomes versus consequences

The terms 'outcome' and 'consequence' are frequently confused and conflated with each other, for both terms signify a result or end of some sort, an effect that results from a cause. Dictionaries often list the terms as synonyms. Either term could fit with the phrase 'fruits of action' used in the Gita. I suggest the following conceptual distinction between the terms: an 'outcome' refers to a planned or hoped-for result that, consciously or unconsciously, shapes the nature of the action, while a 'consequence' is the result that will occur from the action anyway. Freeing action from a desire for outcomes requires discipline, or *yoga*, a term that recurs frequently in the Gita in relation to discussions on *karma* or action. An assessment of consequences is an ethical action, guided by principles such as not wanting to harm any living being or not cause damage to the environment. This evaluative activity, too, requires a kind a discipline or *yoga*.

As a rough analogy to illuminate the point, consider the situation of a doctor who is faced with having to make a decision regarding a patient who is critically ill. While there may be protocols and precedents that the doctor has to follow, and while the patient and his or her family clearly have the final word on the course of action to pursue, it transpires that in this hypothetical situation, the doctor must make a decision on how to proceed. It is not difficult to imagine such a situation arising in the course of a surgery or in the case of a patient being admitted to a hospital in an emergency with no family members at hand to take a decision. The doctor cannot necessarily control the outcome of the action he or she will take, for the patient may or may not survive. Yet, the doctor needs to weigh the consequences of different courses of action, such as whether to perform surgery or not, or what particular surgical procedure to use, or what non-surgical course of treatment to pursue, in light of his or her general knowledge and experience of medicine and understanding of the patient's condition. Wanting a patient to recover, thrive in good health and be able to live a meaningful life is an ideal outcome that all doctors understandably seek, yet that outcome cannot be guaranteed for all patients. A doctor cannot save everyone; indeed, the acceptance of mortality and coming to terms with the fact that they may not be able to save everyone seems to be a part of the journey of becoming a doctor.[28] An obsession with the outcome of saving every patient at any cost may result in harm to the patient, in violation of the Hippocratic oath. Such an obsession may also cloud a doctor's judgment about the best course of action to pursue. This may explain why the goal of prolonging life as an objective in itself, divorced from considerations such as the quality of life of the patient, is a major ethical issue in end-of-life debates.[29]

The enormity of the difficulty of freeing our actions from a concern for outcomes stares us in the face. Even if one is determined to do so, how would one go about this hard task? How does one train the mind to not concern itself with outcomes? The challenge calls to mind the parable of the king who was stricken by an ailment that his physician was unable to cure. Irked at the persistence of the problem and equally annoyed by the physician's abiding inability to alleviate his acute discomfort, the king demanded that he come up with a treatment to address the issue once and for all. The physician, worried that the king's anger might cost him his freedom or his life, racked his brains for a solution. He gave the king what amounted to a placebo, with the requirement that the king should not think of mangoes at any point of time for the medicine to be effective. Of course, once he had put the seed of this idea into the king's head, the king found it impossible not to think of mangoes. Whether the king was eventually cured or not, the physician, at the very least, succeeded in saving his own hide. The kind of discipline asked of the king by the physician will be familiar to anyone who has tried yoga, in the contemporary sense of the term, as the practice of health and mindfulness. In the yoga classes that I have taken, in both the Iyengar and Ashtanga traditions, the injunction to focus my mind and clear it of all extraneous thoughts has perhaps been the hardest part of the exercise. The first time I was asked to attempt to mentally focus in this manner, my mind almost immediately gravitated to the question of what exactly constituted an extraneous thought. Lost in that philosophical musing, I did not hear the teacher's next instruction.

Yet, if met successfully, the practice of negotiating the path between abandoning concern for outcomes while keeping that concern centred on consequences may bring us a rare gift: that of independence of thought. Acting in this manner requires both discipline and some independence of thought to begin with, and each action undertaken in accordance with the principle reinforces and strengthens that independence of thought. Action, as the Gita defines it, is also a practice of mind; one that does not necessarily need to be grounded in any larger religious, spiritual or metaphysical framework. The practice of the concept of *nishkama karma,* based on the distinction between outcomes and consequences, also reminds us of the value of epistemological humility. Humility, as an orientation or dispensation towards the world, is, in fact, the unifying factor across *nishkama karma* and the necessity of acting over choosing inaction. Abandoning concern for outcomes—with the knowledge that attempting to dictate outcomes is a fool's gambit—is an act of humility. Thinking through the possible consequences of our actions is also an act of humility, for thought and action that are grounded in this approach do not privilege our own needs and well-being over those of others.

Just as we cannot control outcomes, though, we cannot always predict the consequences of our actions. Our actions take place in a world of astounding complexity and one peopled by numerous other actors. What we do enters the orbit of other lives and produces effects beyond what we can imagine. What exactly is the object of our consideration, then, when we say that we are considering the consequences of our actions? And how do we go about engaging in any such evaluation, with the knowledge of the limits of our knowledge? Ideally, we want that our actions should harm no one and that they should not cause pain or discomfort to any living being. But, of course, our actions may have consequences that we cannot anticipate, as the great Greek playwrights knew. Agard reminds us of the wisdom of the Greeks on this matter: 'men who admit that consequences will be determined by powers beyond them, realize they have no sure means of knowing what those consequences may be and therefore make their decisions on the basis of what seems to them best.'[30] Faced with the knowledge that each of our actions will set in motion a complex set of effects, and can have positive and negative consequences, we have to choose what to do after evaluating the merits and dangers of each one.

For instance, a simple economic decision about what items to consume, where to buy them from or which companies to boycott and which ones to support will impact people at every stage along the supply chain of the items or corporations in question, even if the impact of one individual's action on the fortunes of a firm or on the American, Indian or global economy is infinitesimal. Given my concerns about Walmart's pay structure and the ethics of the family that owns Walmart, my decision not to shop at any store in the Walmart chain in the US, despite their highly competitive prices, makes no difference to the company itself, which happens to be the largest retailer in the US and one of the biggest corporations on the planet. I do not seek to control the fate of Walmart through this action in any way, but after weighing different options, I personally believe that it is the right course of action for me to take. Someone else may make a similar decision about Reliance in the Indian context, while another person may deem it fine to shop at Reliance, but may choose not to patronise the local kirana store based on another set of ethical concerns. The distinction between outcomes and consequences does not necessarily entail that there is only one right course of action in any situation or with regard to an entire realm of social practice or behaviour. There is no formula for the right action to take for all instances of minor infractions or victimless crimes, for instance.

In fact, the distinction between outcomes and consequences places the onus and responsibility on the individual for pursuing what they believe to be the right course of action. The interpretation of the concept along these lines arguably tilts further in the direction of individual choice than is the case in the Gita, as action in the sense articulated here does not need to be constrained by the obligations of family, caste, class or obligations to religion and nation.

If one were to explore the ethical issues involved in the hypothetical example provided above in somewhat greater detail, a contrarian perspective would hold that any decision to avoid patronising a retailer because of, say, their ethically controversial labour policies is unlikely to have any positive economic impact even if there is a prima facie moral or political case to be made for taking such a stand. World-renowned economists like Jeffrey Sachs argue that the world needs more, not fewer, 'sweatshops' or factories in the developing world that provide goods like shoes, clothing, tablecloths, furniture or electronic components to be consumed globally.[31] These factories, of course, do not pay anything close to the federal minimum wage of $7.25 in the US. The argument offered by Sachs and those of his persuasion is that, exploitative as these sweatshops in Bangladesh and other poor countries may be, without them the sweatshop employees would have no other comparable avenue for employment, and they would be forced into destitution or even more exploitative work and life situations. Sachs and his ilk argue that one could oppose sweatshops in the US because the economy is developed enough to offer people other, relatively more decent, employment opportunities while in Bangladesh far worse fates would await those who do not work in manufacturing products for Western multinationals to be sold in the mega-malls of the US.

There is, however, a counter-argument to the justification for the existence of Bangladeshi sweatshops. My dissertation co-chair at Emory University, Allen Tullos, a labour historian of the US, pointed out to me that the rationale for the value of sweatshops presented by current-day economists mirrored the argument made by nineteenth-century factory owners against offering better working conditions to workers in Waltham, the birthplace of the American industrial revolution.[32] Had the logic of Sachs and those of his view been implemented in nineteenth-century America, as these economists advocate for it to be in Bangladesh and other poorer, developing nations, we would likely not have any workers' rights in the US, nor the eight-hour workday, nor the weekend off work, nor laws against child labour. And, possibly, we would not have had any such laws, imperfect and inconsistently applied as they may be, in any part of the world. In believing that more sweatshops will eventually lead to the reduction of poverty in countries like Bangladesh, Sachs gets trapped in the tricky terrain of the relationship between action and outcomes. But we should not hold that against him. It is perhaps inevitable that one slides down this rabbit hole before clambering out of it, for neither *karma* nor *nishkama karma* are easy concepts to wrap one's head around, given that outcome-oriented practices and behaviours are so deeply ingrained in us.

The French sociologist Bourdieu has an argument about 'disinterested' action that serves as a critique of the proposition of *nishkama karma*, ruling out the very possibility of such an attitude or approach.[33] Bourdieu argues that being vested in some kind of outcome is a minimum precondition for participating in social life, even if we are not consciously aware of such an attachment on our part. Bourdieu's notion of being 'interested' is based on an understanding that we are invested in rewards, outcomes and stakes of different kinds—economic, educational, cultural, political—without necessarily knowing it in any conscious way. This investment in society and its game of rewards, which compels our actions, choices, behaviours and practices, is embodied in our physical being, how we view the world and how we think. Bourdieu argues: 'One can be interested in a game (in the sense of not indifferent) while at the same time being disinterested.'[34] He distinguishes between being consciously or overtly disinterested and being 'indifferent', the latter denoting a state of utter apathy to a situation.[35] Bourdieu's point here is that even an apparent distancing, or what we believe to be our voluntary detachment, from a situation or its outcomes, does not preclude our habituated, deeply ingrained and automatic orientation to act based on calculations about results. Our practices are framed and governed by the struggle and aspiration for specific outcomes. Bourdieu's theory of action rules out the possibility of being detached from outcomes, unless one allows for a moment of enlightenment or self-knowledge in which these unconscious motives that shape and compel one's behaviour become apparent to one.

Once we start seriously considering the prospect of dedicating ourselves to action without any care for outcomes, other niggling questions arise too. Are the desires that drive behaviours aimed at particular goals not the desires that drive the world itself, whether these are the basic needs of food, shelter and clothing or higher-order wants, such as social relationships, romantic love, self-realisation or intellectual fulfilment? In advocating that we free ourselves from goals, outcomes and desires, is the Gita not suggesting an unrealistic, prescriptive and stifling vision of existence, a theological justification for a puritanical and joyless life? In more practical terms, if consumption is the end goal of economic life, as mainstream economics holds, would a society based on the philosophy of the Gita even be viable and sustainable in the modern world?[36] Is it so wrong to want material objects and designer brands? Even if we grudgingly grant, for the sake of argument, that such a want is not in and of itself troubling, on what basis do we determine what is an appropriate amount of consumption, what are legitimate products to purchase and appropriate experiences to invest in beyond the obviously dangerous or exploitative? How do we reconcile any such overarching principle of how everyone must act in their lives with the basic principles of democracy and individual choice?

It is a complicated question whether a preference for certain abstract outcomes to others entirely contravenes the principle of *nishkama karma* as elucidated by Krishna in the course of his teachings in the Gita. Does any trace of hope or desire contaminate the action that one takes in accordance with the principle of *nishkama karma*? Does the Gita rule out the possibility of any kind of disinterested action that may contain a trace of desire in it, paradoxical though this may sound?

For is the desire to avoid all desire not an aporia, a moment when the Gita contradicts itself and the idea of *nishkama karma* opens itself to being deconstructed? A strict interpretation of the concept of *nishkama karma* would rule out any possibility, no matter how minimal, of any kind of desire or wish informing any action. For example, the use of the term 'bondage' as the equivalent of attachment, in Davis's translation, is exactly such a strict reading or interpretation.[37] Is there a way, though, in which one can keep a preference for a particular outcome on the distant horizon without significantly undermining the principle of disinterestedness as a force that guides one's actions? One response to the conundrum is to distinguish between an action that is geared towards, and guided by, desire for a specific outcome—say, an ideal like world peace—and an action that is independent of such motivation yet accompanied by the *hope* that it may lead to that outcome. *Hope*, according to this argument, is to be distinguished from *desire* as Krishna uses the latter term. If we grant such a reading a modicum of legitimacy, then it allows us to imagine as feasible the practice of *nishkama karma* while preserving place for a commitment to some principle or idea that we may deem worthwhile.

Disinterested action, social justice and outcomes

Beyond desires for material objects or ideal states, what do we make of the disinterest towards evil and of judging the moral worth of a person by intention rather than deeds or action that Krishna presents in the Gita? The argument that Krishna presents squarely contradicts modern notions of justice and responsibility.

> The man who is disciplined
> ...is set apart by his disinterest
> toward comrades, allies, enemies,
> neutrals, nonpartisans, foes, friends,
> good and even evil men.[38]
>
> ...
>
> If he is devoted solely to me,
> even a violent criminal
> must be deemed a man of virtue,
> for his resolve is right.[39]

Other than accepting the existence of evil in fatalistic terms as the will of god or in biologically deterministic and crude Darwinian terms as an inevitable truth about a nasty and cruel world, it is hard to find a rationale for adopting a stand of indifference to evil, to not so much as be affected or shaken by evil acts let alone spurred to action in response to them. How can indifference to evil be the right course of action under any circumstances? This, surely, is a crucial question for us to reflect on, given the many acts of barbarism that span the twentieth century, including the genocide in Rwanda, the bloodshed during the partition of the Indian subcontinent, the murder of six million Jews, Roma, people with disabilities, and others considered subhuman by the Nazis, and the lynchings of African Americans by White mobs in the US.[40]

Delinked from outcomes, the concept of *karma* by itself seems politically ineffectual. Think of any of the major social, political and cultural struggles of the twentieth and twenty-first centuries, whether the fight for Indian independence and the other great struggles for liberation from European colonial rule across much of Asia and Africa, the civil rights struggle in the US, the fight for gender equality in different societies, the great movements for securing workers' rights, the environmental and animal rights movements and, more recently, the social movements for LGBTQ+ rights. Each of these movements was motivated by specific goals, and was centred on achieving those outcomes.[41]

In a detailed examination of the political value of the concept of *nishkama karma*, or disinterested action, Mathur argues that from the point of view of concrete political and social change, *nishkama karma* is a conservative doctrine. His first argument is that that the concept, as fleshed out in the Gita, undermines moral autonomy and agency by subjugating it to the metaphysical notion of liberation of the soul, that is, to the idea of *moksha*. His second argument is that given the messy realities of social existence, it is not viable, in practice, to divorce political action from concrete ends or goals.[42] Mathur's solution is to interpret the 'fruit' of action as *personal gain* and to separate that from a *commitment* to sought-after goals:

> Therefore a more sensible and fruitful interpretation of niskama-karma would be to hold that while we should be firmly *committed* to achieve the goal after a rational assessment of the situation, we should *not* be so egoistically *involved* in the issue as to calculate what, in terms of pleasure or pain, prosperity or otherwise, will be its likely effect on our personal fortunes... If the above distinction is kept in view then it will be perfectly legitimate, nay morally indispensable to be *committed* to

the fulfilment of the goal and yet to be detached with respect to its effects on personal fortunes.[43]

This is a valuable reading, and its practical benefits are manifest, especially from the point of view of initiatives related to social justice. However, by way of critique, one can argue that the text of the Bhagavad Gita does not necessarily make a distinction between outcomes or fruits as personal gains and outcomes as benefitting society at large, or between selfish and selfless outcomes. To seek outcomes at all, in the Gita, is in itself an act that is, arguably, selfish. Additionally, the distinction between selfish and selfless outcomes may not be absolute and may itself be subject to varying interpretation as to where the line between selfishness and selflessness is to be drawn. An altruistic act may also be economically beneficial to the person who engages in such an action. Would that count as a selfish or a selfless action? One could argue, further, that if selfless actions, such as engaging in charitable work or helping the poor, give the actor a sense of moral self-worth, they are also selfish acts, even if to a small degree.

Nishkama karma through the lens of deontological versus consequentialist positions

In philosophical terms, the interpretation of *nishkama karma* that I am proposing tries in a modest way to address the paradoxes and contradictions outlined so far. The dual approach of abandoning worry about the outcomes of action but keeping in the foreground a consideration of the consequences of action, to the extent that these are knowable, captures something of two important traditions in the philosophical area of ethics, namely, deontological and consequentialist perspectives. These perspectives are considered antithetical to each other. Deontological positions judge the value of actions because of their innate worth and value, separately from the consequences that might follow from these actions. Actions, then, have intrinsic value (or lack the same) and ethically sound actions to pursue, it follows, are those have that moral worth or value. As a useful definition puts it:

> In deontological ethics an action is considered morally good because of some characteristic of the action itself, not because the product of the action is good. Deontological ethics holds that at least some acts are morally obligatory regardless of their consequences for human welfare. Descriptive of such ethics are such expressions as 'Duty for duty's sake,' 'Virtue is its own reward,' and 'Let justice be done though the heavens fall.'[44]

Such phrases would be familiar to many of us, encountered through the stories that we may have read as children, which ended with a neat moral. These messages are similar to the dictum of the Gita about engaging in action without consideration of the rewards of such action. In contrast to deontological perspectives, consequentialism proposes that 'choices—acts and/or intentions—are to be morally assessed solely by the states of affairs they bring about'.[45] An action, desire or hope must be judged by the actual, concrete result of implementing the position, regardless of whether the hoped for consequence was something superior to or different from to what eventually turned out to be the case.

Aside from the question of whether one *should* pursue actions with an outcome, goal or fruit in mind, there is a rich tradition of work in mythology, literature, philosophy and economics about whether one *can*, in fact, control the outcomes of human action at all. Humans cannot entirely escape their destiny, even if they have some wiggle room in how they face it. The best laid plans of mice and men, the Scottish poet Robert Burns tells us, go astray.[46] The Fates, the three sisters in Greek tragedy, mock human arrogance and undermine the idea of free will, though the possibility of freedom, as Agard notes, is not entirely erased by the determinism of the Greek plays.[47] Macbeth, similarly, cannot stop the prophecy of the witches from coming true, unrealistic though it sounds to his ears. In Thomas Hardy's novels, an indifferent universe manifests itself as chance, accidents and coincidences that lead to tragedy. Meursault, the protagonist of Camus's classic novel, *The Outsider*, is condemned to death for the crime of not crying at his mother's funeral. Beckett's absurdist masterpiece, *Waiting for Godot*, takes the indifference of the universe as axiomatic to the human condition, in which no outcome necessarily makes more sense and is therefore more desirable than any other. If the persona in Dylan Thomas's 'Do Not Go Gentle into the Good Night' asks his dying father to fight the inevitability of death, Mary Oliver's immensely moving poem 'In Blackwater Woods', speaks of the wisdom of letting go as a form of love:

> ... To live in this world

> you must be able
> to do three things:
> to love what is mortal;
> to hold it

> against your bones knowing
> your own life depends on it;
> and, when the time comes to let it go,
> to let it go.

Marx, who by his own reckoning, moved philosophy into the realm of action from contemplation—'The philosophers have only interpreted the world, in various ways; the point is to change it'—also notes the limits of human agency in shaping history.[48] His argument is that humans possess agency, but they can only exercise it within inherited and existing parameters that are not of their own choosing. In his famous quote from *The Eighteeenth Brumaire of Louis Bonaparte*, Marx notes that, 'Men make their own history, but they do not make it as they please; they do not make it under self-selected circumstances, but under circumstances existing already, given and transmitted from the past.'[49] In contrast to the absurdists, existentialists and the Gita, Marx locates the ineffectuality of humans in shaping historical outcomes in the historical experiences of inequality rather than as a given ontological condition or as a metaphysical truth about human existence.

The desire to control outcomes is doomed to failure for more mundane reasons as well, a fact on which the Gita, the classical liberal economist and critic of the heavy-handed state Friedrich Hayek, and any number of therapists who counsel compulsively driven workaholics in Silicon Valley, London or Mumbai would agree. We cannot control how others with whom we collaborate on a project will act any more than we can control the future. We cannot predict or control how people will adopt a particular technological or media product. Consider, for instance, that the radio was intended as a form of business communication, but its many trajectories of adoption, such as in cars, in rural India, or now in the form of digital streaming services like Pandora and Spotify, have far exceeded the roles initially designated and imagined for it. We conduct more and more of our lives each day on our phones, including shopping, videoconferencing, learning a language, watching a film, or reading and forwarding a rumour on WhatsApp. One wonders what Alexander Graham Bell would have made of the queues of Apple product junkies lined up for hours outside Apple stores, hoping to snag the next iteration of the iPhone on the day of its release. Could the inventor of the telephone ever have imagined that the device he created in

1876 would evolve into a mobile Bauhaus-inspired, handheld computer that could perform a dazzlingly wide array of tasks?

The failure of centralised planning in the Soviet Union and, for that matter, the failure of the Soviet Union itself, show that we cannot socially engineer societies in the direction of preordained outcomes, even armed with the might of the state. In such situations, the obsession with the outcome warps both the action and the actor, whether that actor is a state or an individual. A telling example of this inversion where an obsession with the outcome starts influencing the action in perverse ways is Stalin's unfinished, quixotic project to build a railway that would have spanned the breadth of Siberia.[50] In an absurd circle of cruelty, the railway, which was constructed by prisoners, essentially became the impetus to build more prisons for the sake of ensuring that there was no dearth of labour at hand for building the railways. As any Indian who remembers life in pre-liberalisation India will testify, for all the ways in which that social context was immensely rewarding, it was also a laboratory for all kinds of natural experiments that conclusively demonstrated the failure of the social engineering paradigm. Some legacies of that age persist into the present, for instance, in the ban on liquor in states like Gujarat and Bihar. Prohibition, like its counterpart in earlier times in India and in the US, has given rise to a booming black market trade in alcohol and a dangerous industry of illicitly brewed liquor that routinely claims lives. In 2017, the police in Bihar claimed that rats had drunk 900,000 litres of alcohol, which they had seized on grounds of it violating the state's ban.[51] The ridiculous explanation offered to cover up what was obviously a corrupt police racket of selling seized liquor was a telling example of the consequences of trying to control social behaviour or forcibly inculcating virtues such as abstinence from alcohol in a population against its will.

The most egregious recent example in the Indian context of trying to control outcomes and failing miserably has to be the folly of demonetisation, the currency swap implemented by the Indian government in late 2016. The decision rendered the existing ₹500 and ₹1,000 notes illegal, requiring citizens to swap them out at banks by a certain date. These currency notes would be replaced by new ₹500 and ₹2,000 notes. With the old ₹500 and ₹1,000 currency notes amounting to around 86 per cent of India's total currency in circulation, the purported objective was to render 'black money', or unaccounted-for income, worthless, which, Modi claimed, would root out corruption and eradicate terrorism.[52]

In both its implementation and its proposed goals, demonetisation was an utter failure. It led to bank runs that left ATMs drained of cash. Media images of long lines of desperate citizens waiting at banks to change their money were complemented by tragic stories of ill and elderly individuals dying while waiting to change their currency. The move cost India 1.5 million jobs and lowered economic growth by two percentage points. Demonetisation did not remove any percentage of illegitimate notes or unaccounted-for income from circulation; if terrorists, smugglers and general hoarders of such 'black money' had any resources in freshly demonetised denominations, they likely figured out ways to change that money into kosher currency, laundering it into legitimate income in the bargain. Social media at the time was full of the usual loud whispers about powerful Indians with black money, including politicians, industrialists and film stars, having been tipped off about the impending currency swap, giving them ample time to launder their hoarded cash. In a comical attempt to defend the government's actions, economists sympathetic to the BJP and Modi, including those associated with NITI Aayog, the newly formed government agency, wrote regular pieces in newspapers offering new explanations each week about the real goal of demonetisation before eventually conceding that the policy was a failure.[53] Judging by the accounts of the defenders of government policy—and in stark contrast to what Modi himself had claimed in his speeches about demonetisation—there was no single coherent outcome motivating the decision but, rather, several retroactively gleaned goals, including quashing terrorism, accelerating the shift to a digital economy, inducing Indians to stop using cash and so on.

Lest Americans feel too smug about the many failures of the Soviet Union, interpreting it as a victory for some romantic vision of an American way of life, they have a spectacular record of their own failed social engineering projects, of which the most impressive are the many disastrous imperialistic initiatives of the American state across the globe. The most recent of these ventures, of course, has been the war with Iraq, which lasted from 2003 to 2011, overlapping with the ongoing and more nebulously defined 'war on terror'.[54] Like with demonetisation, the planned outcome of the illegal invasion of Iraq was unclear. The dictator Saddam Hussein, a one-time ally of the US and the UK, had long fallen afoul of his supporters in Western liberal democracies. While he did not prima facie appear to have any links with Osama bin Laden, the mastermind of the 11 September 2001 terrorist attacks on the World Trade Center towers in New York, Hussein was marked as a target on grounds of posing a terrorist threat to the US. In an act of collective abdication of responsibility, the majority of the mainstream media in the US swallowed the allegation put forth by the Bush administration that Saddam possessed weapons of mass destruction. Saddam's forces were dethroned by the made-for-television attack carried out by the US-led coalition, which acted in violation of international law and in blatant disregard of massive global protests against war. Saddam was eventually executed by the pro-US Iraqi government that replaced his administration. Over a decade later, Iraq is in a shambles, as is Afghanistan, the target of the other illegal invasion led by the US in response to the 9/11 attacks. The same state of destruction characterises the situation of West Asia, or the so-called Middle East, which has become the site for a proxy war between different sets of adversaries, whether Russia and the US, or Shia and Sunni powers in the region.

Projects to control social outcomes through sheer exercise of force, diktats of state authority or appeals to moralising clearly do not work at the global, national or even local level, whether in India, the US or elsewhere, just as they did not work for the former Soviet Union. Yet, this message has apparently not really got through to the postcolonial Indian state. Does the idea of *nishkama karma*, though, bear any special relevance for Indian society? To what extent does it capture something essential about Indian life?[55] In exceptionalist narratives about the uniqueness of Indian society, the Gita holds the status of not just a foundational text for large numbers of caste Hindus, but is also seen as a sociological reflection of truths about Indian life. Usually, such narratives are laudatory, centred on claims of Hindu tolerance, sacrifice, humility and the like. Yet, how reflective of Indian social reality is the sentiment that *nishkama karma* is an animating philosophical principle of Indian life?

Nishkama karma: An Indian idea?

Contrary to our self-congratulatory image as a people largely uninterested in wealth, acquisition, material objects and consumption in general, Indians are nothing of the sort. Large numbers of Indians do not have the luxury of being conspicuous consumers or of aspiring to wealth, given that they live in conditions of poverty, struggling to make ends meet and to survive on a daily basis. The stereotype of the ascetic, world-denying Indian who towers above the temptations of material pleasures and base desires is grounded in the Orientalist fiction that the East, of which India is a part, is spiritual, while the godless, hedonistic, immoral West is materialistic. The figure of the fasting, self-denying Gandhi clad in his loincloth and living a life of unimaginable simplicity has contributed to this stereotype, one that is perpetuated as much by Indians as it is lapped up by folks from other countries. This is not a statement about Indian greed at all, but about challenging an article of faith that Indians are a less materialistic or more philosophical people than their counterparts in other countries. The fruits of action animate and motivate millions of Indians just as similar goals and aspirations motivate people the world over.

No doubt, Gandhi inspired many in socialist India to live by an ethic of consuming only what they considered absolutely essential, even if they understandably could not live like Gandhi himself. Yet, ample numbers among the middle class in the same socialist India hankered after Western-made goods: Levi's jeans, Nike sneakers, magnetic pencil boxes, Scotch whiskies, Kit Kat chocolates, cartons of Marlboro and cans of Coke were especially longed-for objects, bearing a talismanic power that their humble Indian counterparts lacked. A large number of Indians would have happily traded India's special relationship with the USSR for some kind of basic capitalist existence. The much-lauded Soviet connection guaranteed that Indian kids could get inexpensive copies of Russian fairy tales about Baba Yaga and watch Russian circus performances on Doordarshan, but not much else.

When cars manufactured by Maruti in partnership with the Japanese automobile manufacturer Suzuki were introduced to an India that had only seen Ambassadors, Fiats and Standard Heralds, they became an immediate status symbol, prized as much for their symbolic value as for their practical use value. As was the case during British colonial rule, the preferred educational destination for Indians in the aftermath of Independence continued to be Britain. By the 1970s, though, significant numbers of Indians, especially in the scientific and technical fields, were choosing to pursue higher studies in the US. Either way, by this point of time, Indians were wending their way to nations in the consumption-oriented, transaction-oriented West, where they successfully struck roots. Over the last fifty years, Indians have established wealthy diasporic communities in London, New York, New Jersey and Silicon Valley, whose numbers continue to grow with freshly arrived immigrants each year.

Since economic liberalisation in 1991, the pent-up hunger for consumption has been the force behind the spectacular growth of the Indian economy. Neither the drive for material consumption nor the desire to possess objects is innate to human nature, contrary to what some economists tell us. Economists, sociologists and cultural critics like Thorstein Veblen, Pierre Bourdieu, Raymond Williams and the members of the Frankfurt School have argued that our needs and desires are linked deeply to status and reinforced through social structures and institutions, peer groups and the media. Whether it was the bottled frustration of stymied consumption or a newly learned craving for material goods, as India's role in the global economy took off in the 1990s and oughts, a large number of middle-class and wealthy Indians set about gathering as many goods and enjoying as many experiences as they could, with their labour now remunerated in far more generous terms than had been the case in pre-liberalisation India.

Indian society is obsessively competitive, especially the professional elites and those immediately below them in the class hierarchy who aspire to higher status, security and responsibility.

This is equally true of the Indian diasporic population in Silicon Valley, whose children are reared to win spelling competitions and secure admission to highly sought-after institutions, followed by jobs in equally prestigious corporations. In India, class examination ranks, board exam results and success in competitive exams to get into the Indian Institutes of Technology (IITs), Indian Institutes of Management (IIMs) and the Indian Administrative Service (IAS) are a national obsession. Perhaps things have changed a little now; frowned upon vocations like hotel management, media and advertising, and film-making, which were considered inferior to engineering and medicine and carried a faint whiff of immorality and degeneracy, are now considered more acceptable. But, judging by the tragic news year after year of students committing suicide because of fear of failure in exams or unhappiness with their results, the booming business of brutally demanding and exploitative coaching classes for getting seats in competitive exams, and the abiding idea of the curriculum vitae, or bio-data as it is called in India, as a general measure of the worth of a human being, the ugly national culture of competitiveness still appears to be thriving.

I have now lived long enough in the US to see how the relentless competitiveness in every aspect of life here as well ultimately becomes counter-productive and destructive, whether in academia, finance, technology or other industries. It may result in a culture of high productivity and efficiency, spur profits and keep the spark of innovation alive, but at some point of time the costs that it extracts, many of which may not be directly visible or recognisable, make the real cost-benefit ratio an unattractive proposition. The toll in terms of a lopsided work-life balance, stress, negative impact on one's health and wider lack of social stability is considerable, yet questioning it in any serious manner is considered an act in the order of heresy since it entails questioning the worth of the system of capitalism and challenging the myth of American exceptionalism.

The US, I would contend, is still better than India. The latter, since 1991, reflects some of the worst tendencies of capitalism while also retaining some of the worst tendencies of socialism, particularly with regard to the attitudes and behaviours of the middle class and elites. It is a cliché that India is a society of contradiction but a cliché with more than a modicum of truth to it. Indian society is marked by a stifling collectivism that does not consider the collective good and, equally, shaped by an ultra-competitive each-person-for-themselves culture that nonetheless does not respect individual rights. The romanticisation of the idea of community, seen in the demand for respecting 'community sentiments' at the slightest, usually imagined, provocation, does not, unfortunately, extend beyond the privileging of sectarian identity, for instance, in any abiding initiative of the common good that does not demonise one group or another. It is no accident perhaps that the ultimate paragon of success in today's India is Mukesh Ambani, India's wealthiest man, and by some accounts, the real power behind the Indian prime minister, Narendra Modi. Anyone who has followed the news involving the Ambanis over the last several years will have a clear idea of why it is hard to see Mukesh Ambani as a model of ethical virtue even if he is technically not a criminal.

This culture, ironically, is touted as a meritocracy by those who buy into its myth, their perception marked by an unwillingness and inability to recognise caste, class and religious privilege and by a self-sustaining, historically produced amnesia about the profound inequalities that have shaped Indian social relations. The ideological contradiction makes sense. People need to believe in the essential legitimacy of a system to participate in it and reinforce that legitimacy. This is true for the effective functioning of any institution, social group like one's ethnicity or regional community, form of social organisation like religion, or even the imagined community of the nation.[56] Long story short, as far as I can tell, for the majority of Indians, possibly like people everywhere, *phal* or fruit, outcomes, goals, results do matter and matter a lot. *Karma* is linked to *phal*, even if a decent number of people have some sense, innate or learned, that the means do not always justify the ends.

Action and uncertainty in the age of crisis globalisation

Why should any of this matter now in particular? What import could the doctrine of *nishkama karma* and the conversation between Arjuna and Krishna hold for any of us today, whether in India or elsewhere in the world?

I would argue that they do for three main reasons. First, the ideal model of the individual in our time is the entrepreneur and, even more narrowly, a certain vision of the entrepreneur as the very embodiment of certitude and absolute conviction combined with genius. The notion of *nishkama karma* offers us a sobering and much-needed critique of what is a singularly toxic notion of selfhood that is currently endorsed widely as an aspirational model of being. The fetishisation of the entrepreneur is seen in the hero worship of the likes of Mark Zuckerberg, founder of Facebook; Jeff Bezos, founder of Amazon; Elon Musk, the founder of Tesla and Space X; and Peter Thiel, venture capitalist and investor in several financially profitable ventures. This model of the entrepreneur owes its existence in part to the cult of Steve Jobs. The entrepreneur is a contemporary version of the Malboro Man with a dash of Einstein—a Rambo-like figure with the zeal of a crusader, who fights inefficiency, stasis and competition with data, algorithms and hyper-efficient customer service, seeking to shape the world in accordance with his singular vision. The entrepreneur is almost always male, and represents a new ideal of American and, increasingly, global masculinity.[57]

Certitude has always been a quality associated with conventional notions of masculinity, of course. The hero, sure of himself, even if his rush into battle is an act of folly, is constructed as the ideological antithesis of the weak and wavering woman. From swashbuckling conquerors and historical figures like Alexander the Great to the strong leaders mythologised in national histories like Winston Churchill, or characters in Hollywood cinema like Indiana Jones, the decisive man knows exactly what action to undertake, whether it is to quell adversity, destroy an enemy or rescue a damsel in distress. In the present moment, this figure takes on a more sophisticated avatar as that heroism is fused with the attribute of oracular vision. We want Musk and Zuckerberg to solve the social problems that we think governments cannot solve, be it providing widespread internet access to overcome the digital divide, radically reducing poverty, figuring out how to deliver vaccines to large numbers of people or yoking the backward masses of the world into an enlightened modern sensibility.

The second reason for the value of *nishkama karma* is that in the thick of crisis globalisation, with things falling apart, it would seem intuitively right that political decisiveness is the need of the hour. The Gita, of course, has much to say about the value of both decisiveness and doubt with regard to a decision or an action, so its relevance on the virtue of political certitude should be obvious. This reason is not entirely unconnected from the rationale presented above about the import of the doctrine of action separated from outcomes. Politicians, after all, are entrepreneurs of the self, and the bravado and bluster of political leaders and figures who seem perennially anxious to show that they are always in control, like Trump, Modi, Putin and other strongmen, is not that far removed from the delusional arrogance of a Zuckerberg or the Himalayan self-regard of an Elon Musk. Modi's actions—such as the abrogation of Article 370 and the withdrawal of the special status of Kashmir, demonetisation, military provocations and clashes with China, forced lockdowns in response to the COVID-19 crisis, accompanied by feel-good rituals like getting Indians to clang vessels in unison—may radiate an illusion of strength, but a sombre assessment of their impact shows that beyond appeasing his Hindu base and appealing to a pervasive communalism among a wide cross-section of caste Hindus, his actions have not necessarily amounted to much of value.

In contrast to the unreflexive certitude displayed by the heroes of our age, Arjuna's anguish, doubt and despondency provide a superior ethic for how to be, live and act. Arjuna must go through doubt about engaging in war, even if he is eventually persuaded by Krishna to fight. To not experience such doubt may be the greater sin than to equivocate about fighting. Arjuna's initial action to not fight is, therefore, as correct an action as is his subsequent one of picking up arms to do battle. Herein lies another paradox of the Gita, but like its other paradoxes, it is a productive one. What is unique about the Gita's advice is not the fact that we cannot control outcomes but the demand that we accept and internalise this through discipline and renunciation. If hope, expectation and desire are quintessentially human traits, then it is a fair question to ask if the Gita is demanding that we quash what is fundamentally human about us.

The third reason for the relevance of *nishkama karma* is that the Gita offers a critique of the dominant ideology of our times, the philosophy that underlies the global capitalist system, sometimes called 'neoliberalism'. The economic orthodoxy that informs the functioning of our world is the idea that humans will always act in their self-interest to maximise their gains. Expressed in the technical jargon of social science, *homo economicus* or economic man (or the economic human) is one whose actions are geared towards 'individualistic rational optimization'.[58] The power of this idea or conception of the human to influence and dictate our lives should not be underestimated. Notwithstanding its inability to predict the 2008 global financial crash, the prestige of economics, and of neoclassical economics, remains undimmed as a master discourse to explain human behaviour itself. At least since the inauguration of neoliberalism in the 1980s, during the Reagan and Thatcher eras in the US and the UK, this model of human behaviour has guided policymaking and governance in not just the economic realm but the areas of law and regulation, education, childcare and healthcare as well. Neoliberalism, as the sociologist Pierre Bourdieu suggests in a series of brief, pugnacious essays, is the machine that now produces the world as we know it.[59] The values of productivity and efficiency have become the yardstick to judge all of human behaviour and as the political scientist Michael Sandel argues, we are moving from a model of a society with a market economy to a model of a market society itself.[60]

Yet, this model of human action and behaviour is based on assumptions about human nature that are taken to be axiomatic truths. Yes, we know extreme cases of persons, or types, who maximise their self-interest. In my own professional backyard, so to speak, it is the pompous over-competitive academic, full of his or her own importance but insecure about the recognition that others get and not above sabotaging careers. In the setting of the corporate world, it is the sycophant whose prime talent is careerism, kissing up and punching down. And in politics it is the schemer, survivor and hustler, not above dispatching anyone who gets in his or her way. The Indian reader will readily recognise any number of living and dead Indian politicians who fit this bill, whether Congress members who sing the praises of secularism each day only to jump ship in favour of the BJP's avowed anti-secularism the next, leaders of the BJP whose policies have caused untold harm to social relations and the dignity of Indians even as they tout the virtues of religious patriotism, or the equally opportunistic Johnny-come-latelys of the Aam Aadmi Party.

But the idea that such actions represent a universal model of human behaviour flies in the face of many altruistic, selfless and compassionate actions that each of us can recount: the person who risks career advancement by coming out as a whistleblower; the activist who risks his or her life for a future that he or she may not even be able to partake in; or the ordinary person who displays extraordinary compassion in his or her life, seemingly immune from calculations of what he or she may get in return. In looking for evidence of the complexities of human motivation and behaviour, we could do worse than to turn to literature. Other disciplines as well, like psychology and psychoanalysis, history and anthropology, as much as philosophy, all tell us that rationality, as indeed the conception of the human self, is not a universal constant across time and space. It is socially constructed, deeply contextual and situational.

The only way in which the assumption that self-interest is a governing principle of human behaviour can be defended is through some convoluted argument that all kinds of actions and behaviours are, in fact, self-interested. According to this logic, humans who are self-destructive or enjoy killing others are maximising their self-interest in every bit the same manner and degree as humans who are self-interested in more recognisable and conventional ways. This line of argument, for example, would hold that someone who winds up in jail and on the evening news for destroying public property is maximising their self-interest because they crave attention or feel exhilarated at experiencing the sense of being an outlaw. Another extreme example of the doctrine would describe a person who gives up all their belongings and chooses a life of voluntary poverty, austerity and self-denial as maximising their self-interest because these choices give them deep satisfaction.

The claim may hold in some cases, no doubt, such as in instances when people make sacrifices that ultimately benefit everyone or defer gratification to reap rewards later. But it is a stretch to apply it to all acts of recklessness, selflessness or sacrifice. If a concept is so elastic as to be applicable to practically any situation, it is, in essence, meaningless. The more generous way to read the assumption of self-interestedness as a foundational human attribute is to acknowledge that it is an assumption *required by a model*; for the model to be viable at all, we need to believe that human behaviour can be seen *as if* it is rational and guided by, at the very least, an instinct of self-preservation or, at the other extreme, by a kind of debased, bestial greed, with everything in between included in the category of self-interest.

But whichever kind of reading of the principle we adopt, the assumption that human action and practice is guided by self-interest is one that has had real, material effects on countless lives. It is perhaps the strongest voluntary determinant of the political economy of globalisation. And if social, economic and political structures founded on the principle in turn start shaping people's behaviour by valorising and rewarding extreme self-centredness, the idea of self-interestedness as the fundamental drive underlying human action becomes a self-fulfilling and self-propagating myth. In other words, it is the system that is geared towards producing selfishness that incentivises selfishness, rather than selfishness being the psychological or behavioural foundation of the system. Yet, of course, we also know that every so often this system comes crashing down, as it did in 2008, a result of foolish optimism married to untrammelled corporate greed. Self-interestedness by itself, then, cannot guarantee a stable state of affairs. Marx famously described these periodic meltdowns as an outcome of the contradictions of each stage of capitalism. The contradictory logic at the heart of the market society model that animates the engine of economic globalisation is encapsulated in the twin beliefs that we cannot control outcomes or engineer societies but that minimally regulated markets will function effectively and fairly, thanks to the magical power of human self-interestedness.

Action for a global world: Outcomes versus consequences

In the present, we face another economic crisis, brought about by the COVID-19 pandemic, whose effects will be felt for generations, as was the case with the 2008 financial crisis. For the last year, the US has been the site of a natural experiment about the viability and limits of a model of society that takes human self-interestedness as axiomatic. As the spread of the virus has seemed to be brought under control in other parts of the world, it has continued to wreak havoc in the US. While societies that had initially tamed the spread of the virus have also experienced setbacks, having to grapple with resurgent waves of infections, the response in the US, barring some pockets, has been uniformly ineffectual. As of late January 2021, more Americans have died of COVID-19 than were killed in the Second World War.[61] Unsurprisingly for a society that valorises selfishness, the refusal of many Americans to wear masks has repeatedly been framed as an assertion of individual rights and freedoms against a tyrannical government. The last year has seen quite a few incidents of brutal violence aimed at store employees, cashiers and the like who have asked customers to wear masks in the interests of public health or as enforcement of a store policy. The distinction between not controlling outcomes and being aware of the consequences of one's actions can provide an effective basis for making a case for the value of wearing masks in a global crisis, if there ever was one. Wearing masks, for instance, is an act that primarily protects others—it is effective collectively only to the degree that it is an act that is reciprocated and followed by everyone. If I pass you by on the street within the danger zone of six feet and I do not happen to be wearing a mask, I may infect you if I am a carrier or spreader, even if you happen to be wearing a mask. In the same scenario, by wearing a mask, you have reduced the risk of infecting me, if you happen to be a carrier or spreader of the coronavirus.

If we both were to think of the consequences of our actions, knowing that we may not be able to fully control the outcome, we would both have done our ethical duty, engaged in the appropriate ethical action and taken an important step beyond the blinkers of narrow self-interest. Either of us may still contract the virus, and walking on a street in San Francisco we may not be able to dictate what happens in Ventura county in California, Illinois, or Mumbai. But even with the knowledge that we cannot control outcomes, we may have moved the needle in the direction of fewer lives lost because of the virus.

One can bring this into the fold of 'maximising self-interest' by arguing that wearing a mask is in one's self-interest because by doing so one sends a message to others that one is acting in an altruistic manner, thereby providing them with the incentive to reciprocate. Yet, as pointed above, the opposition to masks by lay people has *also* been defended on grounds of freedom, liberty and rights against government tyranny: in other words, the very principles that adherents of classical liberalism and libertarianism claim as foundational to those discourses. Such an argument, which insists that wearing masks is an act that is *purely* in one's self-interest—and that pure self-interest without consideration for others is all that is required to ensure the effective functioning of society—is an inherently spurious one.

Wearing a mask, which cannot guarantee an outcome but is a decision taken with the horizon of a possible consequence in view, is the kind of ethical action that is consistent with my reading of the concept of *nishkama karma*. It also reinforces an obvious, if often ignored, fact about globalisation as an order that links nations together, which is that the global is not above, prior to or superior to the national or the local. Rather, the global is constituted through the local and national and resides in them. Wearing masks in the US, for instance, is an act that will benefit not just Americans but the rest of the world too, given the massive flows of tourists, students, businesspersons and families between America and the rest of the world. A similar approach can guide our response to seemingly global problems that appear overwhelming, like climate change, war or persistent conflict caused by cultural differences.

4

THE GITA, DIFFERENCE AND UNIVERSALITY IN THE AGE OF CRISIS GLOBALISATION

Difference: An introduction

As a basic definition, difference marks the distance between historically dominant or traditionally privileged forms of identity and their respective opposites—for example, the distance between being male and female, straight and queer, a member of a racial or ethnic majority and one of a racial or ethnic minority. The idea of difference has a long history; one, arguably, as old as the very conception of being. The demarcation between masculine and feminine principles in myth and religion is an example of difference, as is the contrast drawn in the colonising European gaze between the figure of the indigenous savage and the Westerner who represents civilisation. The modern idea of difference unhinges and reclaims the concept from received understandings, strips it of its pejorative content and reframes it in positive terms. Being female no longer needs to be judged by comparison to the experience of malehood. Being Indian or Chinese does not depend on the relationship of Indian or Chinese identity to Western, European or American forms of selfhood.

Queer identity need not take straight identity as a norm against which to measure and assess itself.

In the contemporary understanding of the term, difference shares a foundational relationship with diversity, which is the social fact of the many overlapping and unique ways of being human. Difference bears the same relationship to the principle of inclusion, that is, the acceptance, recognition and equal treatment of humanity in all its diversity. The principle of difference, then, is also fundamentally linked to the notion of equal rights, premised on the recognition of various forms of identity as complete in themselves and deserving of the same protections, privileges and respect as any other. Difference, finally, stands in a complex relationship with the idea of the universal. The fight for the recognition of difference is guided by universal ideas of justice, equality and rights. Yet, difference also serves as a critique of any universal, abstract idea of the human that may take a particular gender, racial group, sexual identity and the like as an implicit norm.

Difference as a key element in thinking about identity emerged roughly in the context of struggles in the 1960s, coincidentally around the same time that the forces we associate with globalisation began to slowly transform the world.[1] Some conception of identity—gendered, cultural, national, class, racial—is essential to all political movements. Movements in the earlier part of the twentieth century, whether for women's rights, civil rights, or independence, however, also strongly emphasised universal principles, such as the goal of legal equality. The success of those struggles arguably enabled the idea of *irreducible* and *unassimilable* difference to take centre stage in the agenda of later identity-based social movements. A number of factors coalesced to produce the emphasis on difference in the realm of social thought and institutionalised knowledge about selfhood and identity. Winkler and Olivier note that:

Since the 1960s, the intellectual landscape of the humanities has been overshadowed by the question of identity and difference—political and national identity, ethnic and racial identity, gender identity and, in philosophy, the question of the identity of the self and of the knowing, acting and desiring subject. This is partly due to the social, cultural and political upheavals experienced in different parts of the globe at the time, for example, the movement of decolonization in Sub-Saharan Africa, the Civil Rights Movement in the USA, or second-wave feminism.[2]

Far from being the fantasy of woolly-headed academics in their ivory towers, as shallow critiques of 'identity politics' hold, the concept of difference emerged organically from struggles on the ground, from the hard-won realisation that concepts of the self that had dominated institutionalised forms of knowledge in disciplines like philosophy, history, anthropology or psychology were inadequate in capturing the diversity of human experience.[3] Received knowledge about the human subject did not capture the historical, sociological and phenomenological experience of what it meant to be Black, female or a colonised subject. This led to a reflexive turn in the human sciences about implicitly or explicitly articulated ideas of the human that permeated scholarship in different disciplines. The reflexive turn also included a look at the fields' own origins and histories, for instance, the colonial narrative of Indian history that continued to inform historiography well after Indian independence, anthropology's construction of the figure of the savage and its complicity with the civilising mission in the early history of ethnography, the erasure of the history of the non-Western world in accounts of modernity and the abstraction of the human self, shorn of history, race and gender, that had dominated much of Western philosophy.[4]

Thanks in part to globalisation and global media technologies, engaging with difference is now an essential and constant part of present-day social reality. The technological, political, economic and cultural processes central to globalisation have enabled the proliferation and recognition of difference along the many axes of human identity—race, ethnicity, nationality, religion, gender, sexual orientation, ability and social class, among others. However, the same processes have made those who symbolise or represent difference more vulnerable to discrimination, intimidation and attack. One way or another, difference cannot be ignored. This grants the principle of difference as well as the bearers of difference more political power in public life but also places them at greater risk because they appear more threatening to those who see difference and its representatives as disruptive of deeply entrenched ideological beliefs, religious dogma or received wisdom.

Both engine and symbol of globalisation, the internet has empowered more groups to speak and share their experiences online, whether these are persecuted religious, ethnic and cultural minorities, invisible and marginalised communities, or individuals or groups stigmatised for their life choices. But the internet has also made such collectivities susceptible to surveillance and persecution by state authorities, extremists and vindictive majorities. The pervasive practice of trolling, an unfortunate and ugly aspect of global internet culture, tends to disproportionately focus on minorities and women as targets. An inescapable fact of life in a global world, difference manifests itself in highly visible and often highly dangerous ways to majorities of one kind or another: in the unfamiliar garb of the Sikh man in the US or the veiled woman in Europe; in the reality of non-binary gender identities that trouble institutions built on normative notions of gender, such as the military or educational system; or the bodies of people with disabilities in settings that are ableist in their design and architecture.

A word of caution is in place here, though. As implied by Winkler and Olivier in the quote earlier, neither globalisation nor global media technologies are the cause of the recently amplified importance of difference in discussions about rights, equality, identity and democracy. To make such a claim would be to fall prey to the most reductive kind of technological and social determinism. The centrality of difference in political struggles, as is the case with the political struggles themselves, is the result of human agency and collective action; globalisation has but provided these struggles and movements new mechanisms, audiences and opportunities. The sociologist Zeynep Tufecki's book, *Twitter and Tear Gas: The Power and Fragility of Networked Protest*, which examines the role of social media in the Arab Spring, the term used for the popular uprisings of the early 2010s in West Asia and North Africa, richly illuminates the capabilities and limitations of such technologically networked political movements.[5] Tufecki's nuanced and insightful analysis is a much-needed and sobering corrective to the grand claims made in Silicon Valley and technocratic circles in general on behalf on Facebook, Twitter and the like as unmanned weapons of democracy that are able to depose dictators, transform societal consciousness in favour of egalitarian values and, in effect, redesign entire societies. While such hyperbolic arguments have been dialled back a bit recently, in the wake of greater awareness about the negative impact of social media on democracy, the fetishisation of technology as an autonomous vector of societal change largely persists in popular and public discourse.

The efforts of international non-governmental organisations like Amnesty International and Human Rights Watch, which are dedicated to the protection of human rights, have also granted visibility and lent vital support to social movements based on difference, whether for women's rights, LGBTQ+ rights or the rights of minorities like Uighurs in China, Hindus and Christians in Pakistan, Yazidis in Iraq or Rohingya in Myanmar. These organisations also speak up for those accused of or punished for blasphemy in theocratic states such as Saudi Arabia. However, states have pushed back against such criticism, invoking the principle of sovereignty against what they label as illegitimate interference in their internal affairs. Nation-states continue to exercise their formidable might to defend and legitimise the oppression of minorities.[6] Indeed, difference has proved contentious and troublesome for the state. Theoretically, states that profess allegiance to the principles of democracy, equality and human rights should grant all citizens the same freedom to dress, behave and worship as they please. Yet, in every such society that calls itself a democracy, whether Switzerland, the US, Turkey or India, the commitment to equality squares uneasily with the concessions granted to ethnic, racial, cultural or religious majorities. The underlying belief at work here is that the society in question has been primarily shaped by the majority, be they White European Christians, Sunni Muslims or caste Hindus. The practices of Shi'a Muslims in Pakistan, Hindus in the UK, or Dalits and Muslims in India, even when tolerated, are assumed to be at odds with the culture of an imagined national community.[7] India stands as a perfect example of a state that has defiantly continued to wield its power against minorities, in recent years very pointedly against its Muslim, Dalit and Kashmiri citizens, while targeting human rights organisations that have been critical of its actions. In September 2020, Amnesty International shuttered its Indian offices after the Modi government raided its premises and froze its bank accounts, punitive measures that Amnesty contends were carried out in retaliation for its criticism of the government's human rights policies.[8] Difference has become an object of contestation, an arena in which the principles of national sovereignty and international commitment to justice clash, a space in which states and communities fight for the right to determine the shape and substance of citizenship, belonging and selfhood.

Difference and Indian identity

The idea of difference has been crucial to the project of modern Indian identity, while also serving as central to the self-image of Indian society and to the perception of India in the eyes of the world. The diversity of Indian society is a well-worn cliché found everywhere from academic discourse to travel guides, which, like other common clichés about Indian pluralistic culture and tolerance, frequently lapses into hyperbole or a reductive exceptionalism. Any number of academic works on Indian history focus significantly on the intricate web of shared identities and differences, histories of conflict and confluence, social tensions and patterns of coexistence among various Indian groups, with regard to language, region, religion, caste, class and gender. Difference and assimilation are a key trope and organising principle of entire strands of Indian historiography, such as Nehru's *Discovery of India* and the Left-nationalist and Marxist schools of Indian history. Difference is the metahistorical trope that informs and animates the historical biography generated by the postcolonial Indian state about itself and the dominant strands of academic history. In his elegant essayistic meditation, *The Idea of India*, the scholar Sunil Khilnani points out that the genius of Nehru's conception of India lay precisely in the fact that it centred the idea of difference itself as the foundation on which Indian national identity was anchored.[9] For Nehru, Indianness could not be reduced to an essential—and essentialist—set of core characteristics. Rather, in his understanding, 'India was a society neither of liberal individuals nor of exclusive communities or nationalities but of interconnected differences.'[10] Nehru's idea of India was radical in that it was an anti-definition, standing the conventional homogenising logic of nationalism on its head. In its historical and sociological dimensions, Indian identity was a matrix of similarities and differences, overlapping practices and family resemblances between and across groups, but not a prescriptive mould into which the irreducibly complex lives of a bewilderingly diverse collection of peoples had to be forcibly fit.

Today, though, the Nehruvian project of managing difference by making it central to Indianness appears like a pale shadow of itself. Somewhat idealised and utopian in aspiration anyway, the Nehruvian vision of India downplayed the homogenising tendencies of Indian political, social and cultural life through history, whether the caste orthodoxies of Brahmins and other caste Indians, the puritanical religious zealotry of rulers like Aurangzeb or the legacies of a collectivist mindset which demanded social conformity in private and public life.[11] It was also often at odds with the ground realities of religious conflict and persistent caste violence across vast swathes of India. Nevertheless, the formidable charismatic authority of the leaders of the Indian nationalist movement, the central role of the Congress party in Indian independence and the euphoria of liberation from colonial rule meant that the model, warts and all, and often far removed from reality, nonetheless, exercised a powerful hold in the imagination of state and society. Even if utterly insincere in intent, the demonstration and performance of Indianness demanded lip service or a perfunctory gesture to the principles of secularism, inclusiveness and pluralism that were at the heart of Nehru's view of Indian society.

The erosion of the legitimacy of Nehru's idea of an inclusive India is the culmination of processes and trends long in the making, which will be familiar to Indian readers, including the anti-Sikh pogrom of 1984 following the assassination of Indira Gandhi, the controversy over the Shah Bano judgement in 1985 and the Rajiv Gandhi government's decision to overturn the ruling of the court by passing the Muslim Women (Protection of Rights on Divorce) Act, 1986, the destruction of the Babri Masjid in December 1992 by a mob of Hindu extremists, the Hindu-Muslim riots that followed and the targeting of Muslims by the Shiv Sena in Maharashtra, and the routine demonisation of Muslim Indians as terrorists in the post-9/11 world.[12] Yet, under Modi's rule in the last six years, these fractures and fissures along the lines of religion and community have deepened to the point of threatening the very edifice on which the postcolonial Indian state stands. The project of Indian secularism appears to be in tatters as a reason of state, and if it has not been completely leached out of Indian society, the shrill cries of advocates of Hindu nationalism easily drown out those who speak up for the equal rights of religious minorities in public spaces, physical or mediated. Almost immediately after the Modi government won the 2014 Indian general elections, Hindu cow-vigilante mobs and self-styled Hindu militia organisations embarked on a spree of violent assaults against Muslims, often based on flimsy accusations that the Muslims in questions had been illegally peddling or eating beef.[13] The casteism at the heart of Hindu nationalism, despite its rhetoric of commitment to an overarching idea of Hindu unity based on the equality of all Hindus, has likewise contributed to an increase in violence against Dalits since the BJP-led NDA government took power.[14] The routinely horrific incidents of sexual violence against women in India that make the papers of the national and international press practically every week have disproportionately involved vulnerable caste communities, a pattern that has persisted under the overly patriarchal and casteist framework of Hindu nationalist ideology.[15] In part, such violence may represent an upper-caste pushback against the caste-based political mobilisation and greater assertiveness by marginalised and subaltern caste groups that have been part of the social churn experienced by India in recent decades.[16] But the ascendancy of Modi has accelerated and concatenated such trends, enabling a counter-revolution by caste Hindus against Dalits in particular. The anti-Dalit violence is also of a piece with the violence against Muslims, meant to drive home the message about who can claim India as their own, who calls the shots in India, and the right claimed by upper-caste Hindus to determine the fates of others in Indian society.

In the aftermath of the BJP's spectacular electoral victory in 2014, the violence against Muslims and Dalits was largely carried out by Hindu groups and individuals who had taken the results of the election as a sign of encouragement to target minorities, assuming correctly that they would not be held accountable for their actions under the new dispensation. In a strategy that allowed them to claim deniability for any violence and its consequences, Modi and other representatives of the Indian state encouraged such actions through their vituperative discourse and dog whistling, while mostly steering clear of direct calls to violence against particular Indian groups.[17] In tandem, Modi, Shah and the BJP have unhesitatingly weaponised the capacities of the state and state institutions to eviscerate the rights of minorities. Since 2014, they have followed the principle of death by a thousand cuts to capture, compromise and undermine state institutions in the sphere of education, economics, judiciary, and even cricket, such that these vital organs of the Indian state have become indistinguishable from the entity that is the BJP. Three recent events, carried out under the Modi–Shah regime, should suffice here to convey the seriousness and success of the Hindu Right project to capture state institutions.

The first is the Modi government's decision in August 2019 to revoke the special status of Kashmir, robbing it of its constitutionally guaranteed autonomy to whatever extent it had existed in practice.[18] The second is the judgement of the Indian Supreme Court in November 2019, granting the disputed site of the Babri Masjid to Hindus, clearing the way for the long-standing dream of Hindu nationalists to build a temple there.[19] In September 2020, an Indian court also acquitted all those accused of the demolition of the mosque in 1992, including BJP leaders like L.K. Advani.[20] Together, the judgment and acquittal ring a death knell for any vestigial belief in the Indian judiciary as custodians of rights for religious minorities. The third event is the Citizenship Amendment Act passed in December 2019. Critics argue that in conjunction with the proposed National Register of Citizens, the recently passed law will disenfranchise Indian Muslims while also denying persecuted Muslims from neighbouring Muslim-majority countries like Pakistan and Bangladesh the opportunity of political sanctuary in India.[21]

Neither the decision of the Supreme Court about the Ayodhya judgment nor the violence against Muslims and Dalits have provoked widespread protests by Indian elites or by subaltern Hindu groups who see themselves as above Dalits in the hierarchy of Hindu caste identities. Numerous cities in India did see significant protests against the new citizenship law, but politicians from opposition parties had to tread a careful line in registering their criticisms for fear of being seen as batting for illegal Muslim migrants from Bangladesh and Pakistan at the expense of the interests of Hindu citizens. The actions of the government regarding Kashmir presented opposition parties with a similar dilemma. Ably assisted by a pliant, jingoistic media whose shrill reporting was indistinguishable from propaganda, the BJP successfully framed the actions and conversation on the subject as a much-needed measure to serve the national interest. Following in the wake of a particularly restive political phase in Kashmir, which had undone the positive steps taken towards political stability by the previous United Progressive Alliance (UPA) government, Modi and the BJP coded their actions as essential for securing the integrity of the nation against the Pakistan-enabled terrorist activities of Muslim Kashmiris. The acceptance, if not approval, of these and other actions of the Modi-helmed BJP government are just more proof of the power of the Hindu nationalist idea of India in the imagination of the Indian people.

The problem of difference in the Gita

These struggles over difference in India and elsewhere appear far removed from the world of the Gita. Like many significant religious and cultural texts, the Gita is often praised for the applicability of its wisdom to society across time and space, with the enduring popularity of the book invoked as proof of the universal relevance of what the text has to say about the human condition, a message that presumably applies to humans in all their diversity. But the Gita is rooted in a world in which modern notions of equality and rights were alien as were the modern ideal of citizenship and the idea of the individual as the sovereign author of his or her life story. The vision of humanity articulated in the Gita is yoked to a divinely sanctioned model of caste and the patriarchal family. The unequal order of things in this material world is an embodiment of the cosmic order. A harmonious consonance between matters on earth and the divine world is essential for social stability. The Gita's messages of universalism may resonate with modern notions of inclusion, but the text also endorses caste inequality and, by extension, the general principle of inequality. If Gandhi found in the Gita the resources for a universal theory of good versus evil and an overarching philosophy of life, for Ambedkar the text remained politically regressive in its valorisation of the inequities of the caste system.

Even if one were to assume, for the sake of argument, that one could work through and reconcile the contradictions of the Gita and see it as a manifesto for the dignity and honour of all human beings, or as a statement of norms by which all humans are to be judged, how would any such reading square with the legacy of caste violence that has been a permanent stain on Indian history? Or, how would such a reading hold as valid, given the history of blatantly exclusionary actions of the postcolonial Indian state, which have reached a crescendo in the past few years? The defence of the Gita's universality, after all, frames it as a uniquely Indian philosophical-ethical statement about the nature and complexity of human beings. If this is indeed the case and if the text is as prominent in Indian life as widely acknowledged, what would explain the gap between the values in the text and the less savoury aspects of the social reality which the text is meant to inform and reflect?

For Indians and observers of India, there is another urgent question raised by the universalism of the Gita. Granting that one finds in the Gita an impulse towards equality as well as its opposite, and granting that the text possesses sufficient semantic plenitude for competing interpretations, why has Gandhi's vision of the Gita—or his vision of Hinduism, for that matter—not been as influential in present-day Indian politics and society as has the weaponisation of iconic, highly visible symbols of Hinduism, including the Gita, through the project of Hindutva or Hindu nationalism? Adherents of Hindutva or Hindu nationalist ideology see absolutely no contradiction in invoking the Gita as proof of their universalism while expressing the most hostile sentiments towards Muslims, Christians and Dalits. On Twitter and Facebook, any number of accounts that identify themselves as Hindu, signalling their adherence to the faith with messages from Hindu texts as part of their profiles, unrelentingly spew bile against minorities, liberals, secularists and anyone that they term 'anti-Hindus'. For all its ubiquity, for all the universality of insight about the human condition that is attributed to it and for all its emphasis on the idea of *dharma*, that is, moral obligation or ethical duty, the Gita, it would seem, has not necessarily contributed to widespread social transformation with regard to caste, gender equality or communal harmony, though it may have undoubtedly led to many individual acts of compassion or been inspirational for any number of people.

Such tensions between the universalism professed in the

text and the realities of patriarchy and caste in the Gita and the Mahabharata are not unique to the Indian context or these works. Texts from other religious and cultural traditions, whether the Bible or the Qur'an, bear the same contradictions with regard to the rights of women, non-believers or non-members of the faith.[22] Democracy and slavery coexisted in the world of ancient Greece; the Enlightenment project and its progeny, including Western liberalism, could live comfortably, even harmoniously, with slavery and colonialism from the seventeenth through the twentieth century; and in the twentieth century, nakedly imperialistic invasions and occupations have been carried out in the name of protecting human rights, often resulting in the death of several orders more of lives than they were meant to save.[23]

These kinds of contradictions are perhaps also not that far removed from the tensions that bedevil almost all modern societies. Inequality, hierarchies and discrimination are not the preserve of the nonmodern and pre-modern alone. India and the US, the two countries in which I have spent my life, are plagued by deep-rooted and pervasive inequalities and injustices, despite being democracies and relentlessly touting themselves as such. European nations that profess secularism and see themselves as the bastion of Enlightenment values invoke the force of the state to protect the Christian heritage of Europe in the face of fears of being overrun by Muslim immigrants. The opposition to admitting Turkey into the European Union goes back close to two decades at the least and shows no signs of abating. While recent reasons offered for its exclusion centre on its poor human rights record, the long-standing refusal to accept Turkey as a European nation is rooted in the idea of a Muslim-majority country as fundamentally incompatible with European values, culture and identity.[24] Violence against women continues to plague societies across the globe, including those that have made great strides towards gender equality in the form of equal protections for women and laws that are gender just.[25] Till relatively recently, the US did not grant equal protections in most spheres of life to LGBTQ+ populations, who are yet to achieve full equality and social acceptance. Obama, touted as a modern icon of liberalism, openly opposed gay marriage while running for president in the 2008 elections, claiming later that his views on the subject had evolved.[26]

At the very least, then, it is an open question whether the universalism of the Gita is able to transcend its endorsement of the hierarchies of caste and family or whether these hierarchies subvert and compromise the universal value of the insights of the Gita. In light of our expanded understanding of difference, diversity and inclusion, it is legitimate to inquire whether a nonmodern and pre-modern text like the Gita can genuinely speak to modern notions of identity and difference that are intimately tied to equality, rights and justice. For the purposes of a book such as this one, which seeks to understand the possible value of the Gita in addressing the most urgent philosophical, political, social and ethical questions of our times, one has to squarely face and grapple with the contradictions of the text as a matter of interpretation, method and ethical inquiry. Any such reading must be scrupulous in refusing to erase or sidestep those aspects of the text that contradict a politics of inclusion and diversity. With this awareness and with the knowledge that the tensions within the Gita—as they appear in the light of modern, present-day standards of equality, rights and justice, or even in their own context—may not be fully resolved, we can approach the text with the possibility and hope that it may still be able to meaningfully contribute to modern-day debates about difference.

Romila Thapar notes that the world of the Mahabharata is one that is transitioning from a system shaped by the bonds of clan society to those shaped by caste norms.[27] The characters in the Mahabharata are required to follow the obligations of clan societies, such as to their kin, but the principle of kingship also requires that the ruler in such a milieu has to endorse the hierarchical logic of caste. Thapar suggests, though, that even clan society designated those who fell outside the clan system as the 'non-caste Other'.[28] In the narrative of the Mahabharata, these communities of forest dwellers, such as the Nishada and the Shabara, bear all the markers of stigma of the dehumanised person. Impure, outcast, shunned and expendable, they are treated by the 'heroes of the Mahabharata . . . as virtually bereft of human value'.[29] Thapar draws attention to the episode in the epic about a Nishada woman and her five sons, who are deliberately burnt alive in a house for the purpose of tricking the Kauravas into thinking that it was the Pandavas who had perished.[30] That the fact of their identity is excised from R.K. Narayan's elegantly succinct rendition of the Mahabharata is telling in itself, possibly reflecting a deeper cultural anxiety about the inescapable reality of brutal caste violence in one of the urtexts of Hindu society.[31] In her foreword to Narayan's version of the Mahabharata, the scholar Wendy Doniger explains the famed Indian author's silence on 'the more controversial issues' of the text, such as the expendability and dispensability of lower-caste lives, as an unease with the ugly, inescapable truth of casteism in Hindu society.[32]

Yet, the politics of difference in the Mahabharata are less straightforward than appears to be the case at face value. Given its sprawling nature and digressions, its status as an open-ended text that has gathered stories in its fold through historical accretion, and its many versions, the Mahabharata also offers a basis for critiquing caste norms, patriarchal gender relations and violence while it endorses the same. The well-known parable of Eklavya richly illuminates this polysemic complexity of the epic. Eklavya was a Nishada prince who desired to learn archery.

He approached Dronacharya, the teacher of the Pandavas and Kauravas, in the hope that the learned guru would take him as a disciple. Dronacharya refused since Eklavya was not of royal blood. Undeterred, Eklavya built a clay statue of Dronacharya, and, using the idol as a proxy for the teacher, mastered the art of archery. It so happened that Eklavya's talents came to the attention of Arjuna. Threatened by Eklavya's abilities, Arjuna voiced his displeasure to Dronacharya, accusing his teacher of reneging on his promise of making Arjuna the greatest archer in the world. Seeking to get to the bottom of the matter, Dronacharya asked Eklavya to reveal the identity of his guru, only to hear the young man take his name. Revealing Dronacharya's statue to the master, Eklavya explained that he had taken the statue to stand in for Drona himself and had accordingly practiced his craft. To keep his promise to Arjuna and to ensure Arjuna's supremacy in archery, Dronacharya asked Eklavya to cut his thumb off and offer it to him as *gurudakshina*, the offering given to a teacher in respect and gratitude. Without hesitation, Eklavya complied with Dronacharya's request.

The parable of Eklavya stands as a critique of the caste order and of the idea of innate Kshatriya nobility or *dharma* that Arjuna and Dronacharya are meant to possess. The story reveals the flaws of jealousy and insecurity that mar Arjuna's character, undermining his claim to possess the equanimity and freedom from desire and passion that Krishna, in the Gita, describes as the hallmark of the most evolved type of man, superior to both the man of base inclination and the man of impulse and passion. *Dharma* and *karma* are at odds in Arjuna's response and actions, as they are in Dronacharya's action of asking Eklayva for his thumb. In displaying the trait of envy and the unseemly desire to be the greatest archer, Arjuna falls short of the standard of desirable princely virtue too. Eklavya's sacrifice is lionised as proof of his noble and pure devotion to

Drona—whose clay statue Eklavya has taken as proxy for the great teacher and guru—but what it speaks most loudly of is the ignobility of Arjuna, the prince and warrior.[33]

The story can also be interpreted as a critique of the caste system. Aside from the instinctive reaction that the story evokes in us of a great injustice having been done to Eklavya, his literal disablement through the cutting off of his thumb can be read as a metaphor for the crippling effects of caste hierarchy and caste discrimination. The act symbolises the destruction of the human that the violence of caste necessarily entails, a reality that all too tragically persists in an India that likes to think of itself as a modern, enlightened, globalised superpower in the making. The act is made more horrific by the fact that Eklavya has to cut off his thumb himself, for that indicates that he has to accept—or has no choice but to accept—the ideological worldview and caste framework that can demand a severing of his self in the name of a ritualistic obligation.

The story of Eklavya shows how ability and merit are not innate functions of caste and birth, but are, in fact, socially produced; in this, the tale is consistent with modern understandings of disability and ability as socially produced conditions rather than definitive characterisations of the limits and capacities of an individual. The 'social model of disability', a paradigm which emphasises the socially produced character of the experience of disability, distinguishes between impairment and disability. Impairment is the fact of a physical condition that is 'non-standard', such as blindness. Such a condition is not necessarily seen in a negative manner by those who are impaired; they do not consider themselves less than others or incapacitated in any way.[34] Disability, however, is the 'disadvantage or restriction of activity caused by a contemporary social organization which takes no or little account of people who have physical impairments and thus excludes them from participation in the mainstream of social activities'.[35] Disability is the product of exclusion, resulting from social structures, practices and spaces that are constructed and function with no recognition of the existence of people who are impaired. Whether it is the education system, the design and architecture of buildings, the experience of watching a film in a cinema hall—all of these produce the condition of disability by shutting out people with impairments. Caste itself, as a form of social organisation to which exclusion is central, is disabling in this sense. Eklavya is first socially disabled when Dronacharya refuses his request to take him on as an apprentice, on the grounds that he is prohibited from teaching anyone other than royalty. Dronacharya's demand of Eklavya that he cut off his thumb is another act of disabling, a symbolic reminder of the power that Dronacharya wields over Eklavya, who belongs to a forest-dwelling tribe. Eklavya's cutting off of his thumb, finally, is an act of literal impairment that also disables him in that it effectively robs him of his exceptional ability as an archer. Eklavya's story, in sum, stands as a withering indictment of caste hierarchy privilege as literally impairing and socially disabling, a two-pronged destruction of the marginalised caste self.

The violence relentlessly meted out to Dalit bodies in postcolonial India relives this dual act of literal and social impairment and disability over and over again.[36] Dalit communities are at the receiving end of literal or physical violence, structural violence that operates as a near-permanent force of exclusion, and symbolic violence, in the form of routine verbal abuse, derogatory slurs and humiliation at the hands of privileged castes. In an article on the 2006 massacre of a Dalit family in Khairlanji, scholar Anand Teltumbde argues that the events of Khairlanji and their aftermath give the lie to any claim that the pervasive casteism of Indian society has diminished over time or that Dalits can hope to receive justice from the Indian state.[37] Crimes against Dalit groups have also been on the rise over the last decade or so, while conviction rates have declined, as a recent report by the National Campaign for Dalit Human Rights documents.[38] There may be no willing Eklavyas in India today, but the idea of innate caste superiority and inferiority retains its hegemonic status among large groups of Indians, despite the increased assertiveness of Dalit groups and communities.[39] In the present world, as in the world of the Mahabharata, the question of difference remains fundamental to identity and is equally inseparable from the matter of rights. The Mahabharata, of course, was not part of a world in which an ideal conception of selfhood would necessarily involve an engagement with a formally articulated framework of human rights. Yet, like any number of pre-modern and nonmodern texts that deal with human suffering, violence and inequity, it does tread into the realm of what we now recognise as a discourse of rights. The denial of freedom, the oppression that is based on social status and position, the violation of the sovereignty of the self, as in the case of Eklavya, Draupadi and other characters in the Mahabharata—all of these intimately mesh together matters of difference, identity and rights.

Difference, identity and rights

The idea of difference forms part of a trio of interlocked concepts, along with identity and rights, that have become fundamental to debates about being and belonging in the modern world. Emerging out of a long history of struggle for individual and collective rights, the idea of difference is essential to modern notions of personhood. The term immediately begs the question, though, of difference *from* what, implying the existence of some norm or benchmark against which an alternate conception of being is to be positioned. An assertion of difference, then, as noted earlier, serves as a critique of the norm while also staking a claim to parity with it.

As a kind of conceptual shorthand, the notion of difference can be parsed into three dimensions. The first aspect of difference posits that with regard to various attributes of identity, such as gender, race or sexual orientation, some categories within that attribute have been historically, legally, socially and culturally considered inferior to others. Women, for instance, have been treated as less than men, people of colour have been labelled inferior to Whites, religious minorities have been designated as aberrant in contrast to majorities and queer people have been treated as deviant in comparison to straight people. Difference has typically, if not always, marked a distance from a norm, operating traditionally or historically as a measure of inferiority. The second facet of difference follows from the first. It is centred on a political claim, specifically, the demand of equality in a limited, legal sense. The argument here is that those forms of identity that have been considered inferior or deviant—whether they are ascribed identities, that is, inherited and given, or adopted identities, that is, a matter of choice or preference— deserve the same legal rights as those identities which embody the norm. Women, Dalits, African Americans and members of LGBTQ+ populations are entitled to the same rights as men, caste Hindus, White Americans and non-LGBTQ+ communities. The third dimension of difference insists on the entitlement to social acceptance, respect and dignity of those who do not fit the norm or dominant social model of identity. The underlying point here is that legal equality is a necessary but insufficient condition to guarantee belonging and participation in social life in its fullness. Men whose self-expression does not conform to conventional notions of masculinity do not in any way warrant being denigrated by society as not manly enough, people in non-heterosexual relationships or marriages have every right to be accepted as legitimate couples, and ethnic or religious minorities like the Kurds in Turkey or Muslims in India should be able to claim the nation in the same sense, beyond the parameters of official citizenship, as Sunni Muslim Turks or Hindus might, respectively, in these countries.

On the one hand, then, the proliferation of identities that has been made possible by the assertion of difference forms the basis for individual self-definition, summed up in statements like 'I identify as x' or 'I don't identify as y'. On the other hand, these identifications, in that they represent membership of a collective, also become the basis for demands for political recognition, rights and dignity, both socially and legally. The fight for the recognition of new categories of identity seeks to place them on par with the accepted conventional divisions of human life, such as man and woman, drawing attention to the assumed norms that inform our use of language, practices and behaviour, dress codes and legal policies. The hope and expectation that people will use the retroactively created category of cisgender, for instance, to specify that they are not transgender, is an example of this shift. The suggested use of the phrase 'people with disabilities', likewise, takes disability not to be the defining mark nor the essential characteristic of a vast range of people who fall under that category but rather as a descriptive term that identifies one important aspect of their being while not seeking to exhaustively represent that being in its fullness.

I recall watching the great British actor Ian McKellen in a television interview several years ago, in which he made the point that being single was an honourable state, as was being married, as was being gay.[40] The statement struck me as especially powerful in capturing the essential equality and dignity of different forms of selfhood and self-expression. The relationship of difference with rights is also elegantly reflected in Justice Albie Sachs's profound insight that human rights are about *the right to be the same and the right to be different*.[41]

The relationship of identity and rights encompasses the principles of both universality and difference. I have the right to be treated just like everyone else regardless of my identity, and be granted the same rights and respect as anyone else. I also have the right to be acknowledged in my *particularity* as an Indian male, a queer person, a Muslim woman or an atheist—without the fact of my identity resulting in any diminution of my universal rights.

Difference and universality

Key to the theory and practice of selfhood in our present time, difference stands in a complex relationship to universality. The idea of difference in its modern sense calls into question whether dominant social models of identity, such as those based on gender, class, race, nationality, ethnicity, sexual orientation or able-bodiedness, can ever be truly universal, that is, if they can ever really encompass the full diversity of human being. The reason for this scepticism about the possibility of inclusive universalism, if one may call it that, is that dominant discourses are closely linked to, reflect and reproduce structures of power. The crucial philosophical question raised by assertions of difference, then, is whether such claims of universality are necessarily bound to privilege some humans at the cost of others, in both conceptual and practical terms, specifically those individuals and groups that possess more power because of an accident of history, brute physical strength, an unjust social order or a roll of the dice. The point of the critique of universalism is that there will always be an implicit norm on which the understanding of universalism is predicated, and that implicit norm will inevitably privilege some groups, forms of being or ways of life over others.

For the Indian context, the question is whether any normative notion of Indian identity that defines Indianness in terms of certain attributes can really ever be universal. Or, will the idea of Indianness, even in its more secular, egalitarian avatars, ultimately always exclude the marginal and vulnerable figure of the Dalit or the Muslim? Can a radically inclusive conception of sexuality truly encompass the full spectrum of sexual identities or will that imperative of inclusion ultimately be limited by the spectre of heterosexual identity as the invisible, privileged norm? Immanuel Wallerstein, for instance, has argued that European universalism is simply another name for a will to imperialist domination. In the name of universalism and universal conceptions of rights, freedom and equality, ironically, non-European peoples have been denied these very rights, freedom and equality.[42]

In practical terms, the problem of the limit of universality takes shape as a question of the adequacy of legal equality for ensuring social equality. The struggles of practically every marginalised group for equal rights, dignity and justice show that legal equality, while absolutely necessary, is by no means sufficient to guarantee social inclusion and full participation and belonging in a society. Women, people of colour, people with disabilities, and others who, for one reason or another, have been considered less than full subjects or individuals, now stake a claim to equal rights, equality of access to all aspects of social life, full participation in civic rituals and the same entitlement to represent community and nation as any other group. Yet, legal equality for women does not mean that women are able to experience the same freedom in social spaces and the same opportunities in the workplace. The routine exclusion, humiliation and brutalisation of Dalits in India, despite legal equality being enshrined in the Indian Constitution at the moment of the birth of the Indian republic, is an especially stark reminder of the inadequacy of legal universalism as a framework for the meaningful recognition of caste difference and full recognition of equality for Dalit groups.

Difference also serves as a permanent critique of the ideal of universality, by reminding us of the legacies of exclusion of various categories of humanity that have been ironically justified in the very name of the universal human. Indigenous and colonised groups treated as inferior, backward savages in need of civilising by Europeans, African Americans denied the status of full citizens in the American Constitution, the permanent state of violence against Dalits in Indian society even after the guarantee of constitutional equality, the inequities of gender sanctioned by religious and secular traditions alike, the violence sanctioned by state and society against people with non-heterosexual identities—all of these are examples of the tragic gap between an ideal state, in which the universal rights and dignity of all humans would be recognised and celebrated, and the sordid realities of inequality, humiliation and oppression that have historically characterised, and continue to mar, human social relations.

Another way to understand the critique of universalism is that any model will contain or constrain all identities according to the same standard. In a limited sense such a model is perhaps universal in that it treats all identities as equal to one another, but at the same time, it does privilege a distinct, if implicit, ideological view of the world. The notion of consumer-citizenship, as a dominant paradigm of identity in much of the Western world—perhaps most powerfully so in America—is a good example of such a universal 'box' which seeks to hold all identities.[43] All identities, in this model, are shaped in the image of consumers. Different social groups are treated as distinct demographics in terms of consumption habits, their identities are commodified as objects and those commodified identities are monetised, for example in television shows based on ethnicity, queerness or immigrant status. Representations of these commodified identities circulate through the culture, and each category of identity becomes one more group in the landscape of global capitalism. Consumer feminism, which promotes the purchase of female-oriented products as a form of women's empowerment, ethnic cuisines linked to cultural groups, with the rarer or more exotic the more sought after, or gay cruises, all of these phenomena reflect a larger model of consumption-based diversity to which difference is indispensable, since it is both the product being sold and the defining characteristic of the audience to which the product is being marketed.[44]

The critique of universalism in both the practice and theory of identity-based movements has contributed to a broader history of struggles for rights and equality. It has been valuable in helping us to think of the condition of human being in radically more expansive ways, creating more space for human freedom. The idea of difference, seminal to such movements, has been an especially powerful tool in these developments. Yet, the emphasis on identity and difference has also been a double-edged sword in that it has sometimes authorised, even valorised, essentialist and simplistic notions of cultural identity. An example of the latter is the deeply problematic position of ignoring and enabling violence against women and honour killings by immigrant communities in Europe in the name of a multiculturalism based on supposed difference from Western norms.

It is a complicated philosophical question whether the overt or implicit critique of universalism that accompanies discussions and debates on difference can coexist with *some* conception of the universal, even in tension, such as the Kantian idea of 'a universalism that transcends self-centeredness and community boundaries'.[45] We can consider universalism, with regard to human identity, as a necessary critical postulate, an ideal like justice or peace that will never be perfectly realised but one that we nevertheless need to strive for in the hope of making meaningful gains towards it. Universal being would then represent a state of existence that does not replace particular identities but exists with them as an ethical code or a particular dispensation towards the world. Regardless of who we are, how we wish to define ourselves and how we want to be seen and identified, this is perhaps a set of norms we can aspire to follow with the welfare of our fellow human beings and the world in mind.

Difference and globalisation

Like modernity, enlightenment, capitalism or any other major historical phenomenon in human affairs, globalisation has not resulted in the eradication of inequalities rooted in difference or other factors. Nor has it resulted in a radical overhaul of human consciousness and sensibility about inequality, difference and being. We have not reached anything near an ideal global state of equality, acceptance of difference or commitment to the dignity and rights of all human beings. Grand claims are often made about the role of the West or of Christianity as the main source of liberal values in our world, arguments that typically lapse into a predictable ethnocentrism, religious triumphalism or rehashing of archaic justifications for imperial rule. In such narratives, an innate and/or acquired disposition for following the rule of law, entrepreneurial ability, commitment to egalitarian values, freedom and the like are attributed to some mystical and essentialist Western way of being or consciousness.[46] These claims do not take much effort to dismantle; liberal justifications for slavery, colonialism and denial of equal rights for women will do that work. The blatant White ethnocentrism, majoritarianism and racism of the Trump years in America from 2016 to 2020 and the fact that a large proportion of American voters still threw their lot in with him in the 2020 elections also show that citizens of Western democracies are not inherently more democratic, egalitarian or committed to human rights than are citizens of other countries. Joe Biden's victory was undoubtedly decisive, with a lead of seven million votes. Yet, Trump still secured 46.9 per cent of the votes cast, compared to Biden's 51.3 per cent. In terms of absolute numbers, Trump also got more votes than Barack Obama, around 74.25 million to Obama's nearly 69.5 million.[47]

I do not wish to propose any sweeping claims about the impact of globalisation—whether one sees the phenomenon as primarily authored by the West or not—on how people across the world think and behave towards those they perceive as different from them. Yet, globalisation has reshaped and impacted the conversation around difference, diversity and identity in a variety of ways. Conceptualised as a particular phase within a broader arc of modernity, globalisation has magnified, complicated and foregrounded the role of difference in many aspects of life across the globe. New forms of identity, new kinds of self-expression and new kinds of collectives, amounting together to a radically new assertion of difference, are now a feature of the global landscape, significantly so in the West but also in other societies. Social movements in the non-Western world that focus on the same general issues and goals as their Western counterparts often do borrow the vocabularies and strategies of the latter, for instance, with regard to non-binary gender or the reframing of disabilities like autism spectrum disorder or deafness as forms of identity rather than ailments to be rectified. Such initiatives in non-Western societies also draw on their own histories of struggles, working within the framework of inherited legacies of both inclusion and exclusion. Advocates for a more expansive definition of gender in the Indian context, for instance, invoke the figure of the ardhnarishvara, an androgynous half-male and half-female form incorporating both Shiva and Parvati as essential to being, as proof that Indian society has not traditionally been hostile to the idea of a non-binary gender.[48] As a case study of gender in Hinduism, conducted under the aegis of the Religious Literacy Project of Harvard Divinity School, notes:

> While recognition of genders outside male and female has only recently been discussed in Western societies, in Hindu society, people of non-binary gender expression have played important roles for over 2000 years. Called the third gender, evidence for their existence in Hindu society can be found in Hindu holy texts like the Ramayana and the Mahabharata, where Hindu hero Arjuna becomes the third gender.[49]

In societies like India, these understandings of difference and identity coexist with and are grafted on to the idioms of political theory and practice formed in the West. The African American struggle for civil rights has been an inspiration for the movement for Dalit rights in India.[50] The Dalit Panthers, for instance, have fashioned themselves along the lines of the Black Panther Party.[51] In the spaces of English-language Indian social media such as Indian Twitter, critiques of Indian patriarchy have deployed the language of the #MeToo movement, founded by Tarana Burke in the US, to hold prominent men accountable for allegations of sexual harassment, abuse and assault.[52] Somewhat less sincerely, Indian celebrities have taken to jarring and incongruous performative displays of 'wokeness' about the general condition of social inequality, though, predictably, the same celebrities are resoundingly silent about Hindu nationalist violence against Dalits and Muslims.[53]

To what extent the diverse forms of being that are visible today have always existed and have just taken on new names and to what extent they reflect new ways of imagining identity made possible by historical developments such as the rise of the nation-state, capitalism and the commodification of identity is up for debate. In one fundamental sense, though, the emergence of a whole new range of identities is linked to the political economy of globalisation, as the historian Perry Anderson suggests in his explanation of the link between the global capitalist economy, identity and culture in his reading of *Postmodernism, or the Cultural Logic of Late Capitalism,* the masterly theorisation of postmodern culture authored by Frederic Jameson, the greatest living Marxist cultural critic.[54] Anderson elucidates Jameson's view of multinational capitalism as the driving force behind the global consumer society of the late twentieth century—the historical moment of postmodernity. A series of new developments differentiate multinational capitalism from earlier paradigms of capitalist production and organisation, including 'the technological explosion of modern electronics, and its role as leading edge of profit and innovation; to the organizational predominance of transnational corporations, outsourcing manufacturing operations to cheap-wage locations overseas; to the immense increase in the range of international speculation; and to the rise of media conglomerates wielding unprecedented power across communications and borders alike'.[55] No aspect of human existence has been left untouched by these transformative changes, at least in developed societies. They have had 'profound consequences for every dimension in life in advanced industrial countries—business cycles, employment patterns, class relationships, regional fates, political axes'.[56] Most significant—and indeed, as Anderson points out, this is one of Jameson's central insights in the text—is the fact that in the era of postmodernity, 'culture has necessarily expanded to the point where it has become virtually coextensive with the economy itself'.[57] There is no aspect of culture—including, crucially, for the purposes of my argument here, *identity*—that functions autonomously from the logic of the economy or is exempt from being commodified and marketed. The role of ethnic fashion, the appetites for foods from different cultures, the massive global markets for media-driven entertainment, the roles of influencers in social media and the virality of silly memes about cats that generate considerable revenue for websites are also examples of this confluence of economy and culture.

While Jameson's focus was on the transformations experienced by the advanced industrial societies of the West, the totalising logic of late capitalist modernity has arguably spread across more of the globe in the two decades since his book was written, though that process has continued to be uneven. The internet, since the early 1990s, and social media, in the last decade or so, have played a crucial role in the ongoing spread of globalisation. With 2.7 billion active users, plus its extensive and controversial data mining and tracking techniques, Facebook mirrors and shapes much of what happens across the world, from Silicon Valley to remote towns and villages in the developed and developing world alike.[58] Google is indispensable to business in non-Western nations as much as in Western nations, and Amazon, like Apple, Facebook and Netflix, has been steadily increasing its presence in countries like India, hungry for the sheer economic power of millions of additional users.

Inverting Jameson's thesis, it is also the case that difference, in the form of a proliferation and diversity of identities, has in turn become a driver of economic globalisation. As new forms of identity and new communities assert themselves in global public space, their cultural practices simultaneously get mainstreamed and find a place in a global marketplace of culture, ideas and identities. Groups that define themselves on the basis of identities that are different from the norm also constitute new economic markets—as a very basic example, consider 'women's products' or goods created for the diasporic South Asian community or cultural experiences marketed to a Muslim minority community in the US. In a globalised world, there is, additionally, an added pressure for each group or community to identify what is unique or special about it lest it appear indistinguishable from other groups or communities. This anxiety drives communities to publicly perform their difference from other groups, typically in mediated spaces like the internet. These performances of identity and belonging create new kinds of audiences and generate fresh streams of online traffic, which can be monetised in the new digital economy of data capitalism.

Two TED talks by Wael Ghonim, an engineer at Google, whose arrest by Egyptian authorities became a matter of international attention, show a shift in his thinking about the impact of the internet on identity. In his first talk, 'Inside the Egyptian Revolution', delivered in March 2011 during the high noon of the Arab Spring, Ghonim describes the internet as a technology that inevitably serves the best of human popular will, bringing people together organically in an idealised imagined community that transcends differences.[59] It is the kind of techno-utopian statement that could only have emerged from Silicon Valley. By the time he delivers a second TED talk, in January 2016, Ghonim has abandoned much of his deterministic optimism about the internet, shifting to a more resigned, sceptical and cautious view of what the platform and technology can actually achieve. Ghonim notes that the popular revolutions in West Asian countries did not result in the hoped for political and social changes, and the internet did not seem to have led in West Asia, or elsewhere, to any kind of drastic improvement of the human condition. In the talk, Ghonim, sober and somewhat chastened, calls for a rethinking of how technology is used and proposes a redesign of social media according to certain principles that could foster productive and inclusive conversations.[60] The internet has also become a key battle zone for skirmishes regarding competing claims to the past, which centre on contested identities, for example, in the argument between Greece and Macedonia about who owns the name Macedonia and who owns the historical memory of Alexander.[61] Facebook and WhatsApp have been weaponised, whether to subvert or influence elections, as in the case of Russian interference and meddling in the US 2016 presidential elections, or to foment violence against minorities, as in the case of Sri Lanka, Brazil and India.[62] In each case, the use of social media tools has resulted in the targeting of specific social groups because of their identity and their difference.

A framework for reading difference in the Gita

The Gita has the rare characteristic of having spoken to a vast number of constituencies across millennia, bringing its insights into dialogue with the concerns of each age and the particular questions of individuals across time. Patton captures it well in this eloquent statement:

> Through the centuries, the *Gita* has remained a relevant text, inspiring militant revolutionaries, non-violent truth-seekers and renouncers of the world. It has enlightened German philosophers such as Schopenhauer and Heidegger; it has inspired Victorian poets such as Sir Edwin Arnold, and it has grounded post-independence philosophers such as Sarvepelli Radhakrishnan. It has become a literary 'site' which decision-makers go to to understand their dilemmas, whether they be Indian women and men leading Gandhi's *satygraha*, twenty-first-century South Asian-American officers deciding to go to war in the Gulf or London housewives with their children deciding how to organize their day.[63]

It seems reasonable to assume, then, that the Gita should have something to say about the centrality of difference to ideas of selfhood in our time and the constellation of identities that dot the landscape of our age. What exactly the Gita says, and where it falls silent in response to some of the more intractable questions raised by the fact of difference, is what the rest of this chapter takes up.

The Gita presents several perspectives on the universality of being, but it is not unequivocally clear whether they amount to a clear philosophical statement or position on human identity and difference. Certainly, one can make a case that the text contains some universal truths about human existence, in the way that one might make that case for other religious texts like the Bible or the Qur'an or even secular classics like Marcus Aurelius's *Meditations*. But the validity of such a claim rests on the extreme generality of some of the ideas in the text and on the kind of reading to which we subject it. We can argue convincingly that the Gita suggests that anguish is part of the human condition, in the picture that it presents of Arjuna's torment, just as we can argue that the Buddhist tenet that life is suffering has an obvious ring of truth to it.

At a more fine-grained level and grasped in its totality, the Gita presents a more complex picture about being, especially when viewed through the prism of modern-day notions of rights and present-day discourses of identity and being. Framed as a self-contained statement about being, the Gita neither rules out nor endorses the principle of difference as central to identity. One can find passages in the text that speak of being in very broad terms, which can be read as a statement of a capacious inclusivity. One can, similarly, find passages in the Gita that emphasise exclusion. A reading of these two types of sentiment brings out tensions that animate the text with regard to the principles of being and identity.

Working through this challenge requires reading the Gita simultaneously as a double text: one, as a historical document of a time and tradition, and secondly, as a contemporary text that, whatever its complexities, is revered as a source of moral and ethical action by millions. The historical text needs to be studied as a record of its time, as a testament of social conditions, for its philosophical and aesthetic value, for its biases as much as for its possibilities, and for the set of relationships that exist between these different facets of the text. As a contemporary statement of values, the text needs to be read in the spirit of critique, to identify its limits and license, to identify its resonances and silences for different constituencies, audiences and communities. The Gita, as noted before, does not present a systematic or coherent philosophical account of being, action or truth. This inconsistency is both a limitation and a strength. These features of the text provide a methodological opening and a basis for a deconstructive reading of the Gita; Barbara Johnson's definition of the philosophical-methodological approach as involving 'the careful teasing out of warring forces of signification within the text itself' is apposite here.[64] The method of reading the Gita *against itself* may, accordingly, provide a path for thinking about difference in the text and thinking about the text through the lens of difference.

I am aware that this reading is not without its problems and that it inevitably runs the risk of trivialising or erasing the fact of casteism as well as endorsing a patriarchal model of family and the society. There is no getting around the fact that the Gita contains discriminatory references, such as the term 'outcast scavengers'.[65] To undertake a reading along the lines above is not to whisk away these problematic aspects of the Gita under some larger narrative of universal being. Rather, it is to point to the fault line of caste as an integral element of the social order that coexists with the philosophical statement of unity within the world of the text. Keeping that schism plainly and clearly in view rather than papering over it is the only ethically appropriate course of interpretation as a form of action or *karma* with respect to the Gita.

Any such reading is also no doubt influenced by the positionality and social location of the interpreter; for those who have experienced caste discrimination as an abiding condition of life or for historically oppressed subaltern caste groups, the Gita's conservatism with regard to the issue of caste may undermine any other message in the text. We know that the Gita was considered a seditious text during British colonial rule because of its inspirational value for anti-colonial revolutionaries and freedom fighters. This may reflect the fact that many of these anti-colonial figures were from privileged caste Hindu backgrounds. For millions of Indians today, the Gita may well operate as a hegemonic Hindu text or mean nothing at all.

Difference and universality in the text of the Gita

In the opening act or first teaching, titled 'Arjuna's Dejection' in the Stoler Miller edition, Arjuna frames his torment at having to go to war with his cousins in terms of a violation of both social order and natural order. Presenting his reasons to Krishna for not fighting his kinsmen, he says:

> When the family is ruined,
> the timeless laws of family duty
> perish; and when duty is lost,
> chaos overwhelms the family.

> In overwhelming chaos, Krishna,
> women of the family are corrupted;
> and when women are corrupted,
> disorder is born in society.

> ...

> The sins of men who violate
> the family create disorder in society
> that undermines the constant laws
> of caste and family duty.[66]

In the Flood and Martin edition, the chain of events that follows from the destruction of family is described in more specific and stronger terms. The family is 'overwhelmed' by 'lawlessness', which situation results in the 'corruption' of women.[67] In turn, 'from corrupted women comes the intermingling of classes'.[68] The Flood and Martin translation sums up the results of such actions thus:

> Those who destroy the family,
> who institute caste mingling,
> cause the laws of the family
> and the laws of caste to be abolished.[69]

The social order is embodied in the patriarchal family, which is the basic unit of the world of the Gita. Beyond the family, the laws of caste are essential to the structure of the social world.

The societal order, in turn, is yoked to the cosmic order. Righteous and honourable actions undertaken by the individual are essential to maintaining both levels of order. Individual autonomy is circumscribed by obligations and requirements, which have an immediate societal import but also metaphysical significance. As with patriarchal traditions across geographical context and time, women are designated as symbols of family and community, and the corruption of women's honour is associated with the degradation of society.[70] The Flood and Martin translation speaks to the threat posed by women gaining agency from 'lawlessness'—that threat is precisely the destruction of the caste order, the very basis of society, through the contact between classes.[71] If the actions of men are constrained by obligations to family and through it to society and a metaphysical notion of cosmic order, women in the world of the Gita do not even possess the agency of contemplating action.

In generally affirming the status quo as ideal, with regard to both caste and gender, the Gita is not a radically disruptive or emancipatory social text, neither, it would seem, by the standards of the time in which it was written nor, certainly, by present-day standards.[72] For B.R. Ambedkar, the radical anti-caste scholar, a political reformer from the so-called 'untouchable' castes and the strongest voice for the centrality of rights in an independent India, the Gita was 'fundamentally a counter-revolutionary treatise', of the order of other ancient Indian texts that qualified as 'bible[s] of counter-revolution'.[73] In his unfinished book, *Revolution and Counter-Revolution in Ancient India*, Ambedkar finds in the Gita, as in other venerated texts in the Hindu tradition, an essentially conservative defence of the principles of caste Hindu society against egalitarian and socially progressive impulses and currents in Indian society.[74] His use of the term 'bible' is not accidental; the Gita, given its status as religious authority, presents a theological justification for the caste order and the condition of inequality that accompanies that order.

Ambedkar's reading is supported by several passages, including the references to caste noted in the passages cited earlier. In the fourth teaching on the theme of knowledge, Krishna, in elucidating aspects of his self, tells Arjuna:

> I created mankind in four classes,
> different in their qualities and actions;
> though unchanging, I am the agent of this,
> the actor who never acts![75]

The structure of the caste system is a reflection of divine order and difference, and so divinely ordained, it is permanent. By implication, an intellectual rejection of the fundamental premise that different categories of humans possess different qualities, or deliberate actions undertaken to directly challenge it, would be an affront to divinity and its embodiment in figures like Krishna.

Even where it seemingly professes equality, the Gita contradicts itself, for example, in the claim in the fifth teaching on renunciation that knowledge leads to an egalitarian vision:

> Learned men see with an equal eye
> a scholarly and dignified priest,
> a cow, an elephant, a dog,
> and even an outcaste scavenger.[76]

Flood and Martin translate the term as 'dog-cooking outcaste', while Patton translates it as 'dog-cooker'.[77] Gandhi, in his explanation of passages from the Gita, renders this passage in the following words:

> The men of self-realization look with an equal eye on a Brahmin possessed of learning and humility, a cow, an elephant, a dog, and even a dog-eater.[78]

Gandhi's explanation of the text focuses on the fact of the sameness of the *atman* or the inner soul of the spirit of all entities. Enlightenment or self-realisation consists of recognising this sameness in all beings, human and non-human. The ignorant cannot recognise this, but 'men of knowledge' can grasp this truth—'Water of the Ganges in separate vessels is Ganges water after all.'[79] Brief as it is, Gandhi's reading does not consider that affirming an essential sameness of being does not negate the fact of hierarchy. The term 'even' is particularly troubling here, for it positions the 'dog-eater' as lower than 'a cow, an elephant, a dog' and at the other end of the pole from the Brahmin. The conception of equality here is incompatible with modern notions of rights as innate, inalienable and given to all human beings by virtue of being human. Equality, rather, lies in the eye of the beholder, in the invisible essence of soul, only made accessible by a theological–spiritual practice.

A similar rhetorical and argumentative claim is seen in the ninth teaching, in which Krishna says:

> If they rely on me, Arjuna,
> women, commoners, men of low rank,
> even men born in the womb of evil,
> reach the highest way.[80]

Scholars have noted that the affirmation of the existing societal order informs the framing of concepts in the Gita, like duty, action and so forth. Mathur argues that, 'The Gita believes in status quo [*sic*] and sets a high value on social stability. It accepts the established social order and derives the *content* of duty from the caste structure and from the notion of different stages of life.'[81] The stages are the four age-based phases of the life of the individual in Hinduism, that of the student, householder, retired person and person who has renounced life. We do not, of course, know the extent to which the model of the four stages of life was followed in practice in the centuries since it was formulated in ancient Indian thought and reinforced through texts like the Gita.

Inasmuch as the assertion of difference is essential to any call or initiative for justice, the Gita, as a 'closed' text or circuit of meaning, cannot accommodate that perspective; its recognition of difference extends only to the different roles ascribed to castes and genders in the idealised vision of Hindu society that it upholds. According to the logic of the Gita, any action geared towards reframing difference in terms that might challenge the existing order would be considered inappropriate. Mathur points out that in this respect the Gita is not unique with regard to the ancient Indian traditions of thought: 'Indian thinkers of the ancient past (including the author of the Gita) adopted, on the one hand, a *static* concept of right action in terms of conventional class duties and caste duties (*svadharma* and *svabhava*), and on the other hand, resorted to a metaphysical explanation for the gross inequalities and manifest injustices of human life in terms of the operation of a mysterious "law" of *karma*.'[82] The same argument can be made with regard to foundational texts from other religious and cultural traditions, though, needless to say, that is no justification for seeking merit in sentiments that endorse any form of inequality. The question for us is how to deal with these inherited and given aspects of inequality, in light of the principles of equality, justice and human rights that discourses and expressions of difference are inextricably bound up with in our own time. The history of how the Gita has been read and claimed by different groups offers some direction in this regard.

Patton suggests that the Gita's history and sociological reality are not fully constrained by either brahmanical ideology or patriarchy. The text, historically, served as a bridge between a high Sanskritic tradition and local and regional traditions that were taking shape in the second millennium; 'its relatively simple grammar and its time-honoured place in culture allowed it to be part of everyday life, and not necessarily only an elitist, brahmanical text.'[83]

Similarly, the text is not the exclusive preserve of men or the literate. As Patton notes, '[t]ransmission of the Gita presumes neither literacy nor patriarchy; it is one of the few "elite" texts that have crossed this particular boundary.'[84]

And finally, while the text occupies a central place in Hinduism, in 'rural India there are also many Hindus who do not treat the Gita as their canonical text'.[85] As a lived text that is embedded in the social practices of many groups, the significance of the complex ways in which the Gita has been transmitted across social barriers exceeds the limitations of the vision *within* the text.

The Gita may also contain the impulse of individuality, which, though still within the framework of religion, provides an alternate philosophical basis to counter its dominant ideological thrust of hierarchical caste order as theologically ordained. As Flood and Martin argue, 'The *Bhagavad Gita* arguably represents a reaction against the orthodox religion of the Brahmins, offering as a substitute a form of religion based on worship of a personal deity or Lord. This religion of devotion is more inclusive than the older sacrificial religion. Indeed, anyone of any social standing, including women and persons of low caste, can approach God through devotion and be accepted.'[86] It may be a stretch to suggest that this is similar to the Protestant idea of the individual communicating directly with god but, at the very least, the Gita contains the seed of the idea of choice of deity to which the individual can devote himself or herself.[87] Gandhi was 'not a textual interpreter' of the Gita.[88] Yet, in in a kind of redemptive reading, he found the Gita to be a source of abiding moral truths and a set of precepts to guide moral action. His orientation towards the Gita and understanding of the text stands as an act of devotion of this kind. It is perhaps this sense of capacious possibility that allows the Gita to be claimed by a range of constituencies and that militates against the gender, caste and societal orthodoxies that the text unequivocally enunciates.

Many of the other passages in the Gita that affirm a universality of being centred on the relationship of the human and non-human, the animate and inanimate, extend to discussions on the spirit of the eternal and the nature of reality itself, requiring us to wade into metaphysical waters. In the eighth teaching, Krishna states:

> Eternal and supreme is the infinite spirit;
> its inner self is called inherent being;

its creative force, known as action,
is the source of creatures' existence.[89]

And in the ninth teaching, Krishna says:

The whole universe is pervaded
by my unmanifest form;
all creatures exist in me,
but I do not exist in them.

Following Krishna's dazzling revelation of his power to Arjuna, and passages of exquisite poetic beauty in which Krishna describes the infinitude of his being, Arjuna acknowledges Krishna thus: 'you are eternity, / being, nonbeing, and beyond.'[90] Thoreau, Gandhi, Aurobindo and many other well-known and ordinary readers have interpreted these passages as a statement of the ineffable, universal spirit that runs not just through all humanity but through all life. Thoreau, for instance, found in the Gita an endorsement of the spiritual force he had discovered in nature. The idea of the experience of the natural world as a religious encounter also resonates with the philosophy of John Dewey.[91]

For Gandhi, the Gita presented an allegorical framework for overcoming the divisions of the self and for battling the demons within oneself, including the evil of prejudice. The Gita offered Gandhi a basis to fight for what was right, including the dignity of all human beings, even if the Gita endorsed a system in which all humans did not possess equal dignity. The universal potential of the text lay in its articulation of such possibilities. Yet, Gandhi was ultimately disappointed in his hope that people would follow his example of recognising the essential humanity and equality of all people beyond the prejudices of religion and caste. The example he set, including as a reader of the Gita, was not—or possibly could not be—widely emulated. Perhaps the shortcomings of Gandhi's approach to the problem of caste in

Hinduism echo a limit of the Gita itself in this regard. Gandhi's inconsistency on the question of caste, or his evolution regarding his understanding of caste, and his utopian faith in the possibility of community reform grounded in faith and spirituality were in stark contrast to Ambedkar's position on legal reform as essential for the objective of combatting caste inequality.[92] Hinduism, as it actually existed, could not or would not remedy the prejudice, injustice and violence of caste discrimination.

Reading the Gita by centring difference

The Gita suggests several possibilities of thinking through difference with regard to its articulation of the principle of being. One reading is that the Gita, by virtue of its definition of 'being' as a quality of the universe, nature or reality, presents a radically non-anthropocentric view of the world. By provincialising human being as just one kind of being, we can argue against other sentiments in the Gita—again, by reading the Gita against itself—to make the claim that there is nothing particularly special about one kind of human being as compared to another. The elevated state of enlightenment, which the Gita valorises as a higher form or condition of being, depends on action and discipline rather than on ascribed identity. The Gita's insistence on the sameness of being can be interpreted as an antidote to the crude social Darwinism of hierarchies of being that influenced nineteenth-century understandings of human identity, the natural world and social development, and whose long shadows continue to cast their pall on the present.[93] Yet, the non-anthropocentrism of the Gita is somewhat limited by the theory of rebirth, which views human existence as a higher form of life than that of other beings.

Two other strategies rest on centring the principle of difference, paradoxically, for an age when the idea of difference has decentred our understanding of human identity. The first strategy involves liberating the concept of *karma* or action from its metaphysical restrictions. This move is consistent with the idea that the significance of an action is dependent on context—recall that the Gita says that inaction can be action and action can be tantamount to inaction. In the context of our world of today, the only acceptable course of ethical action is to completely repudiate the inequalities of the caste system as well as discrimination on grounds of gender or any other axis of identity. The work of Abdullahi An-Na'im with regard to the relationship of Islam, human rights and secularism is instructive in this regard. An-Na'im, in his elaboration of the work of the Sudanese thinker Ustad Mahmoud Taha and in the course of his own work, has called for a reformation of those aspects of Islam, the Qur'an and Shariah that may contradict modern notions of rights, such as, for instance, the distinction between Muslims and non-Muslims, ideas of heresy and punishment, and passages on the guardianship of women and rights.[94]

The second strategy is to propose an unequivocal acceptance of difference as a basic and, indeed, necessary principle of access to the text of the Gita. This involves making the text politically available to interpretation and critique by different groups, across caste, religion, gender, and community of all kinds, a task that is by no means easy since it involves breaking the stranglehold of the Hindu Right over anything deemed to be the cultural property of the Hindus. Over the last two decades, numerous Indian and Western scholars, such as Romila Thapar, Wendy Doniger and Paul Courtright, have faced harassment, death threats and violence for alleged insults to Hinduism in their work.[95] With the ongoing high noon of Hindutva since the election of Narendra Modi in 2014 and again in 2019 in India, the attacks on scholarly autonomy have amplified and the space for any critique of Hinduism has narrowed even further, part of a relentless pattern of clamping down on dissent.[96] Hindus, right-wing, conservative, or otherwise, are not alone in this. There is a long tradition of Indians of different religious, ethnic and regional persuasions taking offence at any perceived intrusion in what they claim is the exclusive property of their community. Sections 153A and 295A of the Indian Penal Code, for instance, criminalise any attempt to offend religious communities or cause disharmony between religious groups.[97] That these colonial-era laws are widely used as a means of muzzling dissent, whipping up communal tensions or generating political capital by unscrupulous leaders will only make the attempt to pry free the Gita from the clutches of the Hindu Right that much harder.

Yet, the Gita is not the exclusive property of any one community nor of self-appointed guardians of the Hindu community nor of conservative Hindus living in Silicon Valley. It belongs, as do other texts from other Indian traditions, to all Indians and all Indians must be allowed to claim it as such. The political theology of Hindu nationalism involves the weaponisation of Hindu texts, a trend inaugurated by the tacky television version of the Ramayana in the 1980s in India. With small initial steps, this phenomenon needs to be countered with a reclaiming of Hindu texts on secular grounds. Even though secularism appears to be in its death throes in India, and even if exceptionalist claims about Indian secularism have always exaggerated its significance in Indian public life, I remain optimistic that Indian society embodies and retains enough of a commitment to that ideal in practice. In its statement on universal being, there is enough of a basis in the Gita to at least provide a basic framework for inclusion that is cognisant and respectful of difference. In the aftermath of the horrors of Partition, the capacious notion of Indian identity articulated by Nehru was essential for the newly independent nation-state to survive. Nehru may have attempted to ground this political idea of Indian identity in India's history, which he detailed in his book, *The Discovery of India.*[98] Yet, more than a historical argument, Nehru's notion of Indian identity represented a radical act of the imagination, of the possibilities of thinking of national belonging beyond the confines of a chauvinistic nationalism. In exhorting us to take the right course of action, the Gita invites us to similarly imagine and act upon a commitment to being and identity that privileges the freedom of difference—even against itself.

5

WAR AND VIOLENCE IN A GLOBAL WORLD

The Gita's Offerings

The Mahabharata is a book about war. And it is a book that is not shy in its descriptions of war, which are able to jolt us even though we live in the historical aftermath of the genocides of colonialism, the massive death toll of the two world wars, the Holocaust, the Partition and the Rwandan genocide. Fed a steady diet of representations of violence in film and television, much of it gratuitous, and subject to new forms of spectacular, unpredictable violence, whether in acts of Muslim terrorism or videos of brutality that circulate on social media, we are nevertheless not completely inured to powerful, if gory, renderings of violence in texts from times far removed from our own. War in the Mahabharata refers to both the dynastic feud between the Pandavas and the Kauravas and the literal battle fought on the field of Kurukshetra between the cousins. The horrors of the scale of war in the Mahabharata are compounded by the sense that humans are entirely at the mercy of the gods. Smith, in the introduction to his translation, speaks of the 'extraordinarily bloody narrative' of the Mahabharata and the 'unmistakable pessimism that underlies it. Not many novels boast

1,660,02,000 deaths … and fewer still attribute the slaughter to the will of the gods.'[1] Thapar notes the 'minute and sometimes gruesome detail' in which the battle of Kurukshetra is described in the epic: 'Arrows tear apart the chests of the warriors, and the free flow of blood creates pandemonium, in which horses and elephants run hither and thither … The more fearful the contest, the more awesome the shaking of the earth and the blazing of the heavens.'[2]

Yet, the fight on the battlefield, which takes up a 'substantial part of the epic', is not just a contest to determine the supremacy of one branch of the family over the other.[3] A large-scale battle fought to the point of one side conclusively vanquishing the other, the great war of the Mahabharata marks a moment of historical transition, of a shift from clan society to caste society and the establishment of a new political order founded on the laws of caste.[4] War, then, holds a third layer of meaning in the epic. In addition to the family feud and the literal battle, it also signifies the violence inherent in the remaking of society through the emergence of a new political order.[5]

The Gita is a book on the edge of war. And like in the Mahabharata, war carries several meanings in the text. There is the war between the Pandavas and Kauravas that is about to be fought on the battlefield of Kurukshetra. There is the war in Arjuna's mind about the right course of action to follow, which sinks him into an abyss of despair, paralysing him into inaction. There is the war within oneself, between the better angels of our nature and their adversaries. There is the war between good and evil in the world. And yet, as Stoler Miller points out in the afterword to her translation of the text, while on 'one level the *Gita* does appear to justify violence', the text 'is not a justification for war, nor does it propound a war-making mystique'.[6] Certainly, there are readers through history who would not agree with this conclusion. Tilak, for instance, argued that the

Gita's treatment of violence provided a rationale for militant anti-colonial action against British rule, a strategy of resistance that he advocated in opposition to the moderate reformism of leaders like Gokhale and other Indians who sought to operate within the limited framework of the meagre rights given to colonial subjects.[7] Ambedkar's critique of the Gita as akin to a 'bible' of counter-revolution, given its insistence on the caste order, is an indictment of the symbolic violence represented by the text.[8]

There is also a narrative incongruity regarding war in the Gita, which relates to its place in the larger epic, possibly indicating that the Gita was added at a later stage to the Mahabharata. The narrative incongruity is paralleled by an ethical ambiguity about duty in the text, and manifests itself in the form of a tension between the idea of *dharma*, or duty, and fidelity to the rules of caste that will form the basis for the emerging social and political order.

> Although the *Bhagavad-gita* in the narrative is placed just before the start of the war, its teaching seems more appropriate to the society that emerged after the war. Arjuna, dismayed by the thought that he would have to kill his close kinsmen, questions the ethics of such an act. The killing of kinsmen seems to have been more heinous in a society where kinship was a primary identity than in a society where kin ties were subsumed in caste. Krishna speaking from the perspective of a caste society explains to Arjuna that as a kshatriya it is his *svadharma*, the social obligation of one's caste, to fight against evil even if it means killing kinsmen. Is the moral dilemma being subordinated to caste duty?[9]

Thapar sees the events in the Gita as a response to Buddhist and Jain ideas of ahmisa, or non-violence.[10] The themes of the Gita can also be placed in a dialogic relationship with the Ashokan model of kingship in which 'the social ethic is not dependent on caste but on the quality of human behaviour as encapsulated in *dhamma*'.[11] Smith suggests that our understanding of the treatment of violence in the Mahabharata and Gita should be framed by the fact that the Mahabharata is in essence a kshatriya text, both in terms of the views of the chief protagonists of the story and the themes, notably violence, with which the epic is concerned.[12] The ethical dilemma that animates the text can be stated thus: 'If doing violence was wrong, leading to bad *karma* and thus more (and worse) rebirths, how is a Ksatriya to behave, given that—whether as warrior in battle or as punishment-inflicting warrior—doing violence is his role in life?'[13] Smith notes that this is a persistent theme in the Mahabharata, most notably in the Gita.[14]

In sum, though, the Gita is not a conventional book about the nature or art of war. It does not outline a philosophy of war or violence. It does not delineate a set of universally applicable principles or conditions that specify when war is appropriate and when it is not. It is not a book on military strategy, like Clausewitz's *On War* or Sun Tzu's *The Art of War*. The Gita does not offer explanations about the nature and source of violence, collective or individual, behavioural or psychological. It does not paint a picture of the horrors of war as a possible antidote to the urge to wage warfare or as advocacy for an ideology of pacifism. The exact perspective of the Gita on literal war and battle remains contested and conflicted, even as the significance of war in the text extends to the allegorical and metaphorical realms.

In critically examining what the Gita has to say about war and violence in the current historical moment, I treat war and violence as a single discursive or conceptual object, that is, as contiguous with each other. War may be thought of as an extreme form of routine violence, and violence, threatened or real, is the heart of war. The wars that the psychic self wages within itself, or is forced to wage with itself as a result of trauma, often result in further violence to the self. In my reading, I consider war in both its literal and metaphorical incarnations. By war in its literal sense, I refer to events involving physical violence, harm and injury to an enemy, whether this is hand-to-hand combat of the kind that Indian and Chinese soldiers have engaged in recently over disputed border territories or the actions of American drones that annihilate civilians in Yemen and the Khyber Pakhtunkhwa areas of Pakistan.[15] By war in its metaphorical and allegorical sense, I refer to the struggles that we face as individuals, communities and societies about how to deal with crises and what decisions to make in the face of competing ethical imperatives. This sense of war also extends to the collective struggles that we may be engaged in for justice, rights and equality. My reading is centred on arguments about two crucial aspects of the Gita's treatment of the themes or war and violence that I consider highly relevant for the world of today.

My first argument is that Arjuna's anguish about going to war represents a critically important message for us, in that it serves as a model for deliberation before we embark on any course of action that may result in harm to another. This becomes especially important in a global world, in which we encounter people from a wide range of backgrounds, experiences and histories. It is ethically incumbent upon us to be reflexive about how our words and actions may affect anyone who is different from us. Equally, in a global world, our actions may impact people we do not know and cannot see, in ways that we cannot imagine. My second argument is that the discourse of war and violence in the Gita represents an exception to other discourses of war and violence with regard to how it thinks of the enemy.

The enemy is defined with an imprecision that has both positive and negative ramifications as far as contemporary warfare is concerned. On the one hand, the Gita does not construct the enemy as subhuman simply by virtue of the fact of being an enemy, as we see in many examples of war and violence in the era of modernity or even earlier. On the other hand, the Gita is not entirely exempt from notions of Otherness, even if those do not strictly apply to the enemy in question. This aspect of the Gita as well as the passages in it that involve general descriptions of evil do mean that the text is not entirely free from the charge of constructing the human as a possible object of violence, symbolic or literal.

My reading of the Gita along these lines proceeds with a description of the major changes in the paradigm of war in the post-9/11 universe, before moving to an elaboration of both key aspects of the Gita's discourse on war. As with earlier chapters, my explication and interpretation of the ideas of the Gita aim to bring text and context into dialogue, identifying both what the Gita has to say and where it does not have more than silence to offer about the condition of contemporary war and violence.

War and violence in the era of crisis globalisation

On 11 September 2001, as two planes hijacked by Saudi terrorists crashed into the Twin Towers of the World Trade Center in New York, the world as we knew it changed irrevocably. American society would be undeniably transformed in the days, months and years to come, as anyone who saw the crashes, replaying endlessly on television, could tell. I had been in the US for a little over a year then, studying at Emory University in Atlanta as a graduate student. At the time, even before the attacks of 9/11, it seemed like we were in somewhat choppy waters in the US, though from the perspective of 2020, such a claim appears remarkably naive. The previous year, 2000, had seen a controversy about the US presidential elections over the results of votes cast in Florida.[16] The dispute was eventually settled by the Supreme Court, which upheld the results and awarded the presidency of the US to the Republican contender, George W. Bush, over his Democrat rival, Al Gore. The dotcom bubble that had started growing in the mid-1990s had finally burst in 2000 as the market corrected for massively overvalued and unsustainable internet businesses, lowering the American economy into a state of recession.[17] And then, like a caesura ripping time and history itself, came the events of 11 September 2001. The 9/11 attacks inflicted a severe trauma on the collective American psyche, perhaps not experienced since the humiliation Americans had faced as a result of their ill-fated adventures in Vietnam in 1965.[18] But Vietnam was different in that the violence, even if it touched countless American families, was out there. Here, the act of terror had occurred on home soil, in the heart of New York, the city most widely associated with the idea of America in the global imagination. The attacks were designed to literally kill and to symbolically wound, aimed as they were at the iconic towers that were as central to New York's identity as the Golden Gate Bridge is to San Francisco or Big Ben is to London.

The attacks brought home to Americans the frightening fact of their vulnerability to danger in a global world, much like that faced by many people across the world as a permanent reality. It also drove home the fact that the status of being the world's sole remaining superpower did not in any way inure Americans from risk. Growing up in India, even with a relatively privileged upbringing, I was used to the possibility of violence erupting into public spaces and everyday life. I hardly know a person in India who has not witnessed a riot first-hand or felt its effects intimately. The intractability of human vulnerability is driven home in a thousand ways when sudden, unpredictable violence strikes—in the debris of lives that a riot leaves behind, the remains of humans, the stains and streaks of blood; the pathos of personal belongings like a locket or ring separated from the hand or neck that wore it, a bag ripped open with its contents spilled out like guts; the burned husk of a bus; smashed windows; a vendor's cart mauled beyond repair. The sparkling clean streets of cities are signs that a riot has taken place there the day before, for otherwise they would still be strewn with the litter of everyday life. In the collective memory of Indians, 1984 in Delhi, 1992–1993 in Mumbai and other cities, 2002 in Gujarat and 2020 in Delhi, along with other dates, translate into an alternate map and genealogy of India, a history and geography whose animating principle is violence against those who are different from one.

But for countless Americans, such as many of my fellow students at Emory University, this kind of unexpected mass-scale violence erupting out of nowhere was unimaginable. Having grown up, as they had, in racially homogeneous suburbs or small towns and cities in the American South and Midwest, where people trusted each other enough to leave spare keys under the doormat, they had taken for granted an everyday sense of security at which an Indian might marvel in awe. To be sure, many Americans, especially racial minorities and those who live in conditions of economic precariousness, face pervasive violence, whether at the hands of the police, in the form of structural violence through neglect, or by virtue of living in crime-ridden, socially devastated neighbourhoods. America has also been plagued by mass shootings, but the propaganda of the powerful gun lobby in the US, the ideological work of the American Right, and the complicity, unwilling or willing, of the media has relentlessly driven home the idea that these killings are infrequent acts of mentally ill, aberrant human beings, exceptions to the majority of responsible gun owners. Part of the shock of 9/11 was the thought that someone *could want to do this to America*, combined with an incomprehensibility about what could compel such an action. That sense of surprise was driven partly by ignorance of America's own complicated history of relentless violence across the world, with its involvement in countless wars, and an internalisation of the idea that the nation-state, in sociologist Max Weber's famous dictum, possesses a monopoly over 'the legitimate use of force within a given territory'.[19] And in part, it was the sheer unreality of the event that stunned the American nation on that day.

These observations may seem ethnocentric, perhaps guilty of the charge of defining the West or America as the only authentic subject of world history. For political violence, terrorist bombings, hijackings of planes and attacks intended for televised public display as much as to murder have, tragically, not been unknown to inhabitants of other countries, even if the suicide mission of flying passenger planes into the World Trade Center was an act of a new order altogether. The previous century did not lack for violence or bloodshed, with two world wars, the Holocaust, the genocides in Rwanda, Armenia, East Timor and Bangladesh, the Stalinist purges and the savagery of persistent violence against minorities everywhere: Druze and Ahmadis in Turkey; Hindus, Christians, Shi'a Muslims and Ahmadis in Pakistan; African Americans and other communities of colour in the US; Dalits and Muslims in India. The viscerally felt sense of surreality that accompanied the event of 9/11, though, gives us a clue as to why the event was significant beyond any simplistic analysis of America's importance to the global world order.

In a 2002 lecture at Emory University, titled 'The greatest sorrow: Times of joy recalled in wretchedness', the writer Amitav Ghosh described the events of 9/11 as an 'epistemological rupture', something that had previously been beyond the bounds of the comprehensible and that had now irrupted into human consciousness as an unavoidable reality.[20] The attacks on the World Trade Center forced us to confront the knowledge of a new, terrible reality. Ghosh compared the impact of the destruction of the Twin Towers with the similar shock caused by the image of Thích Quảng Đức, the 'burning monk', who had set himself on fire in Saigon in 1963 to protest the oppression of Buddhists by the South Vietnam regime.[21] In a haunting essay, 'The falling man', centred on a photograph of a man falling from one of the towers in the aftermath of the attack, the writer Tom Junod suggests that the events of 9/11 robbed us of the power of interpretation, the images associated with the destruction both saying too much and too little.[22]

The terrorist attacks inaugurated a new kind of public violence, to be enacted indiscriminately against civilians, which, in turn, would be met by a new paradigm of state violence. In the two decades since that rupture in history, we have seen these two forms of violence savagely reshape and remake our world, whether in the form of Islamist terrorist attacks in locations across the world, including Paris, London, Mumbai, Barcelona and Berlin, or in the countermeasures taken by states in the name of fighting terrorist violence.

The shock of 9/11 was followed by collective expressions of grief and mourning in the US but also a demand for retribution. It did not take an oracle to divine that America would retaliate; indeed, given the country's history and power, it was almost a foregone conclusion that America would let slip the dogs of war and that international opinion or law would be of little purchase in persuading it to change its mind. Beyond America, the structure of the world, already interconnected in intricate ways through the mechanisms of globalisation, would undergo a radical shift as well. The international order, the realm of international law, the nature of statecraft and sovereignty, the relationship between the state and individual—all would be radically transformed by what would follow. On 18 September 2001, American president George W. Bush decreed as law a resolution that authorised military retaliation against those who had planned the 11 September 2001 attacks. The scope of the law was vast. It provided the administration with a 'legal rationale for its decision to take sweeping measures to combat terrorism, from invading Afghanistan, to eavesdropping on U.S. citizens without a court order, to standing up the detention camp at Guantanamo Bay, Cuba'.[23] The repercussions of such American initiatives for the global order have been truly far-reaching.

First, these kinds of actions have resulted in the de facto jurisdiction of American power over people across the globe, such that the sovereignty of many other nation-states has been rendered a fiction. The lack of clarity about whether the US had permission from Pakistan to enter its territory to assassinate Osama bin Laden on 2 May 2011 is a prime example of this situation. Second, in acting unilaterally, and in asserting the right to act unilaterally, the US dealt a body blow to all projects of universalism and cosmopolitanism and perhaps to the very possibility of such universalist projects, represented, no matter how imperfectly, by the existence of the United Nations or international covenants on rights. The extreme turn towards unilateralism that America experienced during the reign of Donald Trump was set into motion at that moment in the wake of 9/11 when the US decided to ignore the protocols of international law and diplomacy in retaliating against Afghanistan (and later against Iraq). Third, practices like 'extraordinary rendition', in which other nations engaged in torture on behalf of the US, given the prohibition against torture on US soil, severely undermined the painstakingly accumulated gains in the domain of international human rights to protect suspects, dissenters, government critics and anyone who could be designated as an enemy of the state.[24]

A fourth set of major changes pertains to the impact of the internet. Nation-states have utilised the internet as an instrument in the service of the state, deploying new technologies to gather data, track and monitor activities of citizens and non-citizens, including those who are not suspects of any kind, and have created an extensive surveillance network in the bargain. In the US, this system rests on a complex partnership between the government and private enterprise and on a convergence of the imperatives of national intelligence and corporate profiteering. In her detailed examination of the phenomenon, the journalist Julia Angwin describes the US as a 'dragnet nation', one that indiscriminately sweeps up data about all its citizens or all those living within its borders on the assumption that some of them may be involved in suspicious activities.[25] Technologies meant to track shopping habits now serve as potential data points in a brave new world where any deviation from patterns of behaviour, or variations flagged by algorithms, can trigger interest from law enforcement. The new paradigm, in which old ideas of privacy have been founding sorely wanting, is one that does not just apply to foreign intelligence or specific counter-terrorist activities like monitoring chatter on the internet. Instead, as Aaron Bady describes in an incisive essay, the new paradigm of digital tracking of the self now applies to law and order in general, beyond the field of anti-terror intelligence.[26] Information gathered through information sharing environments (ISEs) is shared between local, state and national authorities, and between government and corporate entities. The model of predictive policing inverts the dictum of innocent until proven guilty; rather, everyone is a potential suspect, potential terrorist, potential threat—and some more so than others—unless they can prove otherwise.

Woven in with these changes is the alarming phenomenon of the role of the internet in fomenting violence. The use of the internet as an instrument of abuse and intimidation, which I have described in an earlier chapter, has contributed to direct acts of violence against minorities or groups marked as enemies, whether racial minorities in the US, Dalits in India, or Muslims in Myanmar. Online speech itself is routinely violent, with women and minorities disproportionately bearing the brunt of severe and persistent abuse.[27] The trolls of the Hindu Right and Modi devotees or bhakts in India share with the alt-Right and groups like 4Chan in the US the tactics of ganging up on targets and threatening, harassing and hounding them off digital platforms like Facebook and Twitter. The so-called Big Tech companies hide inconsistently behind the fig leaves of free speech and community standards, allowing the politically powerful and their supporters to express the most extreme sentiments, while penalising the average user for far less flagrant violations. Modi's supporters, who routinely issue rape and death threats online, yet continue to flourish on Facebook and Twitter, are a case in point.[28] The violence of online speech, which is clearly recognisable, yet may not meet legal standards of hate speech in particular contexts, has compelled the journalist and human rights activist Susan Benesch to suggest a third category of speech that she terms 'dangerous speech'. Benesch's thesis proposes that 'a particular type of public speech tends to catalyze intergroup violence, and that this knowledge might be used to prevent such violence'.[29] In his book on free speech in the digital age, Timothy Garton Ash, while acknowledging the power of the internet to give voice to the ordinary person, identifies the problem with internet speech as an absence of clear norms to govern online discourse.[30] Any such set of norms faces the challenge of meeting the requirements of different nation-states with different laws governing free speech plus the problem of enforcing the laws themselves. The internet contributes to the vulnerability that many groups experience in a moment of crisis, but does not necessarily offer us easy solutions.

The gift of Arjuna's anguish

My first thesis regarding the value of the Gita's ideas about war is that it is Arjuna's anguish, even his indecisiveness, that is the more ethically appropriate response to the question of whether to wage war and violence in a world beset with crisis, and one in which we have to live with the possibility of crisis as a permanent reality. Presenting this claim requires the methodological, interpretive and political stance, outlined earlier as well, of reading the Gita against the Gita, and granting Arjuna's doubt epistemological and political parity with Krishna's knowledge and certitude.

In his state of doubt and anguish, Arjuna fits the description of the 'passionate man' in the hierarchy of the three kinds of men described by Krishna—the enlightened man, who treats with an equal eye war and peace, grief and joy, loss and gain; the passionate man, who is invested in an action or outcome to the point where his desire clouds his judgement; and the man of 'dark inertia', gloomy, depressed and given to sloth.[31] The man of passion, in this case, the anguished man, in the figure of Arjuna, occupies the intermediate position in Krishna's hierarchy. In an ideal state of affairs, to become the man of action, such a man must let go of his passions, which will free the way for him to intuit or arrive at the right course of action.

My suggestion is that even if we agree with Krishna's categorisation of the relative value of different states of being or dispensations, Arjuna's state is a necessary step that anyone in a position of power and responsibility must go through with regard to the question of war. In the absence of divine certitude, which humans cannot by definition possess, doubt is the right course of human action. The recent history of the world is proof of the folly of humans acting with that certitude in their surety of the necessity and importance of going to war. The devastation caused to a vast swathe of humanity in West Asia as a result of the illegal invasion of Iraq in 2003 by a US-led coalition is just one recent example of the outcome of such follies. The fiasco in West Asia is but another episode in a history of Western imperial misadventures in which Western nations have arrogated for themselves the role of gods dictating the destinies of lesser beings. I will comment more in a minute on the human cost of America's interventions in West Asia, but let me emphasise that in describing the actions of Americans and their allies against Iraqis as the deeds of gods with regard to men, I do not merely offer a polemical argument but a substantive one.

Looking back at the discussions within the US and beyond in the months leading up to the military intervention in Iraq in March 2003, what stands out is the near-absolute confidence with which the majority of American politicians, liberals and conservatives alike, the media and the general public seemed in absolute agreement about the moral and divine right of the US to invade another country. An insouciance and arrogance permeated the political, policy and public discussions, suffused as they were with an implicit assertion of the right to toy with Iraqi society and an indifference to the value of Iraqi lives. The voices of dissenters and protesters against the war, though they had logic and evidence on their side, along with the conventions of international law and the force of moral argument, did not carry much weight in public debates. Those who shaped and reflected the opinions on the invasion of Iraq that carried the day were persistently and relentlessly wrong, as author Greg Mitchell argues in his damning book, *So Wrong for So Long*.[32]

In one sense, the situation was a reprise of what had taken place in the immediate aftermath of 11 September, when, within a few weeks, the US invaded Afghanistan in retaliation for the terrorist attacks on the World Trade Center. At that time, too, protesters had taken to the streets in the US. Then as well, in violation of international law, the US, with the support of Britain, initiated the attack and subsequent occupation of a country with a campaign of aerial bombing on 7 October 2001.[33] But a reasonably persuasive case could be made for US military action in Afghanistan. For one, Osama bin Laden, the mastermind behind the attacks, and Al-Qaeda, the Islamic terrorist organisation that he headed, had found agreeable hosts in the Taliban, who had imposed their austere and brutal brand of Islam on the inhabitants of their country. Sharing with the Taliban a sense of the US as the enemy and using Afghanistan as a base with their support, Osama bin Laden had invaded a sovereign country. The destruction of the Twin Towers represented an act of terrorism by someone who was technically a non-state actor, but it was also an act of war. As Salman Rushdie observed during a public discussion in San Francisco, the Taliban had effectively hijacked a country, and so was complicit, as a de facto state power, in the assault on the US.[34] The main rationale for opposing a US attack on Afghanistan—a rationale that applies to any act of war—was to prevent civilian deaths. In the case of Afghanistan, as indeed for Iraq, this fact was made more poignant by the reality that the civilians in each country were themselves being oppressed by the leaders in question. Abdullahi An-Na'im, the renowned scholar of Islamic and constitutional law, shared the observation with me that in deciding to attack these countries the US was punishing the people of both lands for the crimes of their oppressors.[35]

The situation with regard to Iraq was far murkier. Saddam Hussein, once an ally of the West who had been given a symbolic key to the American city of Detroit, had no known link to Al-Qaeda or Osama bin Laden.[36] The Ba'athist ideology that he represented was resolutely non-religious, though he was certainly guilty of extreme violence against his own people. There was no evidence of the smoking gun of weapons of mass destruction or nuclear weapons that Saddam was apparently stockpiling. Most tellingly, Iraqis were completely missing from discussions about whether the US should invade Iraq or not. Save for the odd Iraqi expatriate like Kanan Makiya, the advocates of military intervention were almost uniformly American, led by the likes of US vice president Dick Cheney, who proclaimed in oracular fashion that Iraqis would greet Americans as liberators, and other neoconservatives like Richard Perle and Paul Wolfowitz.[37] But even among the arguments made by critics of the planned invasion and occupation of Iraq, the voices and perspectives of Iraqis were conspicuously absent. The fact that the destiny of Iraqis was being discussed largely by people ignorant of the history and realities of Iraqi society and in blatant disregard of the facts was both imperious and imperialistic, a hubristic act of playing god. Close to two decades later, the US has won neither war. Iraq, like much of West Asia, is in a shambles, and there are just about 3,000 US troops left in Iraq.[38] The war in Afghanistan has been a failure too. Instead of replacing the Taliban with a moderate but effective government, as was the naive hope, the US ended its presence in the country by signing a peace deal with the Taliban in March 2020.[39]

In light of the recent and longer history of war, one message rings out clearly from Arjuna's despair: it is not for men to play god with the fates of other men. The message applies to imperialism as well. For what is imperialism if not war on a society—the annihilation of its economic, cultural, political and social characteristics? Despite the fact that Arjuna is eventually persuaded by Krishna to wage war, the moral force of Arjuna's hesitation to fight, his objections against going to war and the sincerity of his doubt remain valid. They are not subsumed or assimilated into the superior or higher reason of the case that Krishna presents. In the particular instance of the battle of Kurukshetra, it may be the case that deciding to go to war is, in the ultimate analysis, the right course of action for Arjuna.

Perhaps if his adversaries, the Kauravas, had experienced the same kind of crisis as Arjuna, an alternate resolution could have been found and the war itself prevented. In such an instance, or in other kinds of situations, the refusal to fight may well have been the right course of action. The Gita does not present a theory of war, as I have mentioned above, yet there is a nascent idea in the text that any case for war must be contextually relevant. Through his own example and in the details of his conversation with Krishna, Arjuna's views seem to share some themes with the 'just war' theory in the Western political tradition about the conditions under which it may be legitimate to fight. In an essay on the topic, Johnson provides a succinct summation of the main criteria for just war:

> The four most important conditions are: (1) the war must be declared openly by a proper sovereign authority (e.g., the governing authority of the political community in question); (2) the war must have a just cause (e.g., defense of the common good or a response to grave injustice); (3) the warring state must have just intentions (i.e., it must wage the war for justice rather than for self-interest); and (4) the aim of the war must be the establishment of a just peace. Since the end of World War II it has become customary to add three other conditions: (1) there must be a reasonable chance of success; (2) force must be used as a last resort; and (3) the expected benefits of war must outweigh its anticipated costs.[40]

The situation in which Arjuna finds himself resonates with the principles of just intentions, last resort and, possibly, just cause, in addition to meeting the qualification of a legitimate sovereign authority. It would be a stretch, however, to find in Krishna's counsel the presence of all these principles as a rationale for war. In that sense, Arjuna's scepticism rings truer than Krishna's certitude to the kinds of ethical conundrums that have marked debates about war, from the medieval to the modern context. The source of Arjuna's anguish, though, presents us with an ambiguity. Is his anguish at the prospect of bloodshed per se, at the inevitable loss of human life that will accompany the battle of the Pandavas and Kauravas, or is the cause of his despair the fact that it is his kin, his cousins, who share the same status of nobility and the same privileges of caste, against whom he will have to wage war? Describing the 'strange pity' that has overcome him, Arjuna tells his charioteer:

> I see omens of chaos,
> Krishna, I see no good
> in killing my kinsmen
> in battle.[41]
>
> …
>
> Honor forbids us to kill
> our cousins, Dhritarashtra's sons;
> how can we know happiness
> if we kill our own kinsmen?[42]

I suggest that one productive way for us to read Arjuna's reluctance to go to war is to see it in terms of what I would call a paradoxical principle of limited universalism. This framework requires viewing kinship in an allegorical sense as extending beyond family to all humankind. In the context of our world, this would translate into acting with a global consciousness, being motivated by a sense of global citizenship and identifying affectively with people beyond different boundaries, not just of the family but also of community, caste, region, religion and nation. I call this universalism limited because the commitment to universalism in the Gita, as discussed earlier, does not eventually transcend its conservative endorsement of the patriarchal family or a model of social order based on caste. Here, too, we can read the Gita against itself, to prioritise its message of unity and the oneness of all beings as a superior principle to that of caste hierarchy—certainly by the standards of modern notions of rights and by the yardstick of intuitive moral sense or fairness as well. A global consciousness of this kind, which thinks of the damage of war beyond a narrow nationalistic frame, and which values the imagined global community over the imagined national community, can serve as an ethical check against any easy or hasty judgement to rush to war.[43] It can also serve as a bulwark against the temptation to arrogate the right to play god in the lives of our fellow human beings simply because they happen to be born in another part of the world.[44]

Clichéd as it may sound, the allegorical reading of humanity as family serves as an antidote to the depersonalisation of war and its twin, the technologisation of war. Neither is unique to the global age—even before the current moment of globalisation, the twentieth century, after all, was already the century of technologised war—but both impulses have been greatly amplified by developments in the post-9/11 era. The history of technologised war could fill several tomes; a select and brief genealogy of four moments will have to suffice here to highlight the transformations that technological development has wrought upon the nature of war and to flag their implications for how we think of the enemy, responsibility, ethics and the code of war. Each of these historical moments profoundly changed the nature of modern warfare. On 22 April 1915, in the course of the First World War, the Germans engaged in the first use of chemical warfare by unleashing chlorine gas on their adversaries, the French.[45] The next such moment of epistemological rupture in the history of war was the bombing of the Spanish town Guernica on 27 April 1937 by Hitler's aerial forces at the request of Franco, the Spanish dictator. The third moment is the US' act of dropping atomic bombs on Hiroshima and Nagasaki on 6 August and 9 August 1945, respectively, a scale of violence so extreme that it cannot be grasped in absolute terms by the human imagination. It is in the details that the truly horrifying nature of the act truly hit home. The heat from the nuclear explosion was so extreme, for instance, that it instantly vaporised people, leaving but their shadows etched on stone as ghostly reminders of the lives obliterated. And the fourth moment refers not to a single instance but to the next step in technologised warfare—the use of drones to bomb suspects and targets remotely, an ironic echo of the act of the terrorists who turned passenger planes into missiles that brought down the World Trade Center towers.

A work of art that responds to one of these moments, the destruction of Guernica, powerfully illustrates the inevitable transformation of the human into an abstract object, a depersonalised target with whom one feels no attachment and who, consequently, can be annihilated without a second thought or remorse. Memorialised in Picasso's masterpiece of the same name, the bombing of Guernica was intended as punishment for the Basque regions that were holding strong in their resistance to Franco's fascist forces. The aerial assault, carried out by planes equipped with formidable technology for the time, was informed by the ideology of 'total war', developed by the German general Erich Ludendorff, which held that 'in war, no one is innocent; everyone is a combatant and everyone a target, soldier and civilian alike'.[46] Resulting in the death of 1,600 civilians, the attack on Guernica was shocking for many reasons: the cold calculation with which civilians were deliberately targeted in an act of collective punishment; the use of military power by a leader against his own people, that too, with the help of a foreign leader; the horrifying experience of terror from the air in which neither home nor public space was safe; and the sheer chaos that enveloped all living beings.

Several of these themes are present in Picasso's painting, which uses a structure of collage, among other techniques, to signal the shattering of reality caused by the bombing. Neither humans nor animals are spared in the violence the painting depicts; life itself, as we know it, is obliterated. The violence is so extreme and isolating that each creature, human or animal, is utterly alone in its pain and suffering, unable to communicate with any other entity. The twisted bodies and unnaturally positioned necks point to the permanent deformity of the possibility of normal everyday social relations. In an exquisitely brilliant reading of the painting, the art historian T.J. Clark tells us that the site of action in the painting is a liminal space between inside and outside.[47] It is neither and both; there is the suggestion of a floor, of a porch perhaps, as well as a light bulb that simultaneously indicates an explosion. Picasso's decision, Clark explains, signals that with the bombing neither the inside of the house—traditionally a space of refuge, symbolic of interior selfhood in the bourgeois imagination—nor public space was safe against the kind of onslaught perpetrated by the aerial bombardment of the town. Clark also explains how Picasso's rendition powerfully communicates the fact that the violence of the bombing in Guernica did not only trivialise life. It also robbed humans of the possibility of a meaningful death, which itself is a source of a meaningful life. Clark describes this cry of Guernica in a remarkable quote:

Life, says the painting, is an ordinary, carnal, entirely unnegotiable value. It is what humans and animals share. There is a time of life, which we inhabit unthinkingly, but also a time of death: the two may be incommensurable, but humans especially—from the evidence of palaeolithic burials it seems a species-defining trait—structure their lives, imaginatively, in relation to death. They try to live with death—to keep death present, like the ancestors whose bones they exhume and re-inter. But certain kinds of death break that human contract. And this is one of them, says *Guernica*. Life should not end in the way it does here. Some kinds of death, to put it another way, have nothing to do with the human as Picasso conceives it—they possess no form as they take place, they come from nowhere, time never touches them, they do not even have the look of doom. They are a special obscenity, and that obscenity, it turns out, has been a central experience of the past seventy years.[48]

That obscenity, which is rooted in the extreme depersonalisation of the human depicted in Picasso's artwork, has been a function of modern warfare at least since the bombing of Guernica. I want to make a conceptual distinction here between depersonalisation and a broader category of dehumanisation, to which I will turn shortly. I understand depersonalisation as a passive type and form of dehumanisation that renders the human being as an abstract entity, a statistic, number or obstacle to be eliminated. Depersonalisation, as *Guernica* depicts it, is closely tied to the technologisation of war, as an almost inevitable consequence of the latter. In turn, depersonalisation enables and legitimises the imperative of ever-greater technologisation of war. Reflected in a neutral vocabulary of terms like 'collateral damage', to refer to civilians accidentally killed in military conflict, or 'friendly fire', to refer to the accidental death of soldiers by their own side, depersonalisation enables an abdication of moral, political and ethical responsibility for death, violence and damage. Death, like warfare itself, becomes remote and distant, as do the humans who suffer and die. And warfare in the abstract becomes the agent and instrument of death, which is now separated from the concrete actions and decisions of human beings.

While Arjuna's arguments do not exactly conform to this modern notion of depersonalisation, his fear of waging war is that it will obliterate the sense of shared personhood with his kin. In fact, the very unit of society and basis for experience of that common personhood in the world of the Mahabharata—family—is at risk from going to battle with his kinsmen. The family is the condition of possibility for that deep affective bond that makes war with one's own so egregious. In Clark's analysis quoted above, the violence of *Guernica* is that it destroys the taken-for-grantedness of life; the source of that taken-for-grantedness in the Gita is the family.

In the post-9/11 global landscape, depersonalisation has been amplified and folded into the repertoire of modern warfare with the extensive use of drones by the US in its endless 'war on terror' that was launched by George W. Bush and continued by Barack Obama. The US might claim moral right on its side in its use of unmanned aerial vehicles, as the official name for drones goes, yet that moral high ground is severely undermined by the large number of civilian deaths, including those of children, caused by its use of drones in areas of Pakistan, Yemen, Libya, Somalia and Iraq.[49] The American invasion of Iraq was inaugurated with the doctrine of 'shock and awe', the policy of 'stunning one's opponent into realising that your might was so enormous, so unbeatable, that the fight was as good as over'.[50] Launched right in time for American prime time television, the war seemed like something out of a Hollywood film or video game, an example of life imitating a postmodern simulation of itself. Far from being quickly and decisively resolved in favour of an American victory, the long-drawn-out wars in Afghanistan and Iraq have extracted a terrible toll in terms of death, suffering and psychological trauma. The scale and nature of the losses experienced by the Iraqis and Afghans are distant and alien to most Americans, whether they occupy formal positions of power or are ordinary citizens. The same holds true for the numerous deaths of civilians by US drones in various locations across the globe. Details of these deaths remain murky, but the troubling matter of accidental civilian deaths, when acknowledged, is usually dealt with by financial compensation.[51] The question of who is ultimately responsible for the deaths caused by the drones—a US military official, the US government or the president of the US—remains unanswered as is the question of how to hold the responsible party accountable.

This situation of a mighty power acting like its own judge, jury, prosecutor, witness and defendant in the matter of conflict resulting in the deaths of civilians speaks to the concept of *dharma* or duty in the Gita.[52] Like *karma* and other terms in the Gita, *dharma* is a hard term to translate, with multiple resonances and shades of meaning. One of its meanings, delinked from a religious anchoring, and particularly relevant in this context, is *dharma* as a sense of ethical obligation. In the absence of any international body that is genuinely able to hold the powerful nations of the world accountable for the consequences of their military actions, which include a staggering toll of over two million dead as a result of America's wars after 9/11, an exhortation to these nations to subject themselves to ethical scrutiny may seem little more than an ineffectual appeal.[53] Still, the power of the ethical, as social movements for political justice, such as the struggle for civil rights in the US, have shown, often far exceeds that of the purely legal, represented as the latter is by the limited framework of international law and international human rights. These frameworks are necessary but not sufficient; the ethical content of such frameworks can only be developed by an examination on the part of each society and its representatives about what their *dharma* is or should be, with regard to important issues and concerns. What forms that *dharma* will take with regard to war and violence in the global era is an open question. But the tragic cost of the wars in the fractured global world of 9/11, the sheer imbalance of power between the stronger and weaker nation-states of the world, the ongoing erosion of rights which threatens to undo the hard-fought gains in the area of human rights since the end of the Second World War and the retreat of international law and of international institutions, all indicate that there is an urgent need for a direct engagement with the question. The Gita cannot provide the answers to this question either for particular nations or for the global community at large. But it can serve as a wake-up call for our collective conscience and as a guide, at least telling us, in Arjuna's example and in Krishna's often-cryptic teachings, how to move towards an answer.

War and the enemy in the Gita

Depersonalisation, the process of rendering a human being into an abstraction, is one mechanism or one step of dehumanisation, the process of rendering a human being into something non-human, something beneath the human. Depersonalisation enables violence on a human being through distance, literal or metaphorical, by a refusal to see, by a rendering invisible; dehumanisation does not shirk its gaze but sees the human as simply flesh-and-blood, devoid of personhood, an object or thing to be actively loathed and exterminated. In account after account of violence and warfare, whether undertaken by states against groups or communities, or between nation-states, or among communities, the dehumanisation of an enemy or adversary has been a prelude to any act of violence. My concluding reflection here examines an ambiguity in the Gita with regard to its understanding of the enemy. As with the case of Arjuna's anguish, the Gita represents a limited universalism in its framing of the figure of the enemy, in which the enemy is not quite dehumanised but perhaps does not entirely escape the fate of being rendered alien. In delineating the contours of its arguments about the enemy, I consider what value the Gita may have for us in a world in where the prospect of violence unsettles our daily lives, through the possibility of terrorism, through hostility directed at us in physical public spaces, or through assaults online.

Whether in insidious and banal form, such as in the routine racism, casteism or ethnocentrism woven into everyday practices in societies, or in wartime propaganda, or in deliberate initiatives of creating an Other with the express aim of inflicting harm upon them, the minimum condition for the exercise of violence is the construction of the enemy as aberrant, deviant, monstrous, savage and uncivilised—all the things that we ourselves are not. The practice of designating groups of people as such is a regrettable feature of life in both ordinary and extraordinary times. Prejudice, ethnocentrism, racism, patriarchy, casteism and homophobia, all these forms of prejudice and exclusion involve the Othering of a group, community or population to a lesser or greater extent. The act of Othering is what contributes to creating and sustaining an idea of the enemy as deserving of violence, and then serves as justification for the most extreme kinds of violence perpetrated on that enemy. The twentieth century, whether at home in India, so to speak, or in numerous other settings, has seen this process play out, in instance after instance of barbaric violence.

The ingenious conceit of *Maus*, Art Spiegelman's semi-autobiographical masterpiece about the Holocaust, based on his father's life as a survivor, is to depict the different sets of characters in the graphic novel as animals.[54] The Jews are drawn as mice, the Germans cats, the Poles pigs, and Americans dogs. The depiction achieves several objectives while forcing us to engage with a series of important questions about the representation of violence. Spiegelman foregrounds the relationship between the ethical and the aesthetic, showing us his own struggle with finding an appropriate idiom to represent the violence of the Holocaust.[55] Riffing on the Nazi slur and long-standing anti-Semitic trope of Jews as vermin, he depicts them as mice and the Nazis as cats. Yet, in also showing us that the animal faces worn by different groups are masks, Spiegelman draws attention to the arbitrary and performative nature of human identity. Finally, in showing the Nazis as cats, naturally prone to hunting mice, Spiegelman drives home the point that the Nazis viewed Jews as prey, as beings whose natural destiny it was to be killed by cats and who were designed by nature to be subordinate to more powerful creatures.

In one stroke of his artist's pen, with this decision, Spiegelman shows us the fiction and reality of how we understand the identity of someone we deem an enemy. The alienness that we ascribe to the enemy is a fiction, based on assigned or imagined traits that designate them as inferior, evil, subhuman and, therefore, deserving of subjugation, violence and death. It is also a brute reality because the depiction of those marked as enemies as inherently alien, sub-human and evil is how they are actually perceived by many; their lives are profoundly affected by it, their rights limited, the movement of their bodies through the world constrained and circumscribed and their existence put at risk. Regardless of how individuals or groups see themselves and define their identities, they have to negotiate the perceptions that other groups of people or society at large may hold about them. I may believe I am a citizen of the world, who has transcended the specific traits of my ethnicity, skin colour, gender and the like, but if others see me through these lenses, and with their accompanying prejudices about the same, then I have no choice but to engage and deal with their notions of who I am.

The trope of the Jew as Other and the mass-scale violence of the Holocaust that it fed into found an echo in other events in the twentieth century. Second World War propaganda, on both the American and the German side, depicted the enemy according to racist tropes.[56] In the days leading up to the 1994 genocide of Tutsis in Rwanda, a Hutu radio channel routinely described Tutsis as cockroaches, calling upon Hutus to eliminate them.[57] In India, the figure of the Muslim as violent, cruel and barbaric dates back at least to the nineteenth-century colonial construction of Indian history. The project of Nehruvian secularism, which sought, in part, to address the trauma of Partition by creating a composite, syncretic Indian identity, was never entirely able to weed out the perception of the disloyal Muslim among Hindu populations. Since the 1980s, these negative images of the Muslim have been given a new lease of life in the resurgent project of the Hindu Right to redefine India as a Hindu nation, a project that has also sought to co-opt the Gita along with other canonical Hindu texts in the service of the ideology of Hindutva. The idea of the Muslim as a treacherous invader disloyal to India has played a central role in mobilising Hindu violence against different Muslim communities in riot after sectarian riot in independent India. In the aftermath of the 11 September 2001 attacks, the Muslim has also been conflated with the figure of a terrorist. Other subcontinental nations are not lagging behind in their descriptions of minorities. Hindus and Christians in Pakistan and Hindus in Sri Lanka and Bangladesh are similarly demonised.

The enemy in the Gita is not a dehumanised Other, in this sense. The obvious explanation for this is that the enemy is Arjuna's kin, and a text that valorises a social order based on the family as the ideal social unit cannot ideologically designate family members as less than human. In Arjuna's view, the folly of his cousins has placed him in a position where *he* might commit evil by combating them, and in turn, will be plagued by evil. If his cousins are guilty of violating the commitment to family, in attacking them Arjuna will also be guilty of the same sin. Being placed in this situation is the source of his anguish. Arjuna expresses these sentiments in his inaugural lament to Krishna, a partial soliloquy that expresses aloud his inner conflict:

> What joy is there for us, Krishna,
> in killing Dhritarashtra's sons?
> Evil will haunt us if we kill them,
> though their bows are drawn to kill.
>
> ...
>
> The greed that distorts their reason
> blinds them to the sin they commit
> in ruining the family, blinds them
> to the crime of betraying friends.
>
> How can we ignore the wisdom
> of turning from this evil
> when we see the sin
> of family destruction, Arjuna?[58]

The mode of allegorical reading I have suggested and explored in the previous chapter on difference, wherein we extend the hospitality and debt owed to members of the family to world at large, applies here as well. Utopian and naive as it may perhaps seems, such an idea is no more or less unrealistic than any other universal proposition, such as the notion of universal human rights. The idea of violence to another as violence to one's own can function as an ideal regulative principle that at least puts the brakes on hasty recourse to violence as an obvious option or easy solution for resolving conflict. For all America's talk of being a beacon of rights and democracy in the world, and for all the grand claims made about the West as the source of liberalism, the inability to consider ordinary Iraqis and Afghans as equal to their own lies at the heart of the violent and foolish American misadventure in both countries.

A related insight about the nature of the enemy that the conversation between Arjuna and Krishna offers us is that the enemy is not an absolute but, rather, is contextually produced. Here, the ideas of *dharma,* or ethically determined or guided duty, and *karma,* or action, point to a counter-intuitive conceptualisation of the enemy that inverts our commonsensical and conventional understanding of the proverbial bad guy. Books on military strategy, past and present, novels about detectives, gangsters and Mafiosi, Hollywood action films, superhero comics and Bollywood potboilers, all suggest the same sequence and strategy in dealing with the enemy: know your enemy and take action accordingly. The successful hero is one who figures out his enemy's Achilles's heel. In a common plot conceit in films that centre on the trope of good versus evil, the protagonist will often initially suffer a loss or defeat, then, humbled by the defeat, he or she will deliberate on the right strategy, which typically involves exploiting a weakness of the adversary. In shows that deal with crime, dogged detectives follow the same logic in developing a psychological profile of a suspect, seeking a chink in his armour and then relentlessly exploiting that to break the suspect down. In the Gita, it is a situation or context that calls upon us to engage in the right action or *karma.* If that action involves resorting to military action or war against an individual or group, then the latter is framed as an enemy in that situation. The contextual production of the enemy has other important implications, too. In not damning an enemy as the essence of evil, the logic of the Gita provides us with a rationale for a response, in war or otherwise, that is proportional, just and ethical. Gandhi's responses to the barbarism of British colonial rule provide an especially salient illumination of the viability of this principle. Gandhi's example shows that rather than some woolly-headed justification for weakness, the idea of strategically responding to a contextually determined enemy is an effective practical mechanism for achieving political objectives.

The Gita, though, as we have seen, is not fully exempt from the charge of designating some groups as an Other. It is open to this criticism on grounds of its agreement with the social order based on caste, as Ambedkar held in his critique of the text. One cannot simply set aside or explain away this fact about the Gita; it remains a limitation of the text. The Gita's endorsement of caste hierarchies does not entirely negate the value of other concepts in the text that serve as a critique of war and violence. In the context of militaristic violence, the Gita does not reflect the operation, seen in wars, the Holocaust, Partition or genocides, of first transforming the enemy into an object, a thing, devoid of humanity, to make palatable, even necessary, the subsequent act of annihilating them. However, there exists an unresolved contradiction in what the Gita has to say about the exercise of routine violence in everyday life and acts of violence in the context of war.

Finally, the Gita reveals the same contradiction with regard to evil. If the enemy is not defined in terms of evil, the Gita nonetheless does have *a* discourse of evil expressed intermittently through the text, such as in the sixteenth teaching or chapter. Within the Gita itself, it is not explained what the source of this evil is, though, ostensibly, it has to do with the cycle of rebirth in which one accumulates sin or the benefits of good deeds. A nebulous, metaphysical notion of evil carries risks in that it can easily be applied to an entire category of people in all kinds of dangerous ways, especially in a world grappling with difference. However, if we read the book along the lines that Gandhi did, suggesting that the capacities for good and evil are a characteristic of all individuals and communities, and not the mark or prerogative of only some communities, we can transform the metaphysical references to evil in the text into a statement of equality. To do so would not be abandoning the fight for justice in a global world. Instead, it would decentre the ethnocentric privilege of powerful nations, communities and individuals as arbiters of morality, harbingers of wars and authors of the fate of their fellow human beings.

CODA

Gandhi, the Gita and Globalisation

Although Gandhi died just before the advent of globalisation—in the sense in which it is used in this book to refer to the changes that transformed the world in the second half of the twentieth century—his own life was a singularly global one. Born in India, he trained as a lawyer in London and was employed in South Africa for close to two decades, before he returned to India. Gandhi's confrontation with the British empire entailed his transformation from a westernised lawyer clad in a suit to the Mahatma in a loincloth. His transformation of Indian anti-colonial resistance into a mass movement, after he became the Mahatma, was no turn to a narrow nationalism. Rather, it was based on a highly original and heterodox understanding of being and human identity, one that challenged the idea of the West as the sole author or originator of universalist conceptions of selfhood and civilisation.

Gandhi remains the most well-known reader of the Gita, and no text was more important to Gandhi than the Gita. He is not a textualist, as Patton reminds us, and we need not hold that against him; leading the greatest non-violent mass social movement in history more than compensates for not analysing texts according to the formalist principles of close reading.[1] Given how crucial an influence the Gita was on Gandhi's thought and practice of politics, his idea of the self and life in general, and given Gandhi's centrality to Indian life during his lifetime and after, he is also likely the most significant and influential reader of the Gita there ever has been. For Gandhi, the doctrine of *nishkama karma*, or action without desire for reward, was the very heart of the Gita, the central animating idea that, in turn, gave meaning to all the other themes and ideas in the book. Gandhi also understood the discussion on war in the Gita primarily as an allegory for the conflict between good and evil, especially as that battle played out within the self.

My reading in this coda, however, centres not on Gandhi's voluminous writings on the Gita but on his remarkable text *Hind Swaraj* or *Indian Home Rule*.[2] Gandhi's critique of British colonial rule, in his writings and his practices, his political strategies and his presentation of selfhood, was embedded in a larger critique of Western modernity. *Hind Swaraj* is an especially significant statement of that critique. *Hind Swaraj*'s debt to important ideas in the Gita, such as *karma* or action, *dharma* or duty, the imperative of undertaking action selflessly and enlightenment as the conquest of one's passions and desires, is evident through the text.[3] In the work, Gandhi also dismantles the fundamental premise of British and Western civilisational superiority, through a withering assessment of Western modernity, the purportedly universal set of values, way of life or condition of enlightenment that the British claimed that they were gifting to Indians. To the extent that globalisation, global modernity or global capitalist modernity, whatever term we use, is a phase of a larger epoch of modernity, Gandhi's critique of modernity bears relevance for it. Additionally, Gandhi's very act of taking on the British empire, in writing as in other forms of action, represents an immensely powerful performative critique of a key aspect of globalisation—global imperialism.[4] For these reasons alone, *Hind Swaraj* and the ideas of the Gita encapsulated within it offer interesting possibilities for understanding what Gandhi might have said about the condition of the world today.

The word 'swaraj' is most literally translated as self-rule and, as the title of the text suggests, refers to the independence, autonomy and freedom that Indians sought from British rule. But the term bears other resonances and meanings as well. Swaraj also refers to the idea of the control of the self, or rule or sovereignty over the self. A central concept in Gandhi's thought, swaraj, for him, stood for the idea that Indians would only be able to meaningfully govern themselves as a sovereign people if they could gain the same sovereignty over their selves at an individual level by mastering their desires, fighting temptations and quelling their baser instincts.

Gandhi's critique in the text is focused on specific modern Western practices, ideas and historical achievements, including parliamentary democracy, the political form of the modern nation-state, and industrial technology. The very presence of the British in India and the inequities of colonial rule were justified by the argument that these practices, ideas and structures represented the superiority of British civilisation to its Indian counterpart, a claim accepted by many educated and enlightened Indians, including those involved in the anti-colonial nationalist struggle. The idea that the British, through their enlightened despotism, had dragged a backward, stagnant nation into modernity, into the inevitable march of history itself—by technological progress, rule of law and liberal ideas—has been used since colonial times to justify even the worst excesses of colonialism, recently, for example, in the writings and pronouncements of apologists for imperialism like Niall Ferguson and Nigel Biggar.[5]

Written in 1909, *Hind Swaraj* takes the form of a dialogue between two characters, the Editor, who is Gandhi himself, and the Reader, who is both Gandhi's friend Pranjivandas Mehta and the typical Indian reader who might read the book. Short in length, the book, however, contains a plenitude of ideas, the complexity of many of which belies the simplicity with which they are presented. Having studied the text in some depth, having read it several times and having taught it, I increasingly see it as, at once, a highly original critique of ideas and assumptions fundamental to the condition of modernity, a tactical intervention against British colonial rule and a compendium of a set of ethical challenges that Gandhi sets for Indians and the British alike. But in its absolute rejection of everything that could even be remotely associated with British rule, the text, on initial reading, gives one pause.

In keeping with Gandhi's philosophical and polemical goal, one of the key themes of *Hind Swaraj* is a blanket repudiation of much that has become universalised about modernity across the world, such as particular technologies and the idea of technological progress, the political system of parliamentary democracy, and the very idea of the modern nation-state, the dominant form of political organisation and sovereignty in the modern world. The railways come in for particularly sharp criticism from Gandhi. Indian ire towards the railways is easily understood. After all, ever since their introduction during colonial times, the railways have been touted as proof of the benefits of colonial rule to a backward, technologically undeveloped society. The claim is easily countered, for instance, in a droll and incisive recent commentary by Indian politician and writer Shashi Tharoor, who notes that the railways were built by the East India Company, the earliest avatar of the British colonial state, for its own benefits and that many countries built railways 'without having to go to the trouble and expense of being colonised to do so'.[6] The critique of the exaggerated benefits of the railways as an emblem of the superiority of Western modernity, science and technology makes sense. But who could disagree with the obvious benefits of Western medicine in fighting disease, especially in a poor country like India, where large parts of the population were routinely inflicted with and died of preventable diseases, even if that wider condition of misery was itself partly a product of colonial rule?

Gandhi's condemnation of science and technology, including their obvious benefits, stood in stark contrast to the much more readily comprehensible and seemingly sensible views of Nehru on the matter. For Nehru, science and technology represented universal knowledge, regardless of their origins, and were an essential instrument not just for material economic prosperity but for social progress as well. Nehru was well known as an evangelist for what he called the 'scientific temper', a cultivated rational sensibility which stood as the antithesis of the superstition and ignorance that were both cause and consequence of India's colonial subjugation and humiliation.[7]

When I taught *Hind Swaraj* in a course at Emory University titled 'From Gandhi to Google: Technology and Nationalism in India from Colonialism to Cyberspace', my students were understandably confused and even disappointed by Gandhi's views. The course, which was based on aspects of my dissertation research, examined the many rich meanings of technology in the Indian nationalist and popular imagination in three phases: the period of British colonial rule and anti-colonial nationalism that lasted from roughly the mid-eighteenth century till the moment of Indian independence in 1947; the post-Independence and postcolonial phase of centralised planning and technological, economic and industrial development from 1947 to 1991; and the current phase since 1991, during which time India has entered the global economy and thousands of highly skilled technology workers from the country have migrated overseas, especially to technology hubs like the Silicon Valley in the US. This last phase also roughly coincided with the emergence of a global internet-based economy, following the invention of the first 'killer app' of the World Wide Web.

The Indian-American students in the class were especially dismayed by the gulf in thinking between Gandhi and Nehru on the subject. Like many Indians and those of Indian origin in the US, they had been taught by their parents and the diasporic Indian community to revere Gandhi. Widely seen as the prime architect of Indian freedom due to his role in mobilising the mass nationalist anti-colonial movement, Gandhi is affectionately known as 'Bapu' and commonly referred to as the 'father of the nation' in India. Indian public life, in fact, is marked by the performance of an excessive hagiographic appreciation of Gandhi, with any criticism of Gandhi resulting in public controversy, censure and proclamations of moral outrage. Gandhi has even been appropriated by some groups in the Hindu Right—an irony, since a Hindu nationalist fanatic named Godse was responsible for Gandhi's assassination. The Indian-American students in my class, like students in India, had also been taught to revere doctors, scientists, technologists and engineers, and to aspire to working in these professions. And now here they were, situated in the West, justly proud of their Indian heritage and values, on their way to becoming scientists and doctors, while Gandhi was bluntly telling them that these vocations were perhaps not worth much to humanity and that the values that these professions represented were at odds with their Indian identities and heritage.

Any reading of Gandhi as a straightforward statement or generalisation, however, is fraught with pitfalls. Gandhi's scathing critique of Western science and technology is part careful analysis of the impact of technology, part strategic polemic, part clarion call to a moral reflection that he demands of Indians. Above all, it is a radical critique of a particular notion of technology—not unique to the context of globalisation but very much a central driver of it—that is in contradiction with a holistic idea of the human or the conception of an indivisible human spirit. Given the fetishisation of STEM, that is, science, technology, engineering and medicine, in Silicon Valley and beyond, the aura of power and desirability around giant technology firms like Google, Facebook, Amazon and Apple, the mythification of the figure of the technological entrepreneur as a kind of seer who will solve all the world's problems, including poverty, illness and climate change, Gandhi's critique is especially apposite for our technology-obsessed global world.

A close reading of one key passage from *Hind Swaraj* will shed light on Gandhi's original and insightful critique of technology and its deep relevance, despite the fact that some of his claims seem peculiar. In a passage that is noteworthy for the jumble of damning accusations that it presents, Gandhi lists numerous specific objections to the railways as an embodiment of Western scientific and technological reason:

> It must be manifest to you that but, for the railways, the English could not have a hold on India as they have. The railways, too, have spread the bubonic plague. Without them, masses could not move from place to place. They are the carriers of plague germs. Formerly we had natural segregation. Railways have also increased the frequency of famines, because, owing to facility of means of locomotion, people sell out their grain and it is sent to the dearest market. People become careless, and the presence of famine increases. They accentuate the evil nature of man. Bad men fulfill their evil designs with greater rapidity. The holy places of India have become unholy. Formerly, people went to these places with great difficulty. Generally, therefore, only the real devotees visited such places. Nowadays, rogues visit them in order to practice their roguery.[8]

The illogical nature of the claims and the neo-Luddite position in the passage befuddled my students, as I am sure they have many a reader in the century plus since Gandhi penned the book.

Gandhi, it should be noted, was no stranger to such statements nor to holding regressive and controversial views on a number of topics, from sexuality to vegetarianism, natural disasters to caste. And, indeed, the statement can be justly interpreted as reductive, simplistic or regressive.

Yet, there is another set of meanings that we can discern in the passage, which has to do with what Gandhi considers the effects of technology on the essence or spirit of the human. The essence of the human, according to Gandhi, lies in its indivisible *and* limited nature. 'Man is so made by nature,' Gandhi says, 'as to require him to restrict his movements as far as his hands and feet will take him ... God set a limit to man's locomotive ambition in the construction of his body. Man immediately proceeded to discover means of overriding the limit.'[9] This is the crux of Gandhi's critique of technology. Gandhi considered human limitations as essential to the state of being human and indispensable for living an ethical life. In enabling a hubristic overreaching by humans, by empowering them to transcend their physical limitations, the railways had disrupted the natural order of social, economic and cultural life. Thanks to the railways, the existence of people would no longer be bound to the structures of local life or to local ethical concerns, to the ecological rhythms of the spaces in which they were rooted. As the cause of such cataclysmic changes, the railways had destroyed much of what was human about human life. Scholars like Ashis Nandy and Gyan Prakash suggest that the attrition of humanness that ensues from technology is what undergirds Gandhi's general objection to technology as well as his opposition to specific technologies like the railways.[10] As different kinds of technology remake our world—whether drones or social media, electric cars or Zoom—in many positive ways, surely, but often in troubling and disturbing ways, it is well worth paying attention to Gandhi's thoughts.

There are strong and compelling objections that one can raise to Gandhi's romantic invocation of the existing Indian social order—the exact point that the Gita, too, is guilty of—notably the fact that this order rested on and perpetuated the violent inequities of caste and gender that Hindu reformers had long battled to change. For Dalit leaders like B.R. Ambedkar, who belonged to a so-called 'untouchable' caste, the very characteristics of modernity that Gandhi found objectionable—the sense of anonymity it conferred on individuals, its disruption of social relationships, the mobility it afforded caste and 'untouchable' minority groups to move from villages to cities—were its most valuable aspects, carrying a powerful emancipatory power for individual rights, as opposed to the tyranny and claustrophobic hierarchies of the Hindu community and Indian social structures. In a related vein, Gandhi is also justifiably open to criticism that he romanticised the notion of community and, like many seminal Indian thinkers and political figures before and after him, saw the community rather than the individual as the unit of Indian social life.

As a broader philosophical argument about technology, though, Gandhi's critique of the railways in the passage from *Hind Swaraj* carries much purchase. His arguments also appear more valid if one interprets them as a universal critique of technology, beyond the role of technology in only an Indian setting. Gandhi's objections to the railways are that, first, they enable actions that can easily be divorced from their consequences or the immediate structures of social obligation and accountability required by the bonds of social life. Rather than provide for members of their immediate community and neighbours, farmers can use the railways to take grain to distant places for the best price, even at the risk of contributing to a famine. The reference here is likely to the many famines that India experienced under British colonial rule, which were caused not just by drought but by British policies and the larger political economy of colonial exploitation. Under the system, Indian raw materials were exported to Britain to be manufactured as mass-produced goods that were then sold back to Indians, in the bargain devastating local economies and industries. This line of argument is linked to Gandhi's related claim in the passage that the railways have enabled a compartmentalisation, commodification and marketisation of human life by separating economic imperatives, motives and objectives from social, ecological and moral concerns. For Gandhi, it was the very unity of the different dimensions of social life, including the economic, social, political, spiritual and ecological, that defined the human spirit. Human existence was meaningless if not lived according to this principle. The separation of different aspects of human existence worked to the advantage of overtly unethical people while threatening to lure others into unethical action as well. Gandhi's perspective on technology here presciently anticipates a seminal insight in Heidegger's essay, 'The question concerning technology', that technology has reframed humans as a 'standing-reserve'.[11] Heidegger argues that the standing reserve is not merely a source of power or human capacity but rather part of an extractive rearrangement of the order of nature, in which humans become a means to a technological end or system.[12]

Some of these objections, as general insights about technology, also apply to the very different technological form of social media that Gandhi and those in his world could not have anticipated. A common and well-founded argument against the negative effects of social media platforms like Twitter and Facebook is precisely that they enable a deeply problematic divorce between action and accountability, in part by enabling the same kind of anonymity and distance that Gandhi found so troubling about the railways. The critique holds for the pervasive online plague of trolling, the epidemic of fake news and the culture of antagonistic polarisation that characterise much online discourse currently. Likewise, the disruptions that Facebook and Twitter have caused to political and social life through their undermining of democratic processes echo Gandhi's claim about the deployment of the railways by the British to keep India under the colonial yoke. His point about rogues exploiting technology calls to mind the use of Facebook by figures like Steve Bannon to attempt to skew the results of the 2016 US presidential elections or the use of WhatsApp by the Hindu Right to plan assaults against Muslims in the last few years.[13]

Gandhi's solutions to the problems posed by Western technology and, more broadly, by Western modernity or, extending the argument, by global modernity, do not appear practical or feasible for our times. For the individual, Gandhi advocated a puritanical moral code of austere existence involving a level of self-denial that would be nearly impossible for the average person to follow today, as it arguably was in 1909 as well. For society at large, Gandhi recommended the rejection of the very idea of the modern nation-state and formal, parliamentary democracy. Instead, in his alternate vision of modern Indian society, the structures of the nation-state and democracy would be replaced by a community of communities, each unit from the individual village onward embedded into a larger circle of community all the way through to the nation, a concentric circle of social networks that would provide stability, order and balance. Yet, even with its flaws and its very pointed criticism of aspects of British colonial rule, Gandhi's message about the threats of a certain vision of technology to human life and the human spirit remains relevant today. We see social media platforms like Facebook running roughshod over democracy across the world. We see them hiding behind cynical invocations of free speech and neutrality in defending their refusal to do anything about the hate speech, abuse and violence to which many of their users resort. We see the abuse of surveillance technologies and data mining in economically exploiting the most painful details and vulnerabilities of people's lives.

The Gita informs Gandhi's critique even if it is not always apparent. Anything man attempts beyond his natural capability is deemed arrogance by Gandhi. Translated into the Gita's framework, such attempts reflect a desire to control things and, therefore, to control outcomes. The naive and simplistic idea that technology can solve social problems, seen in the large claims made about Facebook building a global 'community' or social media causing the Arab Spring, or Elon Musk's idea of colonising Mars, are each a case in point. The hubris that leads humans to develop frameworks for dominion over nature or over other humans exemplifies inaction or incorrect action and an abdication of duty. Gandhi, like the Gita, does not give us readymade or easily applicable answers to these questions. But his exhortation about the need to look inwards and do the right thing, his criticism of Faustian overreaching as misguided, his opposition to violence, his rejection of a narrow nationalism along with his scepticism about the nation-state, all seem curiously timely. The Gita sings to us in many voices, and we should listen to all of them. One of the especially important voices in which it sings is that of Gandhi.

Afterword to the
Indian Paperback Edition

The Gita in a Global World is informed by two main ideas. The first is that we inhabit a particular historical condition—one that I term 'crisis globalisation'—in which greater existential precarity, increased political turbulence and violence, and the threat of difference are the order of the day. The second idea that animates the book is that the Gita offers us a valuable framework for negotiating the ethical challenges posed by this state of affairs. The book attempts to illuminate a manner of thinking, and provide a set of tools and concepts to address the urgent questions we face about the general situation of uncertainty, the realities of violence and war, and living with and respecting those who we see as different from ourselves in terms of their cultural, social and personal identities. The Gita does not have easy or ready answers to all such questions. It also endorses a vision of society founded on gender and caste inequality. Yet, in that it also articulates a philosophy of universal being, the Gita may also offer a vision of a more just and inclusive idea of human belonging.

In the two years or so since this book was published, the thesis of crisis globalisation appears to ring truer and the lessons of the Gita strike one as more salient. Even as the World Health Organisation has officially declared that COVID-19 no longer counts as global emergency, the sense of precarity resulting from the upheavals that the pandemic caused lingers in its wake.[1] But it is not just the trauma unleashed by COVID that is responsible for our predicament of uncertainty. The challenges of war, conflict and violence, as well as the intractable questions of dealing and living with difference, also seem to have been amplified in this short time period.

New international political conflicts have reared up, hydra-headed, even as long-standing problems in the world order appear to have sharpened. In February 2022, Russia invaded Ukraine, inaugurating a new global political crisis. As of April 2023, the war, which shows no signs of ending, had resulted in the death or injury over 350,000 soldiers from both sides.[2] US-China tensions, rooted in rivalry for political, economic and technological dominance, have ramped up to a level that a former American secretary of defence describes as 'dangerous'.[3] The political instability that characterises the current geopolitical landscape is intertwined with national and global economic insecurity.[4] Aside from the human toll, the economic fallout from the Russia-Ukraine war has slowed global growth to merely 3.1 per cent in 2022, impeding the global economic recovery from the troughs of the pandemic.[5] In the US, a stock market boom has been followed by a bear market in equities since the middle of 2022 and by layoffs across several sectors. The European economy has been especially strongly impacted by the Russian-Ukraine war, and like the US, runs the risk of a recession. China and India show stronger promise of an economic rebound, but both countries face challenges as a result of long-term factors as well as the shorter-term impact of the pandemic.

However, if such developments indicate a shift towards a new equilibrium in global power relations—and that might well be a premature judgement, for the end of American hegemony has been confidently proclaimed numerous times in the last several decades—they do not point to deglobalisation but to de-

Americanisation, resulting from some diminution of American power. Despite initiatives like export controls imposed by the Biden administration on sales of technology to China and the CHIPS Act passed by the US in 2022 meant to encourage domestic semiconductor manufacturing, we are unlikely to see a trend of economic nationalism take root internationally.[6] The US and Europe, for instance, are both turning to India as an important political and economic counterweight to China. India's service exports sector is robust, though it is debating the benefits of strengthening its manufacturing sector.[7] India has also exponentially increased its oil imports from Russia, even as the Western world has imposed sanctions on the latter.[8] And while global supply chain problems persist, the objective is to make supply chains more robust and less dependent on any one nation rather than pursue the utopian goal of national self-sufficiency.

The threat of difference—for instance, the fear of 'non-Western' values colonising the world—is but one factor in the conflicts between nations that plague the world today. However, anxieties around difference and the often violent initiatives to discipline or obliterate difference are central to the national domestic political culture of many countries. In India, as the right-wing Bharatiya Janata Party-led government nears a decade in power, the relentless assault on the rights of minorities, particularly Muslims, shows no sign of letting up. Muslims face extreme brutality at the hands of mobs and state authorities alike, in the form of lynchings, riots, and the demolition of places of worship and habitation.[9] In Italy, the far-right government that came to power in 2022 has taken a hard line on immigration, with plans to make the asylum process more difficult.[10] The Italian prime minister, Giorgia Meloni, has a long record of opposing Italian policies on migration, which no doubt played a role in her party's victory. The resurgence of white supremacy during the Trump presidency in the US has not abated, expressing itself in anti-migrant attitudes, mass shootings and newfound stridency as Trump plans to run again in the 2024 presidential elections.[11] As more than one expert has pointed out, though, white supremacy is not just an American but a global phenomenon.[12] Majoritarian attacks on vulnerable ethnic and racial groups, in turn, can be seen as one specific manifestation of a wider backlash against different types of minority communities across the world. In the US, numerous states and governors have imposed policies expressly targeting LGBTQ+ persons.[13] In India, too, as sexual minorities fight for the legal right to marry, the state and a host of religious organisations have joined hands to oppose them in court.[14]

Such developments may seem to point to a rejection of the value of cosmopolitanism, a virtue associated with a world of salubrious cultural encounters and exchange. They may, equally, suggest a rejection of the larger political economy of globalisation that drives migrations of high- and low-skilled workers and refugees across borders. But the reality remains more complicated. Britain's decision to leave the European Union precisely on grounds of such sentiments—Brexit—has negatively impacted both Britain and Europe, hampering trade and impacting travel, with its deleterious effects clearly threatening to significantly outweigh any benefits.[15] Under Rishi Sunak, the UK is now revisiting its plans to scrap a vast number of EU laws.[16] American responses to debates on gender identity and transgender rights are complicated. Nevertheless, a majority of Americans oppose discrimination, with Democrats and younger Americans more likely to see sex and gender as distinct and not necessarily determined at birth.[17] As was the case with gay rights and gay marriage, it is possible that transgender rights may eventually cease to be a politically contentious matter as more young people across political lines endorse inclusive policies on transgender identity. Similarly, while hostility to immigrants is no doubt one reason for the rightward lurch of European societies, it does not entirely negate Europe's relative openness to migrants in recent decades.[18] More restrictive policies are also unlikely to solve Europe's migrant crisis or provide easy solutions to questions of integration, assimilation and belonging that bedevil Sweden, France, Italy and other European nations. Trends reflecting the positive as well as negative effects of globalisation will not be reversed. As the thesis of crisis globalisation suggests, though, the social turbulence caused by these effects will be heightened and debates concerning them will grow more fractious.

Given this state of the affairs, the themes from the Gita that I have examined as sources for ethical action continue to hold power, as they have well before the onset of the era of crisis globalisation. The concepts that are especially helpful in this regard may be enumerated thus: distinguishing between the desire to control outcomes and awareness of consequences; applying the principle of epistemic humility in assessing any situation; valuing doubt as much as unshakeable certitude; balancing action and contemplation; categorically affirming the universalism of the Gita while rejecting its endorsement of caste and gender hierarchy as an ethical choice; and extending the principle of kinship to all humans and, indeed, all living beings.

In the pages of this book, I have argued that implementing these principles in the practice of everyday life can help us to meaningfully manage the challenges of a world in flux, whether we happen to be powerful individuals whose decisions impact large numbers of our fellow beings or ordinary persons whose actions nonetheless still deeply affect those in our orbit. Krishna's advice to Arjuna on the battlefield but also Arjuna's doubts, the unresolved tension between the universalism of the Gita and the hierarchy of clan, kin and caste, a tension that demands us to make a choice about which principle matters more, the understanding that not taking any decision may be the right course of action in some circumstances but that inaction rooted in indifference is never a viable option—these and related ideas can help us navigate not just the literal and metaphorical wars and battles that constitute the stuff of life but also the experience of peace that one day might hopefully constitute a permanent interregnum between conflict.

NOTES

1. INTRODUCTION:
Reading the Gita in a Global Age

1. Uma Majumdar, 'Mahatma Gandhi and the Bhagavad Gita,' *American Vedantist*, 6 December 2014, https://americanvedantist.org/2014/articles/mahatma-gandhi-and-the-bhagavad-gita/, accessed 6 March 2020.
2. Ibid.
3. On the non-cooperation movement, see D.A. Low, 'The government of India and the first non-cooperation movement—1920–1922,' *The Journal of Asian Studies,* vol. 25, no. 2 (1955): 241–259. Shahid Amin's scholarship on the events at Chauri Chaura and their impact on Indian history and society remains unsurpassed. See Shahid Amin, *Event, Metaphor, Memory: Chauri Chaura 1922 –1992*, Berkeley, California: University of California Press, 1995.
4. James Temperton, '"Now I am become Death, the destroyer of worlds". The story of Oppenheimer's infamous quote,' *Wired UK*, 9 August 2017, https://www.wired.co.uk/article/manhattan-project-robert-oppenheimer, accessed 8 April 2020.
5. See '"Seared to death": The atomic bomb attack on Hiroshima,' *Al-Jazeera*, 5 August 2020, https://www.aljazeera.com/news/2020/8/6/seared-to-death-the-atomic-bomb-attack-on-hiroshima, accessed 12 August 2020; The Associated Press, 'AP WAS THERE: US drops atomic bombs on Japan in 1945,' *AP News*, 3 August 2015, https://apnews.com/3fd267ba7b3c40479382189c99172d61/ap-was-there-us-drops-atomic-bombs-japan-1945, accessed 12 August 2020; Seren Morris, 'How many people died in Hiroshima and Nagasaki?' *Newsweek*, 3 August 2020, https://www.newsweek.com/how-many-people-died-hiroshima-nagasaki-japan-second-world-war-1522276, accessed 12 August 2020.

6. R.K. Narayan, *The Mahabharata: A Shortened Modern Prose Version of the Indian Epic*, Chicago, Illinois: University of Chicago Press, 1978, p. xiii.

7. Ibid., p. xvii. The Indian penchant for engaging in and enjoying digressions can, at the very least, be traced back to the world in which the tale of the Mahabharata would have circulated.

8. See John L. Brockington, 'The Bhagavadgita: Text and context,' in *The Fruits of Our Desiring: An Enquiry into the Ethics of the Bhagavadgita for Our Times*, edited by Julius Lipner, Calgary, AB, Canada: Bayeux, 1997, pp. 28–47; reprinted in *The Bhagavad Gita*, translated by Gavin Flood and Charles Martin, New York: Norton, 2015, pp. 135–153.

9. Brockington, p. 137.

10. Brockington states, 'One cannot, it seems to me, sensibly regard the *Bhagavadgita* as both integral to the epic and theologically profound' (p. 137).

11. Narayan, *The Mahabharata*, p. xvii.

12. The well-known quote is cited in numerous places. See the text of Girish Karnad's A.K. Ramanujan Memorial Lecture delivered at Ramjas College, 21 March 2012, which is reproduced as 'Full Text of A K Ramanujan Memorial Lecture 2012 by Girish Karnad' on the South Asia Citizens' website at http://www.sacw.net/article4762.html (accessed 18 October 2020).

13. The following texts are useful resources on Hindu religious visual culture: Richard Davis, *Gods in Print: Masterpieces of India's Mythological Art*, New York: Mandala Publishing, 2012; Christopher Pinney, *Photos of the Gods: The Printed Image and Political Struggle in India*, London: Reaktion Books, 2004; Kajri Jain, *Gods in the Bazaar: The Economies of Indian Calendar Art*, Durham, North Carolina: Duke University Press, 2004.

14. Borges's poetic essay, 'The Thousand and One Nights', describes the processes by which the book of that name, rooted in Indian stories and fables from across the Orient, became part of the Western literary tradition. See Jorge Luis Borges and Eliot Weinberger, 'The Thousand and One Nights,' *The Georgia Review*, vol. 38, no. 3 (1984): 564–574. Borges describes the first translation of *The Thousand and One Nights* as 'a major event for all of European literature' (p. 567). Borges also comments that the text is 'one of the most illustrious books in all literature (and one more appreciated in the West than in the East, so

they tell me)' (p. 568). The Dalai Lama's superstardom in the West roughly mirrors this phenomenon. I have witnessed exponentially greater enthusiasm for the sayings of the Tibetan spiritual leader in the Bay Area in California than I did in Delhi, despite the relative proximity of the Indian capital to Dharamshala, where he resides.

15. Amit Chaudhuri, 'Philosophy without a philosopher in sight,' *Times Literary Supplement*, n.d., https://www.the-tls.co.uk/articles/philosophy-without-a-philosopher-in-sight/, accessed 4 July 2020.

16. The other was, indeed, a hellfire-and-brimstone evangelical, though not quite as persistent.

17. 'Russia court declares Hindu book Bhagvad Gita legal,' *BBC*, 28 December 2011, https://www.bbc.co.uk/news/world-asia-india-16344615, accessed 2 June 2020.

18. Laurie Patton, *The Bhagvad Gita*, New York: Penguin, 2008, p. viii. A word on the convention I have used for translations of the Gita is in place here. I have placed the name of the particular translator as the author for convenience's sake, though the authors of texts like the Gita and Mahabharata are anonymous.

19. I prefer the term 'nonmodern' to 'pre-modern', because the latter suggests a linear and somewhat reductive model of the inevitable development of all societies and humanity (in the aggregate) towards a more advanced state of modernity. The term 'nonmodern', in contrast, suggests an alternative form of life or way of being to the modern that can coexist with the latter and serve as a critique of it as well. In his incisive theorisation of the nonmodern, Nandy has argued that the nonmodern exists as a layer of consciousness in the Indian psyche along with the modern and Western. Indians have absorbed the West psychologically as just one more stratum of consciousness, and the Indian psyche is not exhausted by Western cognitive and affective sensibilities. See Ashis Nandy, *The Intimate Enemy: Loss and Recovery of Self Under Colonialism*, 2nd edition, New Delhi: Oxford University Press, 2009; 'Outside the imperium: Gandhi's cultural critique of the "West",' *Alternatives: Global, Local, Political*, vol. 7, no. 2 (1981): 171–194, 10.1177/030437548100700202, accessed 11 August 2020; 'An anti-secularist manifesto,' *Indian International Centre Quarterly*, vol. 22, no. 1 (1995): 35–64.

20. See Jane Bennett, 'Modernity and its critics,' in *The Oxford Handbook of Political Science*, edited by Robert E. Goodin, New

York: Oxford, 2011; online publication date September 2013, 10.1093/oxfordhb/9780199604456.013.0006, accessed 11 November 2020.

21. The work of the French sociologist Pierre Bourdieu explains the relationship between different types of capital. I have found it very useful as a theoretical framework for understanding the relationship between social structures and individual choices. I have elaborated Bourdieu's concept of different kinds of capital in an essay, 'Neoliberalism as doxa: Bourdieu's theory of the state and the contemporary Indian discourse on globalization and liberalization,' *Cultural Studies*, vol. 17, nos 3–4 (2003): 419–444.

22. Frantz Fanon, *The Wretched of the Earth*, New York: Grove Press, 2005.

23. See Erica Pandey, 'An uncertain future for workers,' *Axios*, 13 November 2009, https://www.axios.com/future-of-work-gig-workers-technology-detroit-ad62cdc2-13e8-4e78-b057-9e82c8f18a20.html, accessed 11 June 2020.

24. Hollie Silverman, 'California wildfires have burned an area almost the size of Connecticut,' *CNN*, 14 September 2020, https://www.cnn.com/2020/09/14/us/california-wildfires-monday/index.html, accessed 14 September 2020.

25. World Health Organization, 'WHO Coronavirus Disease (COVID-19) Dashboard,' updated as of 16 January 2021, 5.52 p.m., https://covid19.who.int/, accessed 16 January 2021, 6.19 p.m., Pacific Standard Time in the US. As of this date and time, the site provides the following information: 'Globally, as of 5:52pm CET, 16 January 2021, there have been 92,506,811 confirmed cases of COVID-19, including 2,001,773 deaths, reported to WHO.'

26. An article in the *Washington Post*, bluntly titled 'The virus that shut down the world', paints a grim picture of the global impact of the pandemic, detailing the havoc caused by the virus to international trade, tourism, business travel and immigration. Anthony Faiola, 'The virus that shut down the world,' 26 June 2020, *The Washington Post*, https://www.washingtonpost.com/graphics/2020/world/coronavirus-pandemic-globalization/, accessed 3 July 2020.

27. Saurabh Trivedi, 'Coronavirus: The story of India's largest COVID-19 cluster,' *The Hindu*, 11 April 2020, https://www.thehindu.com/news/national/coronavirus-nizamuddin-tablighi-jamaat-markaz-the-story-of-indias-largest-covid-19-cluster/article31313698.ece, accessed 7 May 2020; Chitleen K. Sethi, 'Preacher who was Punjab's 1st COVID-19

death could have been a "super-spreader",' 26 March 2020, *The Print*, https://theprint.in/health/preacher-who-was-punjabs-1st-covid-19-death-could-have-been-a-super-spreader/388946/, accessed 8 May 2020.

28. 'COVID-19 vaccines,' *Centers for Disease Control and Prevention*, updated 15 January 2021, https://www.cdc.gov/coronavirus/2019-ncov/vaccines/, accessed 16 January 2021; Jeff Tollefson, 'Why deforestation and extinctions make pandemics more likely,' 7 August 2020, https://www.nature.com/articles/d41586-020-02341-1, accessed 16 January 2021.

29. Wendy Doniger, 'Bhagavadgita,' *Encyclopædia Britannica*, 11 September 2018, https://www.britannica.com/topic/Bhagavadgita, accessed 15 February 2020.

30. Davis, op. cit., p. 4

31. Jan Kott, *Shakespeare, Our Contemporary*, New York: Doubleday, 1964.

32. Davis, op. cit., 15.

33. Davis, op. cit., 6.

34. Ludwig Wittgenstein, *Philosophical Investigations*, 4th edition, 2009, edited and translated by P.M.S. Hacker and Joachim Schulte, Oxford: Wiley-Blackwell, p. 43.

35. Davis, op. cit., 7

36. Gavin Flood and Charles Martin, *The Bhagavad Gita: A New Translation*, New York: Norton, 2015, p. vii.

37. A.K. Ramanujan, 'Three hundred Ramayanas: Five examples and three thoughts on translation,' in *Many Ramayanas: The Diversity of a Narrative Tradition in South Asia*, edited by Paula Richman, Berkeley, California: University of California Press, 1991, pp. 22–49.

38. As noted above, Ashis Nandy's work presents the most persuasive case for this idea.

39. Though I have not explicitly referred to it in the book, I have also drawn on the public domain version of Edwin Arnold's Gita, which is available on the Project Gutenberg site and resource. See Edwin Arnold, *Bhagavad-Gîtâ (from the Mahâbhârata): Being a discourse between Arjuna, Prince of India, and the Supreme Being under the form of Krishna*, Project Gutenberg EPUB (with images), 2013 [1900], http://www.gutenberg.org/ebooks/2388.epub.images. Gandhi's writings on the Gita are conveniently published in the following volume: Mahatma Gandhi, *The Bhagavad Gita According to Gandhi*, edited by John Strohmeier, Berkeley, California: North Atlantic Books, 2009.

Strohmeier's edition is drawn from the *Collected Works of Mahatma Gandhi*, vol. XXXII (1926-27), pp. 94–376, 'Discourses on the Gita.' See p. xiii for more details about the translation from Gandhi's Gujarati translation of the Gita into English. The other translations used are Barbara Stoler Miller, *The Bhagavad-Gita: Krishna's Counsel in Times of War*, New York: Bantam Classics, 1986; Patton, op. cit., 2008; Flood and Martin, op. cit., 2015; Alok Bhalla and Chandra Prakash Deval, *The Gita: Mewari Miniature Painting (1680–1698) by Allah Baksh*, New Delhi: Niyogi Books, 2019.

40. R.K. Narayan, *The Mahabharat: A Shortened Modern Prose Version of the Indian Epic*, Chicago, Illinois: University of Chicago Press, 2013; John D. Smith, *The Mahabharata*, New York: Penguin, 2009.

41. See p. 35, in D.C. Mathur, 'The concept of action in the Bhagvad-Gita,' *Philosophy and Phenomenological Research,* vol. 35, no.1, 1974: 34–45.

42. Patton, op. cit., p. xxix.

43. I have already briefly elaborated on these topics above, and the next chapter on crisis globalisation undertakes a more detailed examination of the same.

44. Ibid.

45. Marcus Aurelius, *The Meditations*, translated by George Long, *The Internet Classics Archive*, http://classics.mit.edu/Antoninus/meditations.4.four.html, accessed 3 September 2020; Jayson Green, 'George Harrison: *All Things Must Pass,' Pitchfork*, 19 June 2016, https://pitchfork.com/reviews/albums/22037-all-things-must-pass/, accessed 5 September 2020.

46. Francesca Antonini, 'Pessimism of the intellect, optimism of the will: Gramsci's political thought in the last miscellaneous notebooks,' *Rethinking Marxism,* vol. 31, no. 1 (2019): 42–57, ff10.1080/089356 96.2019.1577616ff. ffhal-02116010f, accessed 19 September 2020. Antonini notes that Gramsci's formulation was inspired by a saying of the French writer Romain Rolland.

47. Ludwig Wittgenstein, *Tractatus Logico-Philosophicus*, 2nd edition, New York: Routledge, 2001, p. 5.

48. See Ziya Us Salam, 'Unfazed by attack,' *Frontline*, 16 September 2016, https://frontline.thehindu.com/the-nation/unfazed-by-attack/article9050667.ece, accessed 3 December 2019; Elizabeth Redden, 'The religious war against American scholars of India,' *Inside Higher Ed*, 12 April 2016, https://www.insidehighered.com/news/2016/04/12/

scholars-who-study-hinduism-and-india-face-hostile-climate, accessed 4 December 2019.

2. CRISIS GLOBALISATION:
The Current World Order and How We Got Here

1. Yoko Wakatsuki and Nectar Gan, 'Meet the Japanese man who holds the world's only master's degree in Ninja Studies,' *CNN*, 30 June 2020, https://www.cnn.com/2020/06/30/asia/ninja-studies-graduate-intl-hnk-scli/index.html, accessed 2 July 2020.

2. Despite increasing economic prosperity on the whole and raising the living standards of large numbers of people in developing nations, globalisation has led to widening inequality at the national level and created new classes of haves and have-nots, in the richer as well as poorer nations of the world. See François Bourguignon, 'Inequality and globalization,' *Foreign Affairs*, January/February 2016, https://www.foreignaffairs.com/articles/2015-12-14/inequality-and-globalization, accessed 17 September 2019.

3. Maurice Kugler and Shakti Sinha, 'The impact of COVID-19 and the policy response in India,' *Brookings*, 13 July 2020, https://www.brookings.edu/blog/future-development/2020/07/13/the-impact-of-covid-19-and-the-policy-response-in-india/, accessed 16 July 2020; Lauren Frayer and Sushmita Pathak, 'Coronavirus lockdown sends migrant workers on a long and risky trip home,' *npr*, 31 March 2020, https://www.npr.org/sections/goatsandsoda/2020/03/31/822642382/coronavirus-lockdown-sends-migrant-workers-on-a-long-and-risky-trip-home, accessed 1 June 2020.

4. 'SF responds to coronavirus outbreak with Stay Home order,' SF.GOV, 20 March 2020, https://sf.gov/news/sf-responds-coronavirus-outbreak-stay-home-order, accessed 22 March 2020.

5. Sarah Pulliam Bailey, 'Doomsday Clock: Why Americans love apocalyptic predictions,' *The Washington Post*, 25 January 2018, https://www.washingtonpost.com/news/acts-of-faith/wp/2018/01/25/doomsday-clock-why-americans-love-apocalyptic-predictions/, accessed 3 March 2020.

6. 'PM Modi was 'terrific' in allowing export of hydroxychloroquine to US: Donald Trump,' *The Economic Times*, 10 April 2020, https://economictimes.indiatimes.com/news/politics-and-nation/trump-thanks-

india-on-hcq-decision-says-will-not-be-forgotten/articleshow/75056752. cms, accessed 18 April 2020.

7. Reuters and NBC News, 'Germany tries to stop Trump from luring away firm working on coronavirus vaccine,' *NBC News*, 15 March 2020, https://www.nbcnews.com/news/us-news/germany-tries-stop-trump-luring-away-firm-working-coronavirus-vaccine-n1159426, accessed 24 March 2020.

8. Lee Fang, 'The airline industry blocked disclosure of trade data, helping conceal the airlift of N95 masks from the U.S. to China,' 29 June 2020, *The Intercept*, https://theintercept.com/2020/06/29/ppe-china-export-airlifts/, accessed 1 July 2020.

9. Lauren Aratani, 'How did face masks become a political issue in America?' *The Guardian*, 29 June 2020, https://www.theguardian.com/world/2020/jun/29/face-masks-us-politics-coronavirus, accessed 6 July 2020.

10. Rebecca Gordon, 'What the American deep state actually is, and why Trump gets it wrong,' *Business Insider*, 27 January 2020, https://www.businessinsider.com/what-deep-state-is-and-why-trump-gets-it-wrong-2020-1, accessed 15 February 2020.

11. Richard Hofstadter, 'The paranoid style in American politics,' *Harper's Magazine*, November 1964, https://harpers.org/archive/1964/11/the-paranoid-style-in-american-politics/, accessed 27 June 2020.

12. Ibid.

13. Rachael Rettner, 'COVID-19 has fueled more than 2,000 rumors and conspiracy theories,' *Live Science*, 11 August 2020, https://www.livescience.com/covid-19-rumors-conspiracy-theories-infodemic.html, accessed 14 August 2020; Katherine Schaeffer, 'A look at the Americans who believe there is some truth to the conspiracy theory that COVID-19 was planned,' *Pew Research Center*, 24 July 2020, https://www.pewresearch.org/fact-tank/2020/07/24/a-look-at-the-americans-who-believe-there-is-some-truth-to-the-conspiracy-theory-that-covid-19-was-planned/, accessed 14 August 2020.

14. See Cass R. Sunstein, Chapter 3, 'Polarization and Cybercascades,' in *Republic.com 2.0*, Princeton, New Jersey: Princeton University Press, 2009, pp. 46–96.

15. Tanya Lewis, 'Nine COVID-19 myths that just won't go away,' *Scientific American*, 18 August 2020, https://www.scientificamerican.com/article/nine-covid-19-myths-that-just-wont-go-away/, accessed 3 September 2020.

16. See Mike Wendling, 'QAnon: What is it and where did it come from?' *BBC News*, 20 August 2020, https://www.bbc.com/news/53498434, accessed 1 September 2020; Marianna Spring and Mike Wendling, 'How COVID-19 myths are merging with the QAnon conspiracy theory,' *BBC News*, 3 September 2020, https://www.bbc.com/news/blogs-trending-53997203, accessed 4 September 2020.

17. Aleem Maqbool, 'Coronavirus: The US resistance to a continued lockdown,' *BBC News*, 27 April 2020, https://www.bbc.com/news/world-us-canada-52417610, accessed 22 August 2020.

18. Colby Itkowitz, 'Trump again uses racially insensitive term to describe coronavirus,' *The Washington Post*, 23 June 2020, https://www.washingtonpost.com/politics/trump-again-uses-kung-flu-to-describe-coronavirus/2020/06/23/0ab5a8d8-b5a9-11ea-aca5-ebb63d27e1ff_story.html, accessed 27 June 2020; Yasmeen Serhan and Timothy McLaughlin, 'The coronavirus' xenophobia problem,' *The Atlantic*, 13 March 2020, https://www.theatlantic.com/international/archive/2020/03/coronavirus-covid19-xenophobia-racism/607816/, accessed 5 June 2020.

19. Mary Van Beusekom, 'New data highlight deadly COVID-19 impact in NYC,' *CIDRAP*, 23 April 2020, https://www.cidrap.umn.edu/news-perspective/2020/04/new-data-highlight-deadly-covid-19-impact-nyc, accessed 4 August 2020; Mary T. Bassett, 'Just because you can afford to leave the city doesn't mean you should,' *The New York Times*, 15 May 2020, https://www.nytimes.com/2020/05/15/opinion/sunday/coronavirus-cities-density.html, accessed 4 June 2020; Ron Dicker, 'Tucker Carlson blames "diversity" and "wokeness" for coronavirus,' *Huffpost*, 25 February 2020, https://www.huffpost.com/entry/tucker-carlson-coronavirus-diversity_n_5e54f265c5b65e0f11c64b34, accessed 5 June 2020; Jonathan A. Greenblatt, 'Blaming Jews for the spread of the coronavirus is anti-Semitism pure and simple,' *New York Daily News*, 8 April 2020, https://www.nydailynews.com/opinion/ny-oped-jews-coronavirus-antisemitism-20200408-4arvpei6wvd4td7eyqxpjfhaka-story.html, accessed 3 June 2020; Susan Milligan, 'Everybody blames New York,' *U.S. News*, 25 March 2020, https://www.usnews.com/news/politics/articles/2020-03-25/coronavirus-highlights-the-love-hate-relationship-with-new-york, accessed 9 April 2020. On the West Coast of the US, San Francisco, another

global hub, escaped the fate of New York. Though San Francisco's population is roughly a tenth of the population of New York, it shares many characteristics with the latter, including a multi-ethnic demographic, a large population of travellers, and the status of a tourist destination. The proactive stringent measures initially taken by the governor of California, Gavin Newsom, and the mayor of San Francisco, London Breed, to tame the spread of the virus, such as shelter-in-place orders and the subsequent closing of public locations like parks, beaches and non-essential businesses, were the reasons the virus did not get out of control in the city. Consistency, of course, is not the strong suit of those given to prejudiced analysis and seeking to blame minorities for one problem or another.

20. Rajesh Kumar Singh and Nathan Layne, 'New York City's low-income, minority areas hit hardest by COVID-19, Cuomo says,' *Reuters*, 20 May 2020, https://www.reuters.com/article/us-health-coronavirus-usa-new-york/new-york-citys-low-income-minority-areas-hit-hardest-by-covid-19-cuomo-says-idUSKBN22W2IG, accessed 3 June 2020; Serena Gordon, 'Why are minorities hardest hit by COVID-19?' *WebMD*, 6 May 2020, https://www.webmd.com/lung/news/20200506/why-are-minorities-hardest-hit-by-covid-19#1, accessed 11 May 2020; Nendirmwa Noel, 'Minorities, migrants, and social exclusion during COVID-19,' *NYU: Center on International Cooperation*, 12 May 2020, https://cic.nyu.edu/publications/covid-19-minorities-and-social-exclusion, accessed 14 May 2020. Noel identifies the complex interplay of factors that makes minorities across the global particularly vulnerable and susceptible to the dangers of the virus:

> As COVID-19 deaths increased in the United States (US), a disturbing statistical pattern began to emerge—the virus had a disproportionate impact on minority communities across the country. Unfortunately, this trend of disproportionate health impacts is visible across several countries….Ethnic minorities and migrants are also overrepresented in high-risk frontline jobs with low pay, which increases the risk of exposure and feelings of exclusion. This realization has ignited debates about whether government responses to the pandemic give enough consideration to those who are typically excluded and underrepresented in society.
>
> …

Additionally, sudden border closures have left many migrant workers stuck in precarious situations, putting their own health and that of others in jeopardy.

…

COVID-19 policies that ignore the particular experiences of minorities and vulnerable groups could also exacerbate social fractures (Ibid.).

21. Otis R. Taylor Jr., 'Eviction holdouts join exodus from Bay Area over soaring rent,' *San Francisco Chronicle*, 31 December 2018, https://www.sfchronicle.com/bayarea/otisrtaylorjr/article/Eviction-holdouts-join-exodus-from-Bay-Area-over-13498627.php, accessed 13 September 2020.

22. Trump's measures have not delivered the benefits that they promised. Geoffrey Gertz, 'Did Trump's tariffs benefit American workers and national security?' *Brookings*, 10 September 2020, https://www.brookings.edu/policy2020/votervital/did-trumps-tariffs-benefit-american-workers-and-national-security/, accessed 12 September 2020.

23. See Frank J. Lechner and John Boli, 'General introduction,' p. 2, in their edited volume, *The Globalization Reader,* 6th edition, New York: Wiley Blackwell, 2019, pp. 1–6.

24. Jack Lule, *Globalization and Media: Global Village of Babel*, New York: Rowman & Littlefield, 2012, p. 6.

25. See Brian Larkin, 'Indian films and Nigerian lovers: Media and the creation of parallel modernities,' *Africa: Journal of the International Africa Institute*, vol. 67, no. 3 (1997): 406–440; and Deepa Bhasthi, 'Bollywood affair: How Indian cinema arrived in the USSR,' *The Calvert Journal*, 21 August 2015, https://www.calvertjournal.com/articles/show/4569/bollywood-affair-indian-cinema-USSR-raj-kapoor-nargis, accessed 4 June 2020.

26. For examples of such long histories of globalisation, see Manfred B. Steger and Paul James, 'Excavating the long history of globalization,' in *Globalization Matters: Engaging the Global in Unsettled Times*, Cambridge, Massachusetts: Cambridge University Press, 2019, pp. 137–163; Kevin H. O'Rourke and Jeffrey G. Williamson, *Globalization and History: The Evolution of a Nineteenth-Century Atlantic Economy*, Cambridge, Massachusetts: Cambridge University Press, 1999; Peter Vanham, 'A brief history of globalization,' World Economic Forum,

19 January 2019, https://www.weforum.org/agenda/2019/01/how-globalization-4-0-fits-into-the-history-of-globalization/, accessed 11 June 2020; and the resource, 'History of globalization,' *YaleGlobal Online*, n.d., https://yaleglobal.yale.edu/history-globalization, accessed 11 February 2020.

27. Manuel Castells, *The Rise of the Network Society*, 2nd edition, New York: Wiley-Blackwell, 2009.

28. See Manuel Castells, Chapter 6, 'The space of flows,' in *The Rise of the Network Society*, pp. 407–459.

29. Anthony Giddens, *Runaway World: How Globalization is Reshaping Our World*, 1st edition, New York: Routledge, 2002. The book is based on Giddens's lectures as part of the BBC Reith Lectures series. See the site https://www.bbc.co.uk/programmes/p00gw9s1, accessed 2 July 2020.

30. See the following sources from the last three decades for a sample of the range of perspectives on the impact of globalisation on India. The scholarship tends to weigh heavily in terms of topics related to economic globalisation. Rajeev Bhargava, 'India in the face of globalisation,' *openDemocracy*, 26 February 2003, https://www.opendemocracy.net/en/article_1006jsp/; Tarun Khanna, 'China + India: the power of two,' *Harvard Business Review*, December 2007, https://hbr.org/2007/12/china-india-the-power-of-two; Bruce Stokes, 'Unlike the West, India and China embrace globalization,' *YaleGlobal Online*, 18 October 2016, https://yaleglobal.yale.edu/content/unlike-west-india-and-china-embrace-globalization; 'India Overview,' *The World Bank*, updated 25 October 2019, https://www.worldbank.org/en/country/india/overview; Joe Myers, 'India is now the world's 5th largest economy,' *World Economic Forum*, 19 February 2020, https://www.weforum.org/agenda/2020/02/india-gdp-economy-growth-uk-france/, all sources accessed 11 June 2020; Snigdha Poonam, *Dreamers: How Young Indians Are Changing the World*, Cambridge, Massachusetts: Harvard University Press, 2018; Somini Sengupta, *The End of Karma: Hope and Fury Among India's Young*, New York: Norton, 2017.

31. Marshall McLuhan, *The Global Village: Transformations in World Life and the Media in the 21st Century*, reprint edition, New York: Oxford University Press, 1992.

32. Gregory Scruggs, 'What the 'Battle of Seattle' Means 20 Years Later,' *Bloomberg CityLab*, 29 November 2019, https://www.bloomberg.com/

news/articles/2019-11-29/what-seattle-s-wto-protests-mean-20-years-later, accessed 19 June 2020.

33. Ibid.

34. Adam Chandler, 'How McDonald's became a target for protest,' *The Atlantic*, 6 April 2015, https://www.theatlantic.com/business/archive/2015/04/setting-the-symbolic-golden-arches-aflame/390708/, accessed 7 May 2020.

35. See Joseph Stiglitz, *Globalization and its Discontents*, New York: WW Norton, 2002; Nikil Saval, 'Globalisation: the rise and fall of an idea that swept the world,' *The Guardian*, 14 July 2017, https://www.theguardian.com/world/2017/jul/14/globalisation-the-rise-and-fall-of-an-idea-that-swept-the-world; Shanta Devarajan, 'Has globalization gone too far or not far enough?' *Brookings*, 3 September 2019, https://www.brookings.edu/blog/future-development/2019/09/03/has-globalization-gone-too-far-or-not-far-enough/.

36. See, for instance, Barry K. Gills (editor), *Globalization in Crisis*, New York: Routledge, 2011; Patrick Diamond, *The Crisis of Globalization: Democracy, Capitalism and Inequality in the Twenty-First Century*, New York: I.B. Tauris, 2019; the collection of essays on the initiative, 'The Crisis of Globalisation', on the site *Social Europe*; and the podcast episode, 'Episode 72: Flux, Friction and the Next Phase of Globalization,' *Goldman Sachs*, 9 October 2017, https://www.goldmansachs.com/insights/podcasts/episodes/10-06-2017-jose-manuel-barroso.html.

37. Adam Tooze, 'The death of globalisation has been announced many times. But this is a perfect storm,' *The Guardian*, 2 June 2020, https://www.theguardian.com/commentisfree/2020/jun/02/end-globalisation-covid-19-made-it-real, accessed 12 June 2020.

38. Samuel Huntington, 'The Clash of Civilizations,' *Foreign Affairs*, vol. 72, no. 3 (1993): 22–49.

39. 'World Health, Organization, 'WHO Coronavirus Disease (COVID-19) Dashboard,' updated as of 16 January 2021, 5.52 p.m., https://covid19.who.int/, accessed 16 January 2021, 6.19 p.m., Pacific Standard Time in the US.

40. 'COVID-19, MERS & SARS,' *National Institute of Allergy and Infectious Diseases*, https://www.niaid.nih.gov/diseases-conditions/covid-19, accessed 2 June 2020.

41. For a compelling account of the possibility that the spread of virus is the result of a lethal combination of human experimentation and

human accident, see Nicholson Baker, 'The lab-leak hypothesis,' *New York*, 4 January 2021, https://nymag.com/intelligencer/article/coronavirus-lab-escape-theory.html, accessed 5 January 2021.

42. Graham Readfearn, 'How did coronavirus start and where did it come from? Was it really Wuhan's animal market?' *The Guardian*, 27 May 2020, https://www.theguardian.com/world/2020/apr/28/how-did-the-coronavirus-start-where-did-it-come-from-how-did-it-spread-humans-was-it-really-bats-pangolins-wuhan-animal-market, accessed 3 June 2020.

43. Martin Heidegger, *The Question Concerning Technology and Other Essays*, New York: Harper Torchbooks, 1977.

44. Italics in the original. Zygmunt Bauman, *Modernity and the Holocaust*, Ithaca, New York: Cornell University Press, 2002, p. 73.

45. Anthony J. Parel, editor, *Gandhi: 'Hind Swaraj' and Other Writings*, New York: Cambridge University Press, 2011.

46. Francis Fukuyama, 'The End of History?' in *Globalization and the Challenges of a New Century: A Reader*, edited by Patrick O'Meara, Howard D. Mehlinger, and Matthew Krain, Bloomington Indiana: Indiana University Press, 2000, pp. 161–180.

47. Fukuyama, op. cit., p. 162.

48. The idea of the spirit of history is found in Hegel's work, of course. It refers to Hegel's theory of history in which world history was driven by human consciousness and was comprehensible as such. For an incisive reading and critique of Hegel's concept, see Ranajit Guha, *History at the Limit of World-History* (Italian Academy Lectures), New York: Columbia University Press, 2003.

49. See Eva Cossé, 'The alarming rise of anti-semitism in Europe,' Human Rights Watch, 12 June 2019, https://www.hrw.org/news/2019/06/04/alarming-rise-anti-semitism-europe, accessed 7 December 2019; and Pinchas Goldschmidt, 'With anti-Muslim laws, Europe enters new dark age,' *Politico*, 27 July 2018, https://www.politico.eu/article/with-anti-muslim-laws-france-denmark-europe-enters-new-dark-age/, accessed 7 December 2019; and Jonathan Gatehouse, 'EU attacks anti-immigrant "misinformation, untruths and fake news" from far-right,' *CBC*, 6 March 2019, https://www.cbc.ca/news/thenational/national-today-newsletter-eu-migrants-gerald-butts-1.5042495, accessed 7 December 2019.

50. With the defeat of Trump in the 2020 elections and the election of Joe Biden as the president of the US, there is widespread hope and optimism that these trends will be reversed. Yet, how much of the damage will be undone remains to be seen. The proverbial genie of racism is out of the bottle, and it will take an enormous effort to deal comprehensively with it.

51. Evan Hill et al., '8 Minutes and 46 Seconds: How George Floyd was killed in police custody,' *New York Times*, 31 May 2020 https://www.nytimes.com/2020/05/31/us/george-floyd-investigation.html, accessed 2 June 2020.

52. Donie O'Sullivan, 'White Supremacists pose as Antifa online, call for violence,' *CNN*, 2 June 2020, https://www.cnn.com/2020/06/02/tech/antifa-fake-twitter-account/index.html, accessed 3 June 2020.

53. Violence against minorities has become routinised as a part of daily life in Modi's India, as extensively documented in coverage in the Indian and international press. See Harsh Mander, 'New hate crime tracker in India finds victims are predominantly Muslims, perpetrators Hindus,' *Scroll.in*, 13 November 2018, https://scroll.in/article/901206/new-hate-crime-tracker-in-india-finds-victims-are-predominantly-muslims-perpetrators-hindus; accessed 8 July 2020; and Sonia Sarkar, 'Marginalised under Modi: How India's minorities are starting to stand together,' *South China Morning Post*, 23 February 2020, https://www.scmp.com/week-asia/politics/article/3051781/marginalised-under-modi-how-indias-minorities-are-starting-stand, accessed 8 July 2020. Followers of Indian politics, whatever their political leanings, will be intimately familiar with the changed landscape of India in *pax Modica*. Along with the social reality of violence and threats against minorities, dissenters and even those who are no more than mild critics of the Hindu Right, the BJP and Modi, much of the media itself has become complicit in such violence—at worst, by enabling and joining in these attacks or, at best, by refusing to cover or comment on them. Though several others are not far behind, Arnab Goswami of Republic TV is by far the worst example of a media personality who has made a career out of indulging in dog whistling and screaming accusations of disloyalty, anti-national sentiment and treason at anyone he considers an enemy of the state. Conveniently, these targets usually happen to be critics and adversaries of the Hindu Right, the BJP or Mr Modi.

54. I have explored the Indian manifestation of this phenomenon at some length in my recent published book, *The Virtual Hindu Nation: Saffron Nationalism and New Media*, New Delhi: HarperCollins, 2019.

55. Marshall McLuhan and B. R. Powers, *The Global Village: Transformations in World Life and Media in the 21st century*, New York: Oxford University Press, 1989.

56. For Kant's understanding of cosmopolitanism and world society, see Pauline Kleingeld and Eric Brown, 'Cosmopolitanism,' *The Stanford Encyclopedia of Philosophy*, (Winter 2019 Edition), edited by Edward N. Zalta, https://plato.stanford.edu/archives/win2019/entries/cosmopolitanism/, accessed 2 February 2020.

57. The impact of globalisation on poverty is a highly contentious topic. For a sense of the range of perspectives on the matter, see Ann Harrison, 'Globalization and poverty,' Working Paper 12347, *National Bureau of Economic Research*, July 2006, https://www.nber.org/papers/w12347, accessed 4 November 2020; Lauren Chandy and Geoffrey Gertz, 'Globalization reduced poverty,' *YaleGlobal Online*, 5 July 2011, https://yaleglobal.yale.edu/content/globalization-reduced-poverty, accessed 4 November 2020; Dani Rodrik, 'Global poverty among global plenty: Getting globalization right,' *Americas Quarterly*, 23 April 2012, https://www.americasquarterly.org/fulltextarticle/global-poverty-amid-global-plenty-getting-globalization-right/, accessed 5 November 2020; Andreas Bergh and Therese Nelson, 'Is globalization reducing absolute poverty?' *World Development* vol. 62, pp. 42–61, https://doi.org/10.1016/j.worlddev.2014.04.007; 'Rising inequality affecting more than two-thirds of the globe, but it's not inevitable: new UN report,' *UN News*, 21 January 2020, https://news.un.org/en/story/2020/01/1055681, accessed 5 November 2020.

58. J. Clement, 'Number of monthly active Facebook users worldwide as of 1st quarter 2020,' *Statista*, 30 April 2020, https://www.statista.com/statistics/264810/number-of-monthly-active-facebook-users-worldwide/, accessed 4 August 2020.

59. Martin Matishak and Andrew Desiderio, 'Senate intel report confirms Russia aimed to help Trump in 2016,' *Politico*, 21 April 2020, https://www.politico.com/news/2020/04/21/senate-intel-report-confirms-russia-aimed-to-help-trump-in-2016-198171, accessed 14 June 2020.

60. Daniel Avilar, 'WhatsApp fake news during Brazil election "favoured

Bolsanaro",' *The Guardian*, 30 October 2019, https://www.theguardian.com/world/2019/oct/30/whatsapp-fake-news-brazil-election-favoured-jair-bolsonaro-analysis-suggests, accessed 3 June 2020; Priyanjana Bengani, 'India had its first "WhatsApp election": We have a million messages from it,' *Columbia Journalism Review*, 16 October 2019, https://www.cjr.org/tow_center/india-whatsapp-analysis-election-security.php, accessed 2 December 2019.

61. Chris O'Brien, 'Facebook admits it's still being exploited to incite violence in Myanmar,' *VentureBeat*, 22 August 2019, https://venturebeat.com/2019/08/22/facebook-admits-its-still-being-exploited-to-incite-ethnic-violence-in-myanmar/, accessed 11 June 2020; Timothy McLaughlin, 'How WhatsApp fuels fake news and violence in India,' *Wired*, 12 December 2018, https://www.wired.com/story/how-whatsapp-fuels-fake-news-and-violence-in-india/, accessed 10 June 2020; Emily Stewart, 'Can Facebook be trusted to combat misinformation? Sri Lanka's shutdown suggests no,' *Vox*, 23 April 2019, https://www.vox.com/2019/4/23/18511640/facebook-sri-lanka-bombing-social-media-attack, accessed 12 June 2020.

3. BEYOND SELFISHNESS:
Action and Uncertainty in the Age of Crisis Globalisation

1. See Peter Singer, *Marx: A Very Short Introduction*, New York: Oxford University Press, 2001.
2. Tania Murray Li, 'Governmentality,' *Anthropologica* vol. 49, no. 2 (2007): 275.
3. Ibid., 276.
4. My reference here is to the Beatles composition *Let it Be*, the signature song on their album of the same name. Paul McCartney's lyrics in the song go: 'When I find myself in times of trouble/ Mother Mary comes to me/ speaking words of wisdom/ let it be.'
5. Samuel Taylor Coleridge, 'The Rime of the Ancient Mariner,' (1834 text) *Poetry Foundation*, n.d., https://www.poetryfoundation.org/poems/43997/the-rime-of-the-ancient-mariner-text-of-1834, accessed 4 August 2020.
6. See Emily VanDerWerff, 'What day is it today?' *Vox*, 1 July 2020, https://www.vox.com/culture/21287588/what-day-is-it-today-coronavirus, accessed 3 August 2020.

7. Stoler Miller, *The Bhagavad-Gita*, p. 38. The Flood and Martin translation is very similar:

> Your concern should be with action,
> never with an action's fruits;
> these should never motivate you,
> nor attachment to inaction.
>
> (Flood and Martin, *The Bhagavad Gita*, p. 15)

8. Davis, *The Bhagavad Gita*, p. 17.

9. The other explanation that Krishna offers Arjuna to alleviate the latter's anguish about causing the death of his relatives is the idea of the eternal life of the soul. See Davis, op. cit., p. 16.

10. For a useful explanation of the concept of the hermeneutics of suspicion, a phrase coined by the French philosopher Paul Ricoeur, see Rita Felski, 'Critique and the Hermeneutics of Suspicion,' *M/C Journal*, vol. 15, no. 1 (2012), http://journal.media-culture.org.au/index.php/mcjournal/article/viewArticle/431, accessed 3 August 2020.

11. In the pages that follow I do consider perspectives about the limitations of the concept in some detail.

12. See Patton, op. cit., pp. xiv–xxiv for a discussion of the main philosophical themes of the Gita. Patton describes the three main strands of the Gita as the paths of action, knowledge and devotion, respectively (p. xiv). Stoler Miller lists the set of key, interrelated concepts in the Gita as duty (*dharma*), discipline (*yoga*), action (*karma*), knowledge (*jñāna*) and devotion (*bhakti*). See p. 8. The concept of *karma is* also central to the theory of rebirth and the desired liberation of the soul. While the ideas of rebirth and *moksha*, or liberation of the soul, have no special relevance to the condition of globalisation, an acknowledgement of the concepts, at the least, is warranted for understanding the meanings of *karma*.

13. Patton, op. cit., p. xx.

14. Patton, Davis and Stoler Miller all agree on this.

15. Patton, op. cit., p. xx.

16. Davis, op. cit., p. 17.

17. Stoler Miller, op. cit., p. 53

18. Ibid.

19. It is useful to look here at several different translations of the passages

from the fourth teaching that present these ideas, which differ slightly in their choice of words. Stoler Miller's translation is as follows:

> One should understand action,
> understand wrong action,
> and understand inaction too;
> the way of action is obscure.
>
> A man who sees inaction in action
> and action in inaction
> has understanding among men,
> disciplined in all action that he performs. (p. 53)

Flood and Martin translate the passage thus:

> To be enlightened, one should know
> the way of actions, good and bad.
> Non-action one should also know.
> The way of action is profound.
>
> Who in action sees non-action,
> and sees in non-action, action
> is a wise man, is disciplined,
> whole in all actions he performs. (p. 26)

Patton's translation reads as follows:

> One should have watchful insight,
> into action,
> watchful insight,
> into wrong action
> and watchful insight,
> into non-action.
> The way of insight
> is hard to fathom.
>
> Among humans,
> the person who sees
> non-action in action,
> and action in non-action,
> has insight;

> that one undertakes
> all actions,
> steady in *yoga*. (pp. 53–54)

20. Davis, op. cit., p. 17.
21. Flood and Martin translate it as 'darkness' (Flood and Martin, op. cit., pp. 70–71); Stoler Miller translates it as 'dark inertia' (Stoler Miller, op. cit. pp. 119–121), while Patton chooses to use the Sanskrit term *tamas* (Patton, op. cit., pp. 156–157). Bhalla and Deval, drawing on Radhakrishnan's translation, note that, as originally conceived in their divine origins, the qualities operated in concert to produce a harmonious state of reality. Degrading with 'historical time', they are transformed for the worse: 'Sattva loses its luminosity and is tarnished by [*sic*] self's yearning for happiness. Rajas turns into passion and the self's infatuation with the sensuous and the pleasurable alone. Tamas, uninfluenced by goodness and austere self-control, plunges the self into ignorance, folly and lethargic modes of thinking which perpetuate cycles of violence and revenge, anger and misery.' Alok Bhalla and Chandra Prakash Deval, *The Gita: Mewari Miniature Painting (1680–1698) by Allah Baksh*, New Delhi: Niyogi Books, 2019, p. 379. See also S. Radhakrishnan, *The Bhagavadgita*, New Delhi: HarperCollins, 2014, pp. 376 –378, as referenced in Bhalla and Deval.
22. Flood and Martin, op. cit., pp. 70–71; Patton, op. cit., pp. 156–157
23. Flood and Martin, op. cit., p. 19; Patton, op. cit., p. 38; Stoler Miller, op. cit., p. 44.
24. Stoler Miller's translation expresses this sentiment most directly and clearly:

> One who does what must be done
> without concern for the fruits
> is a man of renunciation and discipline (p. 65).

Patton translates it as follows, keeping the term *yoga* to refer to discipline.

> The person who does
> what must be done,
> and does not resort
> to the fruit of action,

is a renunciant
and practitioner of *yoga*,
not the one without a fire
and without rituals (p. 70).

25. Stoler Miller, op. cit., p. 59; Patton, op. cit., p. 60.

26. Stoler Miller, op. cit., p. 135.

27. In the eighteenth teaching, Arjuna asks Krishna to educate him on the 'essence' of renunciation and relinquishment, concepts that are close to each other but do have important differences. See Stoler Miller, op. cit., pp. 135–137.

28. See Atul Gawande, *Being Mortal: Illness, Medicine and What Matters in the End*, New York: Picador, 2015 for a reflection on some of these concerns. It is perhaps not a coincidence that one of the most astute and insightful commentators on human affairs, the great Russian writer Anton Chekov, was a physician.

29. Abhijit Chakravarty and Pawan Kumar, 'Concepts and debates in end-of-life care,' *Indian Journal of Medical Ethics*, vol. 9, no. 3 (Jul–Sep 2012): 202–206, https://pubmed.ncbi.nlm.nih.gov/22864083/, accessed 18 May 2020.

30. See p. 121 in Walter R. Agard, 'Fate and Freedom in Greek Tragedy,' *The Classical Journal*, vol. 29, no. 2 (November 1933): pp. 117 –126.

31. Allen R. Myerson, 'In principle, a case for more "sweatshops",' *The New York Times*, 22 June 1997, https://www.nytimes.com/1997/06/22/weekinreview/in-principle-a-case-for-more-sweatshops.html, accessed 3 August 2020. See also David R. Henderson, 'The Case for Sweatshops,' *Hoover Institution*, 7 February 2000, https://www.hoover.org/research/case-sweatshops, accessed 3 August 2020.

32. Personal conversation with Allen Tullos. See Jeffrey J. Carmel, 'Waltham: cradle of our other revolution,' *The Christian Science Monitor*, 24 March 1983, https://www.csmonitor.com/1983/0324/032449.html, accessed 2 April 2020. Carmel notes that the Boston Manufacturing Company textile mill inaugurated in 1814 was the first 'successful industrial corporation' in America as well as the first 'truly modern production system in the world'. It was also the scene of 'the nation's first industrial strike, when women workers stopped the looms for two days over a pay dispute', a fight that they lost (Ibid.)

33. See Chapter 4, 'Is a disinterested act possible?' in Pierre Bourdieu,

Practical Reason: On the Theory of Action, translated by Richard Nice, Stanford, CA: Stanford University Press, 1998, pp.75–91.

34. Ibid., p. 79.

35. Ibid., p. 77.

36. Christopher D. Carroll, 'Consumption,' *Encyclopædia Britannica*, 22 February 2016, https://www.britannica.com/topic/consumption, accessed 4 August 2020.

37. Davis, op. cit., p. 17.

38. Stoler Miller, op. cit., p. 66.

39. Stoler Miller, op. cit., p. 89.

40. See Hannah Arendt, *Eichmann in Jerusalem: A Report on the Banality of Evil*, New York: Penguin, 2006; Philip Gourevitch, *We Wish to Inform You That Tomorrow We Will be Killed With Our Families: Stories from Rwanda*, New York: Picador, 1999; Amy Louise Wood, *Lynching and Spectacle: Witnessing Racial Violence in America, 1890–1940*, Durham, North Carolina: University of North Carolina Press, 2011.

41. Gandhi, as always, is the exception here in his articulation of the role of *karma* in political action. I will address the Gandhian understanding of political action in the coda to the book.

42. See pp. 35–36 in D.C. Mathur, 'The concept of action in the Bhagvad-Gita,' *Philosophy and Phenomenological Research*, vol. 35, no. 1 (September 1974): 34–45.

43. Ibid., pp. 37–38, italics in original.

44. The Editors of the Encyclopædia Britannica, 'Deontological Ethics,' *Encyclopædia Britannica*, 21 May 2020, https://www.britannica.com/topic/deontological-ethics, accessed 6 August 2020.

45. Larry Alexander and Michael Moore, 'Deontological Ethics,' *The Stanford Encyclopedia of Philosophy* (Winter 2016 Edition), editor, Edward N. Zalta, https://plato.stanford.edu/archives/win2016/entries/ethics-deontological/, accessed 29 July 2020. There is a vibrant debate on the contrasting perspectives of deontological ethics and consequentialism. There are a range of deontological and consequentialist positions within each paradigm as well. The interested reader may consult this excellent introduction on the subject in the *Stanford Encyclopedia of Philosophy*.

46. The exact quote from Burns's poem 'To a Mouse' is: 'The best laid schemes o' Mice an' Men / Gang aft agley.' See Robert Burns, 'To

a Mouse,' *Poetry Foundation*, n.d., https://www.poetryfoundation.org/poems/43816/to-a-mouse-56d222ab36e33, accessed 18 June 2020.

47. Agard, 'Fate and Freedom.'

48. Karl Marx, *The Theses on Feuerbach*, *Marxists Internet Archive*, [1845] https://www.marxists.org/archive/marx/works/1845/theses/theses.htm, accessed 21 July 2019.

49. Karl Marx, *The Eighteenth Brumaire of Louis Bonaparte, Karl Marx 1852, Marxists Internet Archive,* https://www.marxists.org/archive/marx/works/1852/18th-brumaire/ch01.htm, accessed 29 July 2020. I consider Marx's formulation to be the most sophisticated explanation of the relationship between social, political and historical structures, on the one hand, and individual agency, on the other.

50. Lucy Ash, 'Josef Stalin's deadly railways to nowhere,' *BBC*, 7 June 2012, https://www.bbc.com/news/magazine-18116112, accessed 21 December 2019.

51. Elisabeth Sherman, 'Thirsty rats blamed for the disappearance of 900,000 liters of liquor,' *Food & Wine*, 24 May 2017, https://www.foodandwine.com/news/thirsty-rats-blamed-disappearance-900000-liters-liquor, accessed 11 June 2020.

52. See HuffPost Staff, 'Here's the full text of Modi's speech on the discontinuation of ₹500 and ₹1,000 bank notes,' *HuffPost Staff*, 9 November 2016, https://www.huffingtonpost.in/2016/11/08/heres-the-full-text-of-modis-speech-on-the-discontinuation-of_a_21601525/, accessed 3 August 2020; John E. Marthinsen, 'India's Demonetization: What were they thinking?' *Babson College*, April 2017, https://www.babson.edu/academics/executive-education/babson-insight/finance-and-accounting/indias-demonetization-what-were-they-thinking/#, accessed 7 August 2020; and Sneha Alexander and Vishnu Padmanabhan, 'Despite hype, demonetization missed all goals,' *Livemint*, 5 May 2019, https://www.livemint.com/news/india/despite-hype-demonetization-missed-all-goals-1557059532885.html, accessed 7 August 2020; ET Bureau, 'Demonetisation hit growth by 2 percentage points: US study,' *Economic Times*, 19 December 2018, https://economictimes.indiatimes.com/news/economy/policy/demonetisation-hit-growth-by-2-percentage-points-us-study/articleshow/67154320.cms?from=mdr, accessed 8 August 2020.

53. See, for instance, Jagdish Bhagwati, 'War on black money:

Demonetisation is a courageous reform that will bring substantive benefits,' *The Times of India*, 14 December 2016, https://timesofindia. indiatimes.com/blogs/toi-edit-page/war-on-black-money-demonetisation-is-a-courageous-reform-that-will-bring-substantive-benefits/, accessed 11 June 2020; Jagdish Bhagwati, Vivek Dehejia and Pravin Krishna, 'RBI data isn't enough to argue if demonetization was a success or failure,' *The Print*, 5 September 2017, https://theprint.in/opinion/premature-argue-demonetisation-success-failure/9195/, accessed 11 June 2020; Lawrence H. White, 'India's failed demonetization program and its retreating economic defenders,' *Cato Institute*, 28 September 2017, https://www.cato.org/blog/indias-failed-demonetization-program-its-retreating-economic-defenders, accessed 11 June 2020.

54. Jonathan Stein and Tim Dickinson, 'Lie by lie: A timeline of how we got into Iraq,' *Mother Jones*, September/October 2006, https://www. motherjones.com/politics/2011/12/leadup-iraq-war-timeline/, accessed 11 June 2020.

55. Both liberal and conservative discourses about Indian identities, culture, history and society traffic in clichés about Indian exceptionalism. India is not unique in this regard, though. Every nation has its own version of exceptionalism. The Nehruvian model of Indian identity is as guilty of this essentialism as its antithesis, the ideology of Hindutva that since 2014 has replaced the former as the dominant self-image of Indian identity. Conflating a desired political order with the messiness of history, the Nehruvian vision of India reads an idealised secularism into Indian history. Reducing the Indian past to a tension between the imperatives of secularism and sectarianism, the story proclaims secularism to be an essential Indian attribute, which, it is held, will ultimately always triumph over the forces of religious discord. In contrast, Savarkar's idea of India proposes that India has been and is a Hindu nation, and that its Hindu character grants India its essential cultural identity and uniqueness. *Nishkama karma* does not seem to figure in either scheme. Nehru very much hoped that Indians, especially those with the privilege of power or armed with a scientific and technological education, would work for the goal of the development of the nation. And Savarkar, likewise, wanted to militarise Hinduism and create a modern and strong Hindu nation-state founded on the

ideology of Hindutva. Jawaharlal Nehru, *The Discovery of India*, New Delhi: Penguin India, 2008 and Vinayak Damodar Savarkar. *Hindutva: Who is a Hindu?* Nagpur, 1928.

56. This, in a nutshell, is the Gramscian idea of hegemony, or an explanation of why people internalise beliefs and abide by social structures that may not always be in their best interests, whether these beliefs and social structures pertain to class, religious identity or corporate hierarchies. The reductive Marxist reading sees hegemony and a related concept, ideology, as forms of deception, a trick played on unsuspecting masses by those in power. But hegemony is a more sophisticated idea. It does not rule out the fact that people can find genuine fulfilment and meaning while participating in arrangements that work more advantageously for others than they do for them. For an explanation of the concept, see Juan Carlos de Orellana, 'Gramsci on Hegemony,' *Not Even Past*, 26 May 2015, https://notevenpast.org/gramsci-on-hegemony/, accessed 17 January 2020.

57. That this image is a myth, though feted and sustained by Silicon Valley, is made clear by the high rates of stress, anxiety and mental health challenges that entrepreneurs face. They are as much victims of this myth making as are so-called 'wantrepreneurs', aspirants who seek to emulate successful entrepreneurs. See the episode 'Silicon Valley's Secret' on the show *Mostly Human with Laurie Segall*, n.d., https://money.cnn.com/mostly-human/silicon-valleys-secret/ , accessed 7 August 2020.

58. See Dante A. Urbina and Alberto Ruiz-Villaverde, 'A critical review of *Homo Economicus* from five approaches,' *The American Journal of Economics and Sociology*, vol. 78, issue 1 (January 2019): 63–93.

59. Pierre Bourdieu, *Acts of Resistance: Against the Tyranny of the Market*, New York: New Press, 1999.

60. Michael J. Sandel, *What Money Can't Buy: The Moral Limits of Markets*, New York: Farrar, Straus and Giroux, 2013. I do not want to propose an uncritical dismissal of the energies released by the shift to a more market-oriented model of society in India, though a discussion of how the costs and benefits of such a transition have panned out in the Indian context could fill a library of its own. It may also appear to the observer of Indian affairs that even as India has lifted millions out of poverty, it has not shaken off the legacies of either the British colonial state or the developmental mixed-economy postcolonial state.

61. Will Stone, 'COVID-19 deaths draw comparisons to other tragic death tolls,' *NPR*, 26 January 2020, https://www.npr.org/2021/01/26/960631333/covid-19-deaths-draw-comparisons-to-other-tragic-death-tolls, accessed 28 January 2021.

4. THE GITA, DIFFERENCE AND UNIVERSALITY IN THE AGE OF CRISIS

1. I have discussed this at some length in the second chapter of this book.
2. See page 95 in Rafael Winkler and Abraham Olivier, 'Identity and Difference,' *Journal of the British Society for Phenomenology*, vol. 47, no. 2 (2016):95–97, https://www.tandfonline.com/doi/full/10.1080/00071773.2016.1145889, accessed 11 August 2020.
3. The term 'identity politics' is more often than not used in a petty, sneering manner to dismiss new understandings of identity and difference, political movements for rights related to sexual identity, postcolonial rejections of colonial narratives of history and the critique of universalism reflected in such initiatives. Given that its usage so frequently represents lazy intellectual posturing, it is not worth treating it as a meaningful analytic concept. At best, it can be used as a descriptive term.
4. Perhaps no text is more indicative of this remarkable moment in Western scholarship in the second half of the twentieth century than Edward Said's *Orientalism*, though critiques of Western thought, such as in the writings of Gandhi, long predated Said's work. In his work, which drew on the relationship between power and knowledge theorised by Michel Foucault, Said showed how the so-called 'Orient', a term used to cover a vast terrain of highly diverse and individuated non-Western cultures, was both a fiction and a reality. The Orient, Said argued, was an idea that had seized the Western imagination as its Other, and this imagined Orient became the theatre for the exercise of Western power, a pretext for military and economic domination, as well as cultural subjugation. The radical insight of Said's text was to show how the production of Western knowledge, for all its claims of commitment to a liberal and universal idea of the human subject, was deeply implicated in the prejudices of Orientalist discourse. Not only could Western knowledge not break free from the dichotomies of the West as rational, logical, civilised and comprehensible and the East as irrational, mystical, spiritual, inscrutable, barbaric and mysterious—dichotomies that

informed and justified policies of imperialism and colonialism—it was actively complicit in reproducing them. In the bargain, Western knowledge became a handmaiden to Western colonialism even as it claimed to produce objective and scientific accounts of the truth about non-Western and colonised cultures. See Edward Said, *Orientalism*, New York: Vintage Books, 1979.

5. Zeynep Tufecki, *Twitter and Tear Gas: The Power and Fragility of Networked Protest*, New Haven, Connecticut: Yale University Press, 2017. The book is available at the website https://www.twitterandteargas.org/.

6. The German sociologist Max Weber famously defined the state as 'a human community that (successfully) claims the monopoly of the legitimate use of physical force within a given territory', p. 78. See Max Weber, 'Politics as a vocation,' in H. H. Gerth and C. Wright Mills (translated and edited), *From Max Weber: Essays in Sociology*, New York: Oxford University Press, 1946, pp. 77–128.

7. The historian Gyanendra Pandey describes this as the distinction between the unmarked 'axiomatically natural' citizen and the marked 'hyphenated' minority citizens of a state (p. 608). Pandey suggests that this hierarchy of citizenship is central to the very project of the modern nation-state. Gyanendra Pandey, 'Can a Muslim be an Indian?' *Comparative Studies in Society and History*, vol. 41, no. 4 (October 1999): 608–629.

8. Yogita Limaye, 'Amnesty International to halt India operations,' *BBC News*, 29 September 2020, https://www.bbc.com/news/world-asia-india-54277329, accessed 2 October 2020.

9. Sunil Khilnani, *The Idea of India*, New Delhi: Penguin Books, 1999.

10. Ibid., pp. 171–172. The similarity to the structuralist idea, articulated by the linguist Ferdinand de Saussure, of language as a system of differences, is striking. See his *Writings in General Linguistics*, New York: Oxford University Press, 2006.

11. There is, however, a legitimate place for the utopian in our political imaginations. I owe this insight to the historian Sudipta Sen in a personal conversation with him. The fact that Nehru's utopian hopes for India, if nowhere near fully realised, also enabled much of value to be achieved, from securing the foundations for an electoral democracy to establishing a framework for respecting diversity as a social fact,

affirm this point. Some notable achievements of the Nehruvian project include setting up excellent institutions of research and higher education, insisting on keeping the welfare of the marginalised sections of Indian society central to any policy initiative and encouraging a cosmopolitan sensibility among the Indian citizenry.

12. Zakia Pathak and Rajeswari Sundar Rajan, 'Shahbano,' *Signs*, vol. 14, no. 3 (Spring 1989): 558–582; Namita Bhandare, 'Muslim women: a court in their corner,' *LiveMint*, 25 July 2015, https://www.livemint.com/Politics/9xcfehlzEUPgQS5x6GL8PM/Minority-women-A-court-in-their-corner.html, accessed 10 November 2020.

13. Supriya Nair, 'The meaning of India's "beef lynchings",' *The Atlantic*, 24 July 2017, https://www.theatlantic.com/international/archive/2017/07/india-modi-beef-lynching-muslim-partition/533739/, accessed 11 November 2020; Zeba Siddiqui, 'Protests in Indian cities after Muslim man is lynched, Modi says he is "pained",' *Reuters*, 26 June 2019, https://www.reuters.com/article/us-india-protests-lynching/protests-in-indian-cities-after-muslim-man-is-lynched-modi-says-he-is-pained-idUSKCN1TR2AG, accessed 11 November 2020; Lauren Frayer, 'This is it. I'm going to die: India's minorities are targeted in lynchings,' *NPR*, 21 August 2019, https://www.npr.org/2019/08/21/751541321/this-is-it-im-going-to-die-indias-minorities-are-targeted-in-lynchings, accessed 11 November 2020; Priya Chacko and Ruchira Talukdar, 'Why Modi's India has become a dangerous place for Muslims,' *The Conversation*, 2 March 2020, https://theconversation.com/why-modis-india-has-become-a-dangerous-place-for-muslims-13259, accessed 11 November 2020.

14. Meena Kandasamy, 'India's most oppressed get their revenge,' *The New York Times*, 15 May 2019, https://www.nytimes.com/2019/05/15/opinion/india-elections-dalits.html, accessed 20 November 2020. Indo-Asian News Service, 'Attacks against Muslims, Dalits grew sharply in India under Modi: US report,' *India Today*, 10 February 2017, https://www.indiatoday.in/india/story/muslims-dalits-religious-attacks-grew-in-india-narendra-modi-us-report-959959-2017-02-10, accessed 20 November 2020. See also Salil Tripathi, 'Why India has become a different country,' *Foreign Policy*, 27 November 2020, https://foreignpolicy.com/2020/11/27/why-india-has-become-a-different-country/, accessed 27 November 2020.

15. Hannah Ellis-Petersen, 'Dalits bear brunt of India's "endemic" sexual violence crisis,' *The Guardian*, 15 September 2020, https://www.theguardian.com/world/2020/sep/16/dalits-bear-brunt-of-indias-endemic-sexual-violence-crisis, accessed 20 November 2020.

16. For an understanding of the political mobilisation of subaltern castes in the decades after independence, see Christophe Jaffrelot, *India's Silent Revolution: The Rise of the Lower Castes in North India*, New York: Columbia University Press, 2003 and Jeffrey Witsoe, *Democracy Against Development: Lower-Caste Politics and Political Development in Postcolonial India*, Chicago: University of Chicago Press, 2013.

17. Swati Chaturvedi, 'Narendra Modi has gone from dog-whistle to vulture politics,' *The Wire,* 8 May 2019, https://thewire.in/politics/narendra-modi-has-gone-from-dog-whistle-to-vulture-politics, accessed 14 November 2020.

18. Kelly Buchanan and Tariq Ahmad, 'FALQs: Article 370 and the removal of Jammu and Kashmir's special status,' *Library of Congress*, 3 October 2019, https://blogs.loc.gov/law/2019/10/falqs-article-370-and-the-removal-of-jammu-and-kashmirs-special-status/, accessed 19 November 2020.

19. John Sebastian and Faiza Rahman, 'The Babri Masjid and the sound of silence,' *The Wire*, 6 December 2019, https://thewire.in/law/the-babri-masjid-judgment-and-the-sound-of-silence, accessed 22 November 2020.

20. Hannah Ellis-Peterson, 'India's BJP leaders acquitted over Babri mosque demolition,' *The Guardian*, 30 September 2020, https://www.theguardian.com/world/2020/sep/30/india-bjp-leaders-acquitted-babri-mosque-demolition-case, accessed 24 November 2020.

21. Soumya Shankar, 'India's citizenship law, in tandem with national registry, could make BJP's discriminatory targeting of Muslims easier,' *The Intercept*, 30 January 2020, https://theintercept.com/2020/01/30/india-citizenship-act-caa-nrc-assam/, accessed 30 November 2020; Aditi Malik, Shivaji Mukherjee, and Ajay Verghese, 'In India, thousands are protesting the new citizenship law. Here are 4 things to know,' *The Washington Post*, 31 December 2019, https://www.washingtonpost.com/politics/2019/12/31/india-thousands-are-protesting-new-citizenship-law-here-are-things-know/, accessed 23 November 2020.

22. See John Witte Jr. and Frank Alexander (eds), *Christianity and Human Rights: An Introduction*, New York: Cambridge University Press, 2010

and Abdullahi An-Na'im, *Selected Essays of Abdullahi An-Na'im*, New York: Routledge, 2006.

23. The argument has also been made that colonialism or slavery were, in fact, not just compatible with but, indeed, constitutive of universalist projects grounded in liberal values. See Lisa Lowe, *The Intimacies of Four Continents*, Durham, North Carolina: Duke University Press, 2015; Immanuel Wallerstein, *European Universalism: The Rhetoric of Power*, New York: The New Press, 2006; Paulin Ismard, *Democracy's Slaves: A Political History of Ancient Greece*, Cambridge, Massachusetts: Harvard University Press, 2017.

24. For an example of such arguments, see John Casey, 'Turkey is not part of Europe—as the history of our continent shows,' *The Independent*, 10 March 2016, https://www.independent.co.uk/voices/turkey-not-part-europe-history-our-continent-shows-a6923486.html, accessed 4 October 2020; on recent developments, see VOA News, 'Report puts Turkey's EU membership bid in limbo,' *VoA*, 6 October 2020, https://www.voanews.com/europe/report-puts-turkeys-eu-membership-bid-limbo, accessed 8 October 2020.

25. See 'Violence against women and girls: The shadow pandemic,' *UN Women*, 6 April 2020, https://www.unwomen.org/en/news/stories/2020/4/statement-ed-phumzile-violence-against-women-during-pandemic, accessed 5 October 2020.

26. Hunter Schwarz, 'Obama's latest "evolution" on gay marriage: He lied about opposing it, Axelrod says,' *The Washington Post*, 10 February 2015, https://www.washingtonpost.com/news/the-fix/wp/2015/02/10/axelrod-says-obama-lied-about-opposing-gay-marriage-its-another-convenient-evolution/, accessed 11 November 2020.

27. Romila Thapar, 'The epic of the Bharatas,' Seminar 608, 2010, https://www.india-seminar.com/2010/608/608_romila_thapar.htm, accessed 4 October 2020.

28. Ibid.

29. Ibid.

30. Thapar observes, 'As a comment on clan society this requires explanation, unless it can be argued that such episodes were introduced later when the mleccha were treated as less than human.' Ibid.

31. R.K. Narayan, *The Mahabharata: A Shortened Modern Prose Version of the Indian Epic*, Chicago, Illinois: University of Chicago Press, 2013.

32. Doniger notes, 'The total indifference to the fate of low-caste tribals on the part of the Pandavas—and, indeed, on the part of the narrator of the text—has become, in recent years, a point of embarrassment to contemporary Hindus sensitive to the injustices of the caste system,' p. ix. See Wendy Doniger, 'Foreword,' in R.K. Narayan, *The Mahabharata*, 2013, pp. vii–xii.

33. The Indian godman Ravi Shankar has a dubious explanation for why Drona's demand that Eklavya cut off this thumb as *gurudakshina* was a noble act. Such convoluted arguments are a sorry reminder of the justification for caste discrimination and violence that bedevil what Romila Thapar has incisively termed 'syndicated Hinduism'. See 'The story of Eklavya and Dronacharya,' *Wisdom by Gurudev Sri Sri Ravi Shankar*, n.d., https://wisdom.srisriravishankar.org/story-eklavya-devotion/, accessed 5 October 2020; Ruchika Sharma, 'Hindutva calling itself a version of Hinduism is problematic: Historian Romila Thapar,' *Scroll.in*, 4 February 2018, https://scroll.in/article/867440/hindutva-calling-itself-a-version-of-hinduism-is-problematic-historian-romila-thapar, accessed 1 December 2020.

34. Sara Goering, 'Rethinking disability: the social model of disability and chronic disease,' *Current Reviews in Musculoskeletal Medicine*, vol. 8, no. 2 (June 2015): 134–138, published online 11 April 2015, 10.1007/s12178-015-9273-z, accessed 4 December 2020.

35. Mike Oliver, *Understanding Disability: From Theory to Practice,* New York: St. Martin's Press, 1996, p. 22, cited in Goering, 2015.

36. Javid Iqbal Wani and L. David Lal, 'The precarity of Dalit lives in India,' *The Indian Express*, 27 October 2020, https://indianexpress.com/article/opinion/columns/dalit-atrocity-casteism-hathras-thakur-brahmin-rape-6903255/, accessed 4 December 2020.

37. Anand Teltumbde, 'Khairlanji and its aftermath: Exploding some myths,' *Economic and Political Weekly*, vol. 42, no. 12 (March 2007): 1019–1025.

38. Express News Service, 'Atrocities against Dalits see a rise,' *The New Indian Express*, 7 July 2020, https://www.newindianexpress.com/cities/delhi/2020/jul/07/atrocities-against-dalits-see-a-rise-2166477.html, accessed 8 December 2020.

39. Including, it should be noted, among Muslims and Christians who have incorporated the logic of caste in their cultural-religious

frameworks. See Pratik Patnaik, 'Caste among Indian Muslims is a real issue: So why deny them reservation?' *The Wire*, 2 December 2020, https://thewire.in/caste/caste-among-indian-muslims-real-why-deny-reservation, accessed 8 December 2020; Megan Sweas, 'Caste first, Christ second, for some Indian Christians,' *Religion Dispatches*, 9 July 2012, https://religiondispatches.org/caste-first-christ-second-for-some-indian-christians/, accessed 8 December 2020.

40. I cannot recall the particular television show for certain, though it was possibly said in an interview with the now-disgraced journalist Charlie Rose.

41. Justice Sachs is justly celebrated as an anti-apartheid activist, a voice for global human rights and the architect of the first constitution of post-apartheid Africa. I owe the reference and the elaboration of the concept to Professor Abdullahi An-Na'im, Charles Howard Candler Professor of Law at Emory University, Atlanta, and a renowned expert on human rights, international law, Islamic law and constitutional law.

42. Immanuel Wallerstein, *European Universalism: The Rhetoric of Power*, New York: The New Press, 2006.

43. See Frank Trentmann and Kate Soper (eds), *Citizenship and Consumption*, New York: Palgrave Macmillan, 2008.

44. Hadley Freeman, 'From shopping to naked selfies: how "empowerment" lost its meaning,' *The Guardian*, 19 April 2016, https://www.theguardian.com/world/2016/apr/19/from-shopping-to-naked-selfies-how-empowerment-lost-its-meaning-feminism, accessed 9 August 2020.

45. See Garrath Williams, 'Kant's account of reason,' *The Stanford Encyclopedia of Philosophy* (Summer 2018 Edition), edited by Edward N. Zalta, https://plato.stanford.edu/archives/sum2018/entries/kant-reason/, accessed 15 August 2020.

46. The journalist Andrew Sullivan's arguments are a perfect example of such apologetics. In a 2018 article, Sullivan writes:

> It is Christianity that came to champion the individual conscience against the collective, which paved the way for individual rights. It is in Christianity that the seeds of Western religious toleration were first sown. Christianity is the only monotheism that seeks no sway over Caesar, that is content with the ultimate truth over the immediate satisfaction of power. It was Christianity that gave us

> successive social movements, which enabled more people to be included in the liberal project, thus renewing it. It was on these foundations that liberalism was built, and it is by these foundations it has endured.

See Andrew Sullivan, 'America's new religions,' *New York*, 7 December 2018, https://nymag.com/intelligencer/2018/12/andrew-sullivan-americas-new-religions.html, accessed 9 December 2020.

47. See Sophie Lewis, 'Joe Biden breaks Obama's record for most votes ever cast for a U.S. presidential candidate,' *CBS News*, 7 December 2020, https://www.cbsnews.com/news/joe-biden-popular-vote-record-barack-obama-us-presidential-election-donald-trump/, accessed 9 December 2020.

48. The Editors of Encyclopædia Britannica, 'Ardhanarishvara,' *Encyclopædia Britannica*, 8 April 2015, https://www.britannica.com/topic/Ardhanarishvara, accessed 10 December 2020.

49. 'Hinduism Case Study- Gender,' *Harvard Divinity School Religious Literacy Project*, 2018 https://rlp.hds.harvard.edu/files/hds-rlp/files/gender_hinduism.pdf, accessed 13 August 2020.

50. See Gyanendra Pandey, *A History of Prejudice: Race, Caste, and Difference in India and the United States*, New York: Cambridge University Press, 2013.

51. See the chapter 'Caste, race, and Black power in India,' in Nico Slate, *Black Power Beyond Borders: The Global Dimensions of the Black Power Movement*, New York: Palgrave Macmillan, 2012, pp. 127–143.

52. Gurvinder Gill and Imran Rahman-Jones, 'Me Too founder Tarana Burke: movement is not over,' *BBC News*, 9 July 2020, https://www.bbc.com/news/newsbeat-53269751, accessed 3 August 2020. See also Scroll Staff, 'MJ Akbar defamation case: Priya Ramani says disclosure of sexual harassment was for "public good",' *Scroll.in*, 6 September 2020, https://scroll.in/latest/972332/mj-akbar-defamation-case-priya-ramani-says-disclosure-of-sexual-harassment-was-for-public-good, accessed 8 December 2020.

53. Sumedha Bharpilania, 'Bollywood actors are talking about Black Lives Matter and Indians are calling out their double standards,' *Buzzfeed*, 6 June 2020, https://www.buzzfeed.com/sumedha_bharpilania/bollywood-actors-are-talking-about-black-lives-matter-and, accessed 7 August 2020.

54. See pp. 54–66 in Perry Anderson, *The Origins of Postmodernity*, New York: Verso, 1998, for an extended discussion. See also Frederic Jameson, *Postmodernism, or the Cultural Logic of Late Capitalism*, Durham, North Carolina: Duke University Press, 1989.

55. Anderson, *The Origins of Postmodernity*, p. 55.

56. Ibid.

57. Ibid.

58. J. Clement, 'Number of monthly active Facebook users worldwide as of 2nd quarter 2020,' *Statista*, https://www.statista.com/statistics/264810/number-of-monthly-active-facebook-users-worldwide/, accessed 9 August 2020.

59. Wael Ghonim, 'Inside the Egyptian revolution,' *TED*, March 2011, https://www.ted.com/talks/wael_ghonim_inside_the_egyptian_revolution?language=en, accessed 7 November 2019.

60. Wael Ghonim, 'Let's design social media that drives real change,' *TED*, January 2016, https://www.ted.com/talks/wael_ghonim_let_s_design_social_media_that_drives_real_change/transcript?language=en, accessed 7 November 2019.

61. See Kostas Zafeiropoulos, 'Alexander the bot: The Twitter war for the Macedonian soul,' *BalkanInsight*, 18 December 2019, https://balkaninsight.com/2019/12/18/alexander-the-bot-the-twitter-war-for-the-macedonian-soul/, 12 June 2020; Joanna Kakissis, 'For two countries, the dispute over Macedonia's name is rooted in national identity,' *NPR*, 24 February 2018, https://www.npr.org/sections/parallels/2018/02/04/582506402/for-two-countries-the-dispute-over-macedonias-name-is-rooted-in-national-identit, accessed 24 July 2020.

62. See Amalini de Sayrah, 'Facebook helped foment anti-Muslim violence in Sri Lanka. What now?' *The Guardian*, 5 May 2018, https://www.theguardian.com/commentisfree/2018/may/05/facebook-anti-muslim-violence-sri-lanka, accessed 4 June 2019; Paul Mozur, 'A genocide incited on Facebook, with posts from Myanmar's military,' *The New York Times*, 15 October 2018, https://www.nytimes.com/2018/10/15/technology/myanmar-facebook-genocide.html, accessed 3 June 2019; and Timothy McLaughlin, 'How WhatsApp fuels fake news and violence in India,' 12 December 2018, https://www.wired.com/story/how-whatsapp-fuels-fake-news-and-violence-in-india/, accessed 3 August 2020.

63. Patton, *The Bhagavad Gita*, p. viii.
64. Barbara Johnson, *The Critical Difference: Essays in the Contemporary Rhetoric of Reading*, Baltimore, MD: Johns Hopkins Press, 1980, p. 5.
65. Stoler Miller, *The Bhagavad-Gita*, p. 61.
66. Stoler Miller, op. cit., pp. 28–29.
67. Flood and Martin, op. cit., p. 8.
68. Ibid.
69. Flood and Martin, op. cit., p. 8–9
70. The construction of women as symbols of community honour is seen in a wide variety of contexts. Examples include racial miscegenation laws in the US, which criminalised interracial marriage between Blacks and Whites, honour killings among South Asian communities or assaults against women in civil war. During any kind of inter-group violence, women disproportionately bear the brunt of brutality, since denigrating women is seen as humiliating the enemy community to which they belong. Ironically, this accompanies the idealisation of women as symbols of race, ethnicity, nationality or, more broadly, community. In the South Asian context, the savage sexual violence to which women were subjected during the upheavals of Partition is one of the most horrifying instances of the objectification and dehumanisation of women in the history of the region. Urvashi Butalia's landmark work *The Other Side of Silence*, an oral history of women's experiences of sexual violence during Partition, contains account after harrowing account that testifies to this phenomenon. See Butalia, *The Other Side of Side: Voices from the Partition of India*, Durham, North Carolina: Duke University Press, 2006.
71. Flood and Martin, op. cit., p. 8.
72. Mathur, 'The concept of action in the Bhagvad-Gita,' p. 35.
73. See chapter 9, 'Krishna and his Gita,' in B.R. Ambedkar's unfinished book, 'Revolution and Counter-Revolution in Ancient India,' n.d., available at http://www.ambedkar.org/ambcd/19C.Revolution%20 and%20Counter%20Rev.%20in%20Ancient%20India%20PARTIII. htm#a9, accessed on 11 August 2020
74. Ibid.
75. Stoler Miller, op. cit., p. 33.
76. Stoler Miller, op. cit., p. 61.
77. Flood and Martin, op. cit., p. 3; Patton, op. cit., p. 66.

78. The source I have used is *Mahatma Gandhi, The Bhagavad Gita According to Gandhi*, edited by John Strohmeier, Berkeley, CA: North Atlantic Books, 2009, p. 82. Strohmeier's edition is drawn from the *Collected Works of Mahatma Gandhi*, vol. XXXII (1926-27), pp. 94–376, 'Discourses on the Gita.' See p. xiii for more details about the translation from Gandhi's Gujarati translation of the Gita into English.

79. Ibid.

80. Stoler Miller, op. cit., p. 90.

81. Mathur, 'The concept of action in the Bhagvad-Gita,' p. 34, italics in original.

82. Mathur, 'The concept of action in the Bhagvad-Gita,' p. 40.

83. Patton, op. cit., p. xxx.

84. Patton, op. cit., p. xxxi.

85. Patton, op. cit., p. xxx.

86. Flood and Martin, op. cit., p .xiv.

87. Marion Goldman and Steve Pfaff, 'Martin Luther's spiritual practice was key to the success of the Reformation,' *The Conversation*, 24 October 2017, https://theconversation.com/martin-luthers-spiritual-practice-was-key-to-the-success-of-the-reformation-83340, accessed 8 November 2020.

88. Patton, op. cit., pp. xxviii–xxix.

89. Stoler Miller, op. cit., p. 79.

90. Stoler Miller, op. cit., p. 104.

91. See Scott Stroud, 'Orientational meliorism, pragmatist aesthetics, and the "Bhagavad Gita",' *The Journal of Aesthetic Education*, vol. 43, no. 1 (Spring 2009): 1–17, http://www.jstor.com/stable/40263701, accessed 5 August 2020.

92. Dhrubo Jyoti, 'Gandhi, Ambedkar, and the 1932 Poona Pact,' *Hindustan Times*, 1 October 2019, https://www.hindustantimes.com/india-news/gandhi-ambedkar-and-the-1932-poona-pact/story-5WuyrphB8OwtRp5lC9XQGP.html, accessed 3 November 2020.

93. On social Darwinism, see J.A. Rogers, 'Darwinism and social Darwinism,' *Journal of the History of Ideas*, vol. 33, no. 2 (April–June 1972): 265–280.

94. See Mahmoud Mohammed Taha, *The Second Message of Islam*, translated by Abdullahi An-Na'im, Syracuse, New York: Syracuse

University Press, 1996; Abdullahi An-Na'im, *Toward an Islamic Reformation: Civil Liberties, Human Rights, and International Law*, Syracuse, New York: Syracuse University Press, 1996.

95. Redden, op. cit.

96. See Sumit Ganguly, 'India's democracy is under threat,' *Foreign Policy*, 18 September 2020, https://foreignpolicy.com/2020/09/18/indias-democracy-is-under-threat/, accessed 9 December 2020.

97. Section 153A of the Indian Penal Code deems it a crime to promote 'enmity between different groups on grounds of religion, race, place of birth, residence, language, etc.' See 'Section 153A in the Indian Penal Code,' *Indiankanoon*, n. d., https://indiankanoon.org/doc/345634/, accessed 17 August 2018. Section 295A ventures into the realm of the sacred, criminalising the act of harming, damaging or defiling 'any place of worship, or any object held sacred by any class of persons', once again locating claims of injury in membership of a group, community or collective. 'Section 295A in the Indian Penal Code,' *Indiankanoon*, n.d., https://indiankanoon.org/doc/305995/, accessed 17 August 2018.

98. Jawaharlal Nehru, *The Discovery of India*, New Delhi: Penguin Random House India, 2008.

5. WAR AND VIOLENCE IN A GLOBAL WORLD:
The Gita's Offerings

1. Smith, *The Mahabharata*, xiv. Smith's point calls to mind Shakespeare's words in *King Lear*: 'As flies to wanton boys are we to th' gods; They kill us for their sport.'

2. See p. 1831 in Romila Thapar, 'War in the 'Mahabharata,'' *PMLA*, vol. 124, no. 5 (October 2009): 1830–1833.

3. Ibid.

4. Thapar, 'War,' p. 1830.

5. Colonialism stands as the clearest example of the violence inherent in such an act of political reordering.

6. Stoler Miller, *The Bhagavad-Gita*, p. 149.

7. For a fine analysis of Tilak's reading of the Gita, see D. Mackenzie Brown, 'The Philosophy of Bal Gangadhar Tilak: *Karma* vs. *Jnana* in the *Gita Rahasya*,' *The Journal of Asian Studies,* vol. 17, no. 2 (1958): 197–206, accessed 30 August 2020, doi:10.2307/2941466.

8. See chapter 9, 'Krishna and his Gita,' in B.R. Ambedkar, 'Revolution and Counter-Revolution in Ancient India,' available at http://www. ambedkar.org/ambcd/19C.Revolution%20and%20Counter%20 Rev.%20in%20Ancient%20India%20PARTIII.htm#a9.

9. Thapar, 'The epic of the Bharatas.'

10. Ibid.

11. Ibid.

12. Smith, *The Mahabharata*, pp. xii–xiii.

13. Ibid.

14. Smith, *The Mahabharata*, xiii.

15. See James Palmer and Ravi Agrawal, 'Why are India and China fighting?' Foreign Policy, 16 June 2020, https://foreignpolicy.com/2020/06/16/ why-are-india-china-fighting-ladakh-skirmish/, accessed 7 June 2020; and Human Rights Clinic, 'Counting Drone Strike Deaths,' *Columbia Law School*, October 2012, https://web.law.columbia.edu/sites/default/ files/microsites/human-rights-institute/files/COLUMBIACountingDrones Final.pdf, accessed 4 June 2020.

16. See Thomas E. Mann, 'Reflections on the U.S. 2000 presidential election,' *Brookings*, 1 January 2001, https://www.brookings.edu/articles/ reflections-on-the-2000-u-s-presidential-election/, accessed 11 December 2020.

17. Ben Geier, 'What did we learn from the dotcom stock bubble of 2000?' *Time*, 12 March 2015, https://time.com/3741681/2000-dotcom-stock-bust/, accessed 11 December 2001.

18. See David Kieran, 'Why Americans still can't move past Vietnam,' *The Washington Post*, 10 October 2017, https://www.washingtonpost.com/ news/made-by-history/wp/2017/10/10/why-americans-still-cant-move-past-vietnam/, accessed 11 December 2020.

19. André Munro, 'State monopoly on violence,' *Encyclopædia Britannica*, 6 March 2013, https://www.britannica.com/topic/state-monopoly-on-violence, accessed 7 June 2020.

20. I had the privilege of attending the lecture. The exact phrase, 'epistemological rupture' was coined by the French philosopher Gaston Bachelard. See Hub Zwart, 'Iconoclasm and imagination: Gaston Bachelard's philosophy of technoscience,' *Human Studies*, vol. 43 (2020): 61–87.

21. See 'The Burning Monk: Malcolm Browne, 1963,' *Time*, http://100photos. time.com/photos/malcolm-browne-burning-monk, accessed 7 July 2020.

22. Tom Junod, 'The falling man: An unforgettable story,' *Esquire*, 9 September 2016, https://www.esquire.com/news-politics/a48031/the-falling-man-tom-junod/, accessed 2 August 2020.

23. 'The U.S. war in Afghanistan: 1999–2020,' *Council on Foreign Relations*, n.d., https://www.cfr.org/timeline/us-war-afghanistan, accessed 3 June 2020.

24. Max Fisher, 'A staggering map of the 54 countries that reportedly participated in the CIA's extraordinary rendition program,' *The Washington Post*, 5 February 2013, https://www.washingtonpost.com/news/worldviews/wp/2013/02/05/a-staggering-map-of-the-54-countries-that-reportedly-participated-in-the-cias-rendition-program/, accessed 4 June 2020.

25. Julia Angwin, *Dragnet Nation: A Question for Privacy, Security, and Freedom in a World of Relentless Surveillance*, New York: St. Martin's Griffin, 2015.

26. Aaron Bady, 'World without walls,' *MIT Technology Review*, 25 October 2011, https://www.technologyreview.com/2011/10/25/190229/world-without-walls/, accessed 4 June 2020.

27. See Spandana Singh and Dillon Rosen, 'Perspectives and policies on the digital safety of vulnerable communities,' *New America*, last updated 13 December 2018, https://www.newamerica.org/millennials/reports/perspectives-and-policies-digital-safety-vulnerable-communities/, accessed 11 December 2020; and 'Twitter still failing women over online violence and abuse,' *Amnesty International*, 22 September 2020, https://www.amnesty.org/en/latest/news/2020/09/twitter-failing-women-over-online-violence-and-abuse/, accessed 11 December 2020.

28. Tim Hume, 'Modi might be the only world leader whose Twitter use is more problematic than Trump's,' *Vice News*, 31 January 2018, https://www.vice.com/en/article/zmqaq3/modi-might-be-the-only-world-leader-whose-twitter-use-is-more-problematic-than-trumps, accessed 9 December 2020.

29. 'What is dangerous speech?,' n.d., https://dangerousspeech.org/about-dangerous-speech/, accessed 4 September 2020.

30. Timothy Garton Ash, *Free Speech: Ten Principles for a Connected World*, New Haven, Connecticut: Yale University Press, 2017.

31. Stoler Miller, op. cit., p. 132.

32. Greg Mitchell, *So Wrong for So Long: How the Press, the Pundits—and the President—Failed on Iraq*, New York: Union Square Press, 2008.

33. 'The U.S. war in Afghanistan: 1999–2020,' https://www.cfr.org/timeline/us-war-afghanistan.

34. The event was a discussion at the Herbst Theater in San Francisco, organised by City Arts in the summer of 2008 that I had attended.

35. Personal conversation.

36. Alexandra R. Moses, 'Saddam once received key to Detroit,' *AP News*, 26 March 2003, https://apnews.com/1b90335d077473f45a97694 1bac5a2aa, accessed 13 June 2020. See also Patrick Cockburn, 'Revealed: how the West set Saddam on the bloody road to power,' *Independent*, 29 June 2007, https://www.independent.co.uk/news/world/revealed-how-the-west-set-saddam-on-the-bloody-road-to-power-1258618.html, accessed 13 June 2020.

37. Faiz Shakir, 'Cheney, five years ago: "We will, in fact, be greeted as liberators",' *Thinkprogress*, 14 March 2008, https://archive.thinkprogress.org/cheney-five-years-ago-we-will-in-fact-be-greeted-as-liberators-4df9079115f8/.

38. 'US to withdraw 2,200 troops from Iraq by end of September,' *BBC News*, https://www.bbc.com/news/world-middle-east-54085129, accessed 11 December 2020.

39. See Office of the Spokesperson, 'Joint statement on the signing of the U.S.-Taliban agreement,' *U.S. Department of State*, https://www.state.gov/joint-statement-on-the-signing-of-the-u-s-taliban-agreement-2/, 9 March 2020, accessed 14 July 2020.

40. James T. Johnson, 'Just War,' *Encyclopædia Britannica*, n.d., https://www.britannica.com/topic/just-war, accessed 17 July 2020.

41. Stoler Miller, op. cit., p. 27.

42. Stoler Miller, op. cit., p. 28.

43. The reference here is to Benedict Anderson's seminal work on nationalism, *Imagined Communities: Reflections on the Origins and Spread of Nationalism*, London: Verso, 2016.

44. Joseph Conrad's well-known quote from his masterpiece, *Heart of Darkness*, may be apt here: 'The conquest of the earth, which mostly means the taking it away from those who have a different complexion or slightly flatter noses than ourselves, is not a pretty thing when you look into it much.' Joseph Conrad, *Heart of Darkness and Other Tales*, New York: Oxford University Press, 2008, p. 107.

45. Gerald J. Fitzgerald, 'Chemical warfare and medical response during

World War I,' *American Journal of Public Health*, vol. 98, no. 4 (April 2008): 611–625.

46. 'Guernica: the Spanish civil war,' *PBS*, n.d., https://www.pbs.org/treasuresoftheworld/a_nav/guernica_nav/gnav_level_1/1acivil_war_guerfrm.html, accessed 2 June 2020.

47. Clark presents his reading of *Guernica* in chapter 6, 'Mural' of his book, *Picasso and Truth: From Cubism to Guernica*, Princeton, New Jersey: Princeton University Press, 2013, pp. 235–282.

48. Clark, ibid., pp. 247-248

49. See the resource, 'The drone war' on *Propublica*, https://www.propublica.org/series/drones, accessed 23 July 2020.

50. Oliver Burkeman, 'Shock tactics,' *The Guardian*, 24 March 2003, https://www.theguardian.com/world/2003/mar/25/usa.iraq1, accessed 7 August 2020.

51. Cora Carrier, 'What does the U.S. pay for accidentally killing a civilian in a drone strike?' *The Atlantic*, 5 April 2013, https://www.theatlantic.com/international/archive/2013/04/drone-strike-compensation/316588/, accessed 11 June 2020.

52. I owe this point about imperial power being accountable to no one but itself to Abdullahi An-Na'im. I have not referred as much to the idea of *dharma* as to related ideas like *karma*, since one meaning of *dharma* as sacred or religious duty runs the risk of taking us down the rabbit hole of religion, a hermeneutic consequence I have wished to avoid in this book. To recall my argument, my concern about invoking religion is that it becomes what I call a 'sponge concept', to which anything and everything can be attributed because of a superior, and, ultimately, incomprehensible force.

53. This is a conservative estimate. By one assessment, the civilian death toll in just Iraq is 2.4 million. See Medea Benjamin and Nicolas J.S. Davies, 'The staggering death toll in Iraq,' *Salon*, 19 March 2018, https://www.salon.com/2018/03/19/the-staggering-death-toll-in-iraq_partner/, accessed 12 December 2020.

54. Art Spiegelman, *The Complete Maus*, New York: Pantheon, 1996.

55. For a comprehensive examination of this question, see Dominick LaCapra, *Representing the Holocaust: History, Theory, Trauma*, Ithaca, New York: Cornell University Press, 1994.

56. See Sam Keen, *Faces of the Enemy: Reflections of the Hostile Imagination*, New York: Harper & Row, 1991.

57. Kennedy Ndahiro, 'In Rwanda, we know all about dehumanizing language,' *The Atlantic*, 13 April 2019, https://www.theatlantic.com/ideas/archive/2019/04/rwanda-shows-how-hateful-speech-leads-violence/587041/, accessed 12 December 2020.

58. Stoler Miller, op. cit., p. 28.

CODA:
Gandhi, the Gita and Globalisation

1. Patton, *The Bhagavad Gita* p. xxix.

2. *Mahatma Gandhi, The Bhagavad Gita According to Gandhi*, edited by John Strohmeier, 2009. M.K. Gandhi, *Hind Swaraj and Other Writings*, ed., Anthony J. Parel, Cambridge, UK: Cambridge University Press, 1999.

3. Clara Joseph argues that *Hind Swaraj* is indebted to Gandhi's reading of the Gita. See Clara A.B. Joseph, 'Dialogue in Gandhi's *Hind Swaraj or Indian Home Rule* or the Reader as Truth-Seeker,' in *Theology and Literature: Rethinking Reader Responsibility* in Williams Ortiz Gaye and Clara A.B. Joseph, editors, New York: Springer, pp. 119–145.

4. At the height of its powers, the British empire covered a quarter of the world's landmass, its extensive dominion perhaps the reason for the saying that the sun never set on the British empire. The tongue-in-cheek response to that has been the retort that this is so because not even god trusts an Englishman in the dark. See Editors of Encyclopædia Britannica, 'British empire,' *Encyclopædia Britannica*, 6 April 2020, https://www.britannica.com/place/British-Empire, accessed 19 July 2020.

5. Ferguson is an unapologetic defender of imperialism and colonialism. See Priyamvada Gopal, 'The story peddled by imperial apologists is a poisonous fairytale,' *The Guardian*, 27 June 2006, https://www.theguardian.com/commentisfree/2006/jun/28/comment.britishidentity, accessed 17 December 2020. Biggar, likewise, in a long-standing tradition, sees the British empire as a largely benign force for good, aside from, as he put it without a shred of irony, 'the occasional massacre'. See https://www.thehindubusinessline.com/news/free-speech-row-british-academia-rally-around-indian-origin-cambridge-lecturer/article23530188.ece, accessed 10 August 2020. Zareer Masani's recent defence of Macaulay is another example of the never-finished project of rehabilitating the

reputation of British imperialists. Zareer Masani, *Macaulay: Pioneer of India's Modernization*, New York: Random House, 2012.

6. Shashi Tharoor, '"But what about the railways…?" The myth of Britain's gifts to India,' *The Guardian*, 8 March 2017, https://www.theguardian.com/world/2017/mar/08/india-britain-empire-railways-myths-gifts, accessed 8 June 2020.

7. For an examination of the idea of the scientific temper, see Rajendra Prasad, 'The debate on scientific temper,' *Social Scientist*, vol. 10, no. 1 (January 1982): 56–60.

8. Gandhi, *Hind Swaraj*, p. 47.

9. Gandhi, op. cit., p. 51.

10. See Ashis Nandy, *Traditions, Tyranny, and Utopias: Essays in the Politics of Awareness*, New Delhi: Oxford University Press, 1987, p. 138; and Gyan Prakash, *Another Reason: Science and the Imagination of Modern India*, Princeton, NJ: Princeton University Press, 1999, p. 217.

11. Martin Heidegger, 'The question concerning technology' in *The Question Concerning Technology and Other Essays,* translated by W. Lovitt, New York: Harper and Row, 1977, pp. 3–35. See pp. 17–19 for the concept of 'standing-reserve'.

12. The search for different forms of energy, including renewable energy, a main global priority for fighting climate change, also fits this paradigm.

13. See Carole Cadwalladr, '"I made Steve Bannon's psychological warfare tool": Meet the data war whistleblower,' *The Guardian*, 18 March 2018, https://www.theguardian.com/news/2018/mar/17/data-war-whistleblower-christopher-wylie-faceook-nix-bannon-trump; Vijayta Lalwani and Shoaib Daniyal, 'From Planning Murder to Praising Modi: WhatsApp Chats Offer a Window into the Minds of Delhi Rioters,' *Scroll.in*, 8 July 2020, https://scroll.in/article/966775/from-planning-murder-to-praising-modi-whatsapp-chats-offer-a-window-into-the-minds-of-delhi-rioters, accessed 4 August 2020.

AFTERWORD TO THE INDIAN PAPERBACK EDITION

1. Maria Cheng and Jamey Keaten, 'WHO downgrades COVID pandemic, says it's no longer emergency,' *AP News*, 5 May 2023, https://apnews.com/article/who-declares-covid-emergency-over-pandemic-8b6445735df5218b5d9d6ec32fa047ca.

2. Timothy Frye, 'Casualties won't topple Putin: But they will make his

job much more difficult,' *Foreign Policy*, 10 April 2023, https://foreignpolicy.com/2023/04/10/russia-ukraine-casualties-putin-war-military-politics/.

3. Sumathi Bala, 'U.S.-China relations are going downhill with "no trust" on either side, Stephen Roach says,' *CNBC*, 28 March 2023, https://www.cnbc.com/2023/03/28/us-china-ties-on-dangerous-path-with-no-trust-on-both-sides-roach-cohen.html.

4. International Monetary Fund, *World Economic Outlook: A Rocky Recovery*, Washington, D.C, April 2023, https://www.imf.org/en/Publications/WEO/Issues/2023/04/11/world-economic-outlook-april-2023.

5. Brian Michael Jenkins, 'Consequences of the War in Ukraine: The economic fallout,' *The RAND Blog*, 7 March 2023. https://www.rand.org/blog/2023/03/consequences-of-the-war-in-ukraine-the-economic-fallout.html.

6. Gregory C. Allen, 'In tech war with China, the U.S. is finding friends,' *Time*, 23 February 2020, https://time.com/6257857/us-china-tech-war-semiconductor/; Vishnu Kannan and Jacob Feldgoise, 'After the CHIPS Act: The limits of reshoring and next steps for U.S. semiconductor policy,' *Carnegie Endowment for International Peace*, 22 November 2022, https://carnegieendowment.org/2022/11/22/after-chips-act-limits-of-reshoring-and-next-steps-for-u.s.-semiconductor-policy-pub-88439.

7. Siddhi Nayak and Shivangi Acharya, 'Analysis–India's surging services exports may shield economy from external risks,' *US News*, 3 April 2023, https://money.usnews.com/investing/news/articles/2023-04-03/analysis-indias-surging-services-exports-may-shield-economy-from-external-risks.

8. Rakesh Sharma, 'India now buying 33 times more Russian oil than a year earlier,' *Bloomberg*, 16 January 2023, https://www.bloomberg.com/news/articles/2023-01-16/india-now-buying-33-times-more-russian-oil-than-a-year-earlier.

9. Danylo Hawaleshka, 'The rise and rise of Islamophobia in India,' *Al Jazeera*, 18 April 2023, https://www.aljazeera.com/gallery/2023/4/18/history-illustrated-the-rise-of-islamophobia-in-india.

10. BBC News, 'Giorgia Meloni: Migrants' fears over Italy's new far-right prime minister,' 22 October 2022, https://www.bbc.com/news/world-africa-63330850.

11. Robin Young, Lynn Menegon, and Grace Griffin, 'White supremacy poses increasing threats in the U.S.: "We are dealing with a massive movement",' *WBUR*, 7 July 2022, https://www.wbur.org/hereandnow/2022/07/07/white-supremacy-patriot-front.

12. Chandran Nair, 'Racism in America should not take center stage in the fight against white supremacy,' *Time*, 20 July 2021, https://time.com/6082168/white-privilege/; Daniel Geary, Camilla Schofield and Jennifer Sutton, 'Toward a global history of white supremacy,' *Boston Review*, 16 October 2020, https://www.bostonreview.net/articles/daniel-geary-camilla-schofield-jennifer-sutton-toward-global-history-white-supremacy/.

13. Annette Choi, 'Record number of anti-LGBTQ bills have been introduced this year,' *CNN*, 6 April 2023, https://www.cnn.com/2023/04/06/politics/anti-lgbtq-plus-state-bill-rights-dg/index.html.

14. Joe Wallen, 'LGBTQ+ couples in India await the Supreme Court's decision on same-sex marriage,' *NPR*, 9 May 2023, https://www.npr.org/2023/05/09/1174752874/india-same-sex-marriage-case-supreme-court.

15. Hanna Ziady, 'Brexit has cracked Britain's economic foundations,' CNN, 24 December 2022, https://www.cnn.com/2022/12/24/economy/brexit-uk-economy/index.html.

16. Adrian Browne, 'Brexit: Call for rethink on ditching thousands of EU laws,' *BBC*, 22 December 2022, https://www.bbc.com/news/uk-wales-politics-64051226.

17. Kim Parker, Julia Menasace Horowitz, and Anna Brown, 'Americans' complex views on gender identity and transgender issues,' *Pew Research Center*, 28 June 2022, https://www.pewresearch.org/social-trends/2022/06/28/americans-complex-views-on-gender-identity-and-transgender-issues/.

18. European Commission, 'This is how Europeans perceive migrants,' *European Website on Integration*, n.d., https://ec.europa.eu/migrant-integration/newsletter/how-europeans-perceive-migrants_en.

Acknowledgements

I would like to thank those to whom I owe my most essential debts in making this book possible:

Jagat Pal Chopra and Urvashi Chopra,

Gitanjali, Arihaan and Riley,

Govind Shahani and Roshan Shahani,

Subhrasheel (Noah) Roychowdhury,

Abdullahi An-Na'im, Cindy Patton, Allen Tullos, Phillip Wong, Zhang Hong Mei and Laszlo Szabo,

Ajitha G.S., Dipanjali Chadha, Saurabh Garge, Gavin Morris and all the other good people at Westland Books.

www.ingramcontent.com/pod-product-compliance
Lightning Source LLC
LaVergne TN
LVHW011003200726